BETRAYAL

BETRAYAL

HOW BLACK
INTELLECTUALS
HAVE
ABANDONED
THE IDEALS
OF THE CIVIL
RIGHTS ERA

HOUSTON A. BAKER JR.

COLUMBIA UNIVERSITY PRESS

NEW YORK

COLUMBIA UNIVERSITY PRESS

Publishers Since 1893

New York   Chichester, West Sussex

Library of Congress Cataloging-in-Publication Data

Baker, Houston A.

   Betrayal : how black intellectuals have abandoned the ideals of the civil rights era /
   Houston A. Baker Jr.

      p. cm.

   Includes bibliographical references and index.

      ISBN 978-0-231-13964-9 (cloth : alk. paper)—ISBN 978-0-231-51144-5 (e-book)

      1. African American intellectuals—Political activity. 2. African Americans—
   Civil rights. 3. Civil rights movement—United States.   I. Title.

E185.615B27 2008

323.1196'073—DC22

                                                                    2007031662

Columbia University Press books are printed on permanent and durable
acid-free paper. This book is printed on paper with recycled content.

Printed in the United States of America

C 10 9 8 7 6 5 4 3 2 1

BOOK DESIGN BY VIN DANG / JACKET DESIGN BY JAMES VICTORE

To race women and race men of countless generations who have preserved our redemption songs

And, as always, to Charlotte, for caring

No failure in America, whether of love or money, is ever simple; it is always a kind of betrayal, of a mass of shadowy, shared hopes.

GREIL MARCUS, "Robert Johnson," from *Mystery Train*, 1976

CONTENTS

PREFACE | *xi*

Introduction: Little Africa | *1*

Jail: Southern Detention to Global Liberation | *17*

Friends Like These: Race and Neoconservatism | *45*

After Civil Rights: The Rise of
Black Public Intellectuals | *71*

Have Mask, Will Travel:
Centrists from the Ivy League | *99*

A Capital Fellow from Hoover: Shelby Steele | *127*

Reflections of a First Amendment Trickster:
Stephen Carter | *157*

Man Without Connection: John McWhorter | *173*

American Myth: Illusions of
Liberty and Justice for All | *197*

Prison: Colored Bodies, Private Profit | *203*

Conclusion: What Then Must We Do? | *213*

NOTES | *219*
REFERENCES | *227*
INDEX | *233*

IN THE SPRING OF 1968, in Memphis, Tennessee, Dr. Martin Luther King Jr. joined city sanitation workers locked in a heated struggle for equal rights. Dr. King found a familiar geography in Memphis; he was on the ground, in the South, in fierce contest with forces of injustice. Yet again he had been called to champion the lives and cause of those blacks farthest down—garbage men, cleaning women, practical nurses, and underpaid day laborers. It is precisely King's alliance with the working-class black majority that makes him perhaps the twentieth century's most striking exemplar of the "race man." In this book I offer an account of Dr. King's model black public intellectualism. I argue that King and the movements of which he was a critical part helped raise the variable of "race" to global revolutionary significance. After revisiting Dr. King's labors and establishing the global efficacy of his comprehensive, activist black public intellectualism, I turn a critical gaze on the written words of King's black intellectual successors. In my view, many of the proclaimed successors of the post–Civil Rights era have been treacherous in their betrayals of the ideals, social commitments, and best energies of the Civil Rights and Black Power movements.

Two categories of black public intellectuals in particular have garnered extraordinary levels of media exposure in the United States during the past few decades: black centrists and black neoconservatives. Though these intellectuals have been prolific, their writings have seldom been subjected to rigorous textual analysis or critical rhetorical scrutiny. The claims of these centrist and neoconservative intellectuals to speak authoritatively about and for "the race" have yet to be amply critically challenged. An informed critique of the centrist and neo-conservative black public intellectual texts that have gained fame and wide recognition in our era is long overdue.

The ubiquity and accrued cultural currency of black public intellectuals in our era has helped foster a myth of racial progress. Under strict analytical scrutiny, however, the writings of black centrist and neoconservative intellectuals often reveal themselves to be far from progressive, and in no way allied to the best practices and ideals of race men and race women of countless American generations. The written words of post–Civil Rights era black public intellectuals often go against the grain of a fruitful deployment of race as an analytical category, and I believe they ultimately represent a manifest betrayal of the legacy of Dr. Martin Luther King and the magnificent accomplishments of the Civil Rights and Black Power movements. In the pages that follow, I summon my personal experience in the offices of autobiographical critique, and my vocational and professional aptitude as a reader and analyst of written texts to substantiate my claim that *betrayal* has often marked the works of hand of post–Civil Rights era black public intellectuals.

There is today a monumental divide between black intellectuals and the black majority. Who could imagine, for instance, an Ivy League black centrist public intellectual flying coach to Memphis to stand in perilous solidarity, harmony, and allegiance with striking black garbage men? Martin Luther King Jr. brilliantly and ethically sutured the divide between his own Ph.D. and Nobel laureateship and the black majority. He knew that unless the black majority moved upward in tandem with what W. E. B. Du Bois called "college-bred black men and women," there would be no true racial progress in America. Through the force of his oratory, writing, preaching, and body-on-the-line commitment, King declared there could be no genuine racial progress in America if the black majority did not achieve such cardinal privileges of modernism as dignified labor recompensed by just wages; adequate and affordable housing; safe mobility on U.S. streets and interstate highways; access to empowering education for a new global service economy. King knew, to be sure, that select black individuals might well achieve redounding fame. He realized as well that an ever-expanding black middle class would increasingly come to occupy profitably race-oriented, affirmative action jobs. Select citizens of the new black middle class would probably even find themselves in the media spotlight on a regular basis. But King, like many thousands gone, knew that "the race" at its majority level would reap virtually no benefit whatsoever from the luxurious homes, sleek cars, punctilious fashions, and media celebrity of a new black elite. And certainly, if any of this elite were ever to decide to vilify the black poor, distort the legacy of Civil Rights and Black Power in ahistorical writings and lectures, or put themselves shame-lessly at the service of those who "despitefully use" the black majority, what verdict could there be but *betrayal?* As a classic Langston Hughes quip has it: "I love Ralph Bunche. But I can't eat Ralph Bunche for lunch." The intel-lectual charisma, financial success, media revelry, and celebrity book sales of an elite black few does virtually nothing to feed the desires and needs of the black majority.

By the time of his assassination in Memphis, Dr. King had matured far, far beyond the mellifluous orator who delivered "I Have a Dream" at the National Mall. His philosophy, ideology, activist logistics, coalitional politics, and personal conviction had progressed. One reason King's soul and vision had to expand was to answer the instructive challenge to Civil Rights leader-ship that had been issued by Black Power. For, if one closely watches video records of the Memphis sanitation workers' strike, one sees fierce young black men in front of the television cameras. Their fists are clenched. They are shouting "Black Power!" By 1968 King had become not only a tacit ally of Black Power but also a powerful new model of the race man. The struggle for which King stood would come to mold him into a global black intellectual revolutionary. His assassination, then, was not simply a blow to black Ameri-can leadership. His murder marked (as we in our present weary, cynical, and leaderless time must know) a worldwide and enduring crisis. King's death brought a profound close to the global activist, public sphere intellectual la-bors of one of the most astutely committed race men to emerge from the ranks of Afro-America.

Still, America's collective memory of King captures only a reductive, freeze-frame, ahistorical notion of his life and labors. Willfully ignoring (or simply misreading) the expansive final years of his revolutionary shifts of consciousness, many Americans still envision King—like a closed video loop—forever speaking dream cadences at the National Mall. King's true legacy is far greater and far more progressive than this restrictive historical notion allows.

This book presents an extended and carefully articulated critique of the centrist and neoconservative texts and textual practices that have distorted Dr. King's brilliant black public intellectual legacy. In it I offer specific analyses of the works and words of orators, scholars, pundits, and writers who have, in my opinion, misread *race* and the lives of race men and race women. In the pages that follow, I insist that, in the first and final instances, the rhetoric, writings, and public personae of black centrist and neoconservative intellectuals have served profoundly to verify and confirm white America's betrayal of Dr. King's black intellectual legacy, as well as the larger polity's betrayal of the interests of the black majority to whom King granted unyielding allegiance. Black neoconservatives and centrists in their writings have been determined, it seems, to refuse to acknowledge the preeminence of "race" (at its black majority level) as the sine qua non of Dr. King's public life.

Like the dominant white culture, black neoconservatives and centrists claim that King's oration on the National Mall defined him as a man who assumed the ethical high ground and implicitly gave voice to a triumphal "antirace" American consciousness and agenda as prelude to a "nonracial" utopia. Something on the order of the following might characterize the disingenuous claims of black neoconservative and centrist intellectuals with respect to Dr. King's legacy: "Race is dead. Long live the King!" At best this is a mischaracterization of what Dr. King factually declared and achieved. King stood so firmly against a triumphal antiracial and utopian grain, in fact, that he was *not* invited to the White House with so-called race leaders on the day following the march on Washington. He was denied entrée because he was considered too militant—not a quiet, respectable, peaceful, and accommodating black presence fit for fruitful race relations in the United States. True to his calling as a genuine race man, after the march King left the nation's capital for Birmingham, Alabama, where he resumed his group work of bringing in the funk, bringing in the noise of black rebellion.

The archconservative hypothesis—that freeze-frame reduction of King's life to his dreamy moment at the Mall—is the utterly derivative ground for most black neoconservative and centrist intellectual denunciations, vilifications, and counterfactual accounts of Black Power in America. In the following pages this will become abundantly clear. But let me offer a brief word of explanation here.

Certain cadres of post–Civil Rights era black intellectuals characterize Black Power as sort of a dread serpent in the garden of interracial brotherhood they insist was the telos of King's dream. Frozen in his historical tracks, King is held by such latter-day black intellectuals to have shared no positive or affirming traffic whatsoever with this serpentine Black Power. Hence, Black Power—divorced by centrist and neoconservative fiat from Dr. King's actual historical alliance with and endorsement of major tenets of the movement during the final years of his life—is caricatured as a fanatical, alien black phoenix rising fiendishly from ashes of the "good Negro" martyr. Neoconservatives textually disinherit Black Power from all family resemblance to the work and thinking of Dr. King. This is the treacherous design of black and white men and women who wish ardently to preserve King in amber at the National Mall.

I feel it is critical at the outset of the present book to state that ideologically, intellectually, and fiscally the black public intellectuals whose texts are critiqued in the following pages are not sui generis. They did not miraculously emerge from the brow of an American Zeus with the serendipitous zing of Athena. No, they are not original in that way. The appearance of this cadre of black public intellectuals, in fact, can justly be read as epiphenomenal, secondary, and derivative. They are the paid by-products and black afterthinkers of American neoconservatism at large. A loosely scripted—but adamantly defended—body of ideas called "neoconservatism" achieved its most exalted status during the presidencies of Ronald Reagan and George Herbert Walker Bush. This neoconservatism (first named as such by the sociologist Michael Harrington in a linguistic act of derision) was christened in the 1970s. The ideational and cognitive congeries that make up neoconservatism represent a thick, murky admixture of belief in limited government, individual responsibility, penurious social services; correlated with frail social safety nets, neoliberal economics, empiricism (buttressed often by dry, retrogressive, rational positivism) in scholarship, universalism in axiology, an almost religious faith that magnetic corporate enterprise and profits should be attached to all human enterprise; and, finally, free market codes of ethical conduct that translate as "caveat *everybody*, because it is all about the money!"

Think tanks financed by the adherents and supporters of neoconservatism are indisputably the home bases and production sites for black public intellectuals such as Shelby Steele and John McWhorter. Their texts are analyzed in this book. Since I devote an entire chapter to American neoconservatism as a countercurrent to Civil Rights and Black Power in America, I will not elaborate further here. I do, however, want to add that Ivy League black centrist intellectuals are often indistinguishably proximate in their articulations to black neoconservatives.

Sponsorship of black centrist intellectuals and their texts proceeds primarily from an American academy that was, ironically, unequivocally altered and made amenable to black scholarly presence (and black monthly paychecks) by activist Black Power and black studies rebellion. With a less than surprising lack of charity, black centrists have served as the chief denigrators of both Black Power and black majority–oriented black studies. Black centrist intellectuals, that is to say, have ungenerously, and sometimes flamboyantly, orated and acted up against the very black hands that have fed them.

In this book I always ground my analyses in critical, rhetorical, cultural studies readings of actual texts published by the black intellectuals I critique. I base what I think are earned conclusions on the evidence of words and texts my subjects have themselves written, lent authorial signature to, allowed publicly to be marketed and distributed under their imprimatur. I am a confident, certified, and practiced reader and interpreter of textual argument, implicit textual values and implications, and the ever-varying significations of written words in their multiple contexts of reception. I thus have no scholarly reservations whatsoever at taking post–Civil Rights era black public intellectuals at their word.

I freely (and without the least bit of disciplinary hesitation) state that the present book is not bound by methodological protocols considered de rigueur by a number of putatively empirically based scholarly disciplines that have been vastly influential in the modern academic world. Neoconservatism gained more currency than it justifiably deserved through resort to regressions, correlations, and a certain social scientism that claimed empirical truth about "man" as its exclusive province. The quest for such confident disciplinary certainty traces back at least as far as Saint Simon, and it has produced quite impressive experimental, statistical, and observational protocols as bases for policy recommendations. Despite some recent critiques of the "sciences of man," the social sciences continue to offer solid modes for understanding contours of the worlds in which we exist. But, I am not a social scientist, nor was I meant to be. The analyses of the present book do draw upon social scientific observations, but they are not grounded in such practices.

Let me be clear, then: I have great respect for the best of the sciences of man. But I make no claim in my present analyses to findings equivalent to those of the great American father of sociology, W. E. B. Du Bois, in his statistical and Germanic profundity of on-the-ground research and causal speculation about modes and possibilities of black life in the United States.

I take heart, however, in the fact that while Dr. Du Bois is remembered and extolled for his empirical research, he is equally cherished for his skillful, analytical, creative, interpretive brilliance with respect to the sung, written, chanted, preached, moaned, and orated textual records of Afro-American life and culture. His most memorable writings were never simply a matter of superimposing methods grounded in limited Western conceptions of, say, "man," "human," "history," "society," and so on. That is precisely why, in my opinion, Du Bois's compeer James Weldon Johnson declared that the sage of Great Barrington created what never existed before: a *black* intelligentsia. One might note that Weldon Johnson's formulations had as much to do with Du Bois's mentorship of the textual creativity of the Harlem Renaissance as it did with his contributions to the modern advent and progress of the black social sciences.

I hope the analyses that occupy the following pages square in some good measure with the hermeneutical and poetically interpretive protocols of Dr. Du Bois. I buttress my arguments with ample references to and citations from the best sociological, historical, political science, and economics scholarship that has marked recent decades. I can find no textually based and expansively eloquent critique—empirically elaborated—in the social or political sciences of the betrayal effected by black centrist and black neoconservative intellectuals. Adolph Reed is a contemporary hero in this vein, and Harold Cruse is his more than fit predecessor. But during the past several years we have had titles such as *Yo' Mama's Disfunktional!* and *Nigger* as guiding lights in black history and Harvard law; they have scarcely been of comfort or analytical use to my present project.

I claim (I think fairly) that Dr. King's ultimate demands for world justice included (1) equality of results in matters of race relations, (2) reparations in the form of affirmative action and economic restitution for black Americans, and (3) unyielding commitment to anti-imperialism as well as opposition to U.S. Pax Americana campaigns for global supremacy. Even in the face of this historically verifiable, cogently articulated, courageously, and decidedly racially inflected agenda, black neoconservative and centrist intellectuals disarmingly argue that what Dr. King most ardently desired was *only* the promised potential of a "dream deferred" and happy interracial brotherhood located somewhere in a southern American promised land. I forgo ad hominem sensationalism, generalized condemnation, and scintillating innuendo where black neoconservatives and centrists are concerned. The following pages represent a rigorous, scholarly reading practice seasoned with wit. They are meant to garner urgent reader attention, reclaim a legacy, and inscribe my adamant *j'accuse* at an enormous betrayal of black liberation work in America. My best energies are always dedicated in the following pages to what we ideally all hold in common. By this I intend a strict dedication to textual evidence and a stern commitment to the best practices of the humanities as they have been pursued from the ancients to fortunate survivors and continuing scholars who now work in public concert against the well-financed and scarcely ethical offices of neoconservatism's continuing culture wars against the academy. The present book is my critique of those who have betrayed Dr. King's legacy. It is, I think, time they were "outed" as nostalgic, black, money-hungry reactionaries who are fully allied with the worst offices of white American power brokers, publishers, newspapers, media moguls, Internet magnates, and Ivy League universities that are, in any cultural capital and economics of the public sphere models of analysis, principally responsible for such intellectuals' esteem, wealth, and harm to the black majority.

ACKNOWLEDGMENTS

WHEN A BOOK IS years in the making, its author's indebtedness is epic. I envision legions. I know I shall never be able to do justice to the marvelous help I have received. But I shall do my best. Acknowledgments begin with those who were of invaluable assistance at the University of Pennsylvania. I was at Penn when the idea of the present book was born. My colleagues Manthia Diawara and Michael Awkward were the first and most generous scholars with whom I discussed the book's possible contours. I profited in the first stages of writing from the unfailingly brilliant support of Henrietta Stephens, my administrative assistant at the Center for the Study of Black Literature and Culture (CSBLAC). Ms. Stephens provided editorial suggestions. She patiently and with good humor processed endless drafts of my early chapters. Cathy Cooper and Aquanda Boone of CSBLAC were also instrumental in moving the book forward in the early stages. I profited often in Philadelphia from my scholarly conversations with Professors Marjorie Levinson, Margreta DeGrazia, and Wendy Steiner. Professor Eric Cheyfitz also read early drafts of several chapters and provided encouraging scholarly feedback. With astute assistance from Professors Wendy Steiner and John Richetti, I was granted leave to research the first phases of the book.

I have almost no words to describe the loyal and professional support of my agent Jane Dystel. She has been kind, steadfast, and stern in her advice through all phases of this project. Her associate Miriam Goderich has also been of remarkable assistance. Miriam offered splendid editorial guidance. Publishing today seldom blesses one with such invaluable agents.

Since a great part of the book's final labor was accomplished at Duke University, I have many to thank in Durham. I begin with my incomparable colleague Professor Priscilla Wald. Priscilla was unfailingly enthusiastic about the project from the moment I described it. She provided editorial assistance and good cheer with her usual generosity of spirit. Then, there were the brilliant, generous, and courteous graduate students that Priscilla and I had the good fortune to mentor at Duke. They were the heart and soul of the American Literary and Cultural Studies enterprise in Durham. Instrumental in making the present book better were Nicole Allewaert, Lauren Coats, Nihad Farooq, Erica Fretwell, Alexis Gumbs, Keith Jones, Bart Keeton, Vincent Nardizzi, and Eden Osucha. I have cited the contributions of Alexis Gumbs and Eden Osucha in the text itself. I must add here, though, that without the labors of Lauren Coats on *all* aspects of the project, this book would be but a shadow of its present self.

At Duke, my administrative assistant Lincoln Hancock was a superb master of the arts of editorial emendation and manuscript preparation. He read every word of various chapters (sometimes—with patient fortitude—more than once). He provided many a felicitous alternative to rough patches of my prose. Most importantly, he was a stalwart friend during trying times. It is truthful to say this book would not have been so well completed had it not been for Lincoln Hancock.

Through its various offices, Duke provided leave support and research funding to forward the work of the present book.

My abiding friends at Duke—those who always have and continue to encourage my scholarly and intellectually activist work—include Maureen Quilligan, Michael Malone, Ken Wissoker, Cathy Davidson, Richard Powell, and C. T. Woods-Powell. Life and survival at Duke would have been impossible without them.

A number of universities in the United States and abroad provided opportunities for me to present intellectual arguments and ideas from the book. Especially noteworthy are the hospitable occasions at various universities in Taiwan. I visited Taiwan at the invitation of its government, but that invitation was prompted by the efforts of my gracious colleague and friend Professor Yu-Chung Lee.

Thanks to the Fulbright Foundation and its fiftieth-anniversary initiative I was able to offer lectures and accounts of ideas from my book in progress at a number of intellectually exciting venues in Brazil.

In Portugal, the University of Coimbra was wonderfully welcoming and receptive to ideas and arguments critical to the shape and progress of my book.

In the United States, I remember with deep appreciation the invitation of President Joan Hinde Stewart of Hamilton College. She and her faculty made it possible for me to present a formal lecture on black neoconservative intellectuals in beautiful sunset light of one of the most impressive campus chapels I have ever entered.

I also enthusiastically thank Professor Carole Boyce-Davies of Florida International University. She graciously provided a forum for my ideas with an audience of African New World Studies faculty and students. Professor Heather Russell Andrade of Florida International University's faculty has been a staunch supporter and astute adviser on the form and argument of the book since that forum. Professor Andrade has, in generosity of time and intellect, been kind enough to read with deft critical attention a great portion of my manuscript in progress. Her advice has been invaluable.

Professors Mary Beth Rose, Stanley Fish, and Walter Michaels oversaw a fine presentational occasion for my ideas at the Institute for the Humanities located at the University of Illinois at Chicago.

The School of Criticism and Theory (SCT) and its fellows, in the vein of formal university hosts, offered several occasions for me to present formative ideas from my book. Professors Steven Nichols and Dominick LaCapra of SCT especially are to be thanked for providing space and time at their home institutions.

In the last instance, however, it is all about the sense of an ending. Without the magnificent endorsement, support, resources, and encouragement of Vanderbilt University, the present book would never have been completed. Certainly, it would never have come to a close in such an invigorating, collegial, academic environment. I thank Chancellor Gordon Gee, Provost Nicholas Zeppos, Dean Richard McCarty, and Chair of English Jay Clayton for bringing me on board as a faculty member at Vanderbilt. These kind souls have cleared leave time, provided generous research funding, and offered every encouragement for me to move through the book's final stages. As importantly, they have run magnificent interference for me against the everyday intrusions of the outside world. I have never before in my academic career been afforded the order of scholarly generosity and institutional courtesy characterizing my new Vanderbilt home.

The possibility of such a fine home began with my treasured and brilliant colleague Professor Dana Nelson. Professor Nelson and I were scholarly collaborators and visiting coeditors of *American Literature* at Duke in the late nineties. We have many common intellectual interests. When Professor Nelson took the initiative to forward my name for a Distinguished University Professorship at Vanderbilt, things happened efficiently and fast. I am well pleased with my life in the South and at Vanderbilt University. My hope is that Professor Nelson and I shall work together for many, many years on projects and issues that will advance the ethical, material, and intellectual lives of all Americans.

I am almost without adjectives to describe the resolute kindness, professional courtesy, scholarly acumen, and unfailing efficiency of Jennifer Crewe, my editor at Columbia University Press. In my estimation, Jennifer is one of the most remarkable people in publishing today. Her choice of Anne R. Gibbons as copy editor for the present project is proof in point.

I know that if I spent the remainder of my scholarly career attempting to devise adequate ways to thank my wife, Professor Charlotte Pierce-Baker—who is a tenured, full professor of women's and gender studies at Vanderbilt University and the redoubtable author of *Surviving the Silence: Black Women's Stories of Rape*—for her contributions to my intellectual and scholarly life, I would be unsuccessful. Charlotte is my first and best editor. She is my best friend. I would say so much more, but when Professor Pierce-Baker read my first draft of the present acknowledgments, she said: "Enough already!"

BETRAYAL

THE FIRST HOME I remember was in "Little Africa." Little Africa was in Louisville, Kentucky. It was a seemingly endless tangle of unpaved streets and makeshift houses isolated in the deep west end of the city. It was a bleak compound of blackness where white faces were as rare as unicorns. Everyone did some kind of work. But their jobs were usually under the radar of anything resembling a decent, living wage; jobs were part-time, nonunion, unregulated, one-shot seasonal, or domestic moneymakers. Paychecks and their nets were as unpredictable as English weather.

Little Africa was not cohesively working class in the manner of Allentown, Pennsylvania, during its boom years, or Brooklyn, New York, in its rags-to-riches American fantasy. There were not a lot of mythic success stories in our world. In Little Africa, "Give us, Lord, our daily bread" was not a summons for a heavenly handout, but an earnest, quotidian prayer for ten cents to purchase a loaf of Bond Bread from my family's store, Baker's Market.

Baker's Market was a solidly framed and brightly painted place—my mother and father had secured its title through sheer moxie. The store's previous (white) owner had grown tired of marginal profits and other downsides of conducting business in the ghetto. My father, with his solid business acumen and savvy ear to rounds of the black world, got an inside tip about the owner's dissatisfaction and acted on it.

My mother and father were among the select number of African Americans of their generation privileged to earn not only bachelors but also advanced graduate degrees. They were blessed and aided by the generous backing of my maternal grandparents in purchasing their first home and, I suspect, in their acquisition of Baker's Market. I did not know in my youth that we Bakers were differently gifted from the general population of Little Africa. To my young mind, my parents' bearing toward and relationship with their clientele offered no hint of class tension. Their avoidance of displays of assumed superiority made a great deal of sense. They knew that in segregated Louisville, Kentucky, there were few places where they could establish a successful black business. Little Africa was one such locale, and alienating customers through condescension would have been the most extreme folly. But in retrospect, I know my family's situation was markedly different from that of others in Little Africa. My parents, after all, *owned* the grocery store; they also had significant educational and business reserves to fall back on. Still, the fact that their ownership and business options in a segregated Louisville, Kentucky, were limited to the black ghetto made their advantages seem slightly more than window dressing in the defining economies of race and class in America—especially the American South.

We moved to Little Africa in 1951. I was eight years old. Our house (my first remembered home) was a one-story frame dwelling. It was only about seven hundred square feet, divided into four small bedrooms and one tiny bath. But it had electricity and ample insulation, and my older brother and I luxuriously shared one bedroom reserved for us. The house had been built by my maternal grandfather and a cousin. It was located just behind Baker's Market. Next door, my friend Dewy, who was a master of all things mechanical and thought up the best games, lived with his large family in a dilapidated structure lit by coal oil lamps and lacking indoor plumbing. To the rear, Mr. Johnson raised hogs in a small, grassy enclosure he referred to as his "stockyard." When breezes were mischievous, we shared more of Mr. Johnson's stockyard than we wished.

I knew the geography of Little Africa by scent and sense. I listened hour by hour and day by day to black people. I'm sure if someone dropped me off back in Little Africa today, I could still walk its geographies and share its storied textures with the bearing of a native. But we of Little Africa were "inside" a place that Louisville's ordinary white people knew was scarcely fit for dignified human habitation—not even close to an amply resourced American citizenship. Certainly any ordinary white citizen, after overcoming initial shock at the bleak mayhem of our lives, would have concluded we must have done something incomparably evil to deserve such a fate as to be in Little Africa. After all, there are so many who believe that the poor, as a result solely of their own deviance, will always be a burden to society. This seems to remain a conservative American conviction with respect to places like Little Africa.

Louisville's daily, segregated life (in combination with its saturate air of bourbon and tobacco) was a frightening whirr of bullies (both black and white) and soul-killing violence. I shuddered with dark premonition that I might—in the blink of a southern segregationist eye—be run over by something, shot by somebody, stopped and searched at random, punched squarely in the face for no reason. Irrational as those fears now seem, I suspect there was something in my subconscious apprehension of Little Africa that reinforced such trepidation. Even at that young age I knew that fear and trembling are not abnormal responses to the terrors of white supremacy: Jim Crow, colonial malfeasance, apartheid brutality. Inside Little Africa—locked within the black vale and veil of desolation—we learned lessons not only in humility, resistance, and holiness, but also the rudiments of a justified terror before the worst offenses of "whiteness" in America. Perhaps pioneering American frontier dwellers might have felt something akin to that fearful caution known to the denizens of Little Africa. Every prairie occasion in the Old West was, after all, a challenge to bizarre notions of a violent manhood; the frontier was bloodily exclusionary in its definitions of national citizenship and human well-being (ask the few remaining American Indians). I want to clear up one semantic notion at this point. There is no such thing as second-class citizenship. The phrase is a nonsense utterance. Either one is a citizen, or one is not. Exclusion is a flagrant denial of citizenship.

I know my youth in segregated Louisville scarred me in permanent ways—ways that contradict any kind of glibly disingenuous assertion that oppression leaves no permanent mark upon the oppressed. The psychological effect of white supremacy in the United States is irreversible, and, in my view, unforgivable. No late apologetics can erase mental terror and tangible scars. If not the mind, the body always remembers. Much like the Afro-American writer Richard Wright during his Mississippi youth, I lived childhood in a haze of anxiety, confusion, and dread. My early days were spent in a state of constant emergency. My spirit and imagination were enduringly under assault by white power in its myriad dimensions.

The abject struggle for daily bread in Little Africa was like flame to a tinderbox. It spawned frustration and produced an impulsive need to strike out at whatever was nearby, at hand. Everyone in the compound was, of course, black. Therefore, it was permanently the case that someone black seemed always ready in my youth to maim, cut, shoot, or mutilate some *other* black one, equally desperate, locked in the cell of Little Africa's labyrinth of misery. Frantz Fanon speaks of the "native" who tolerates from dawn to dusk white superiority and abuse, but then, in the shantytown black bar after dark reacts with unmeasured violence against a fellow black for the most trivial of offenses. Fanon is concerned with the psychology of such black violence. Economically, one might be compelled to ask: Where can the native vent his rage and hope to stay alive but in a place like Little Africa? White supremacy contains native violence in its own compounds by killing natives or locking them away—permanently.

Baker's Market was one of the few commercial establishments that broke the winding networks of unpaved roads and derelict houses in Little Africa. Lights were almost always on; windows shone with neon Pabst Blue Ribbon and Falls City signs casting deep blue and sharp red into the night. The store stayed open late on weekends (especially payday Fridays and "out to play" Saturdays) and it boasted one of the few pay phones within a mile radius.

Bloodied warriors of segregated life in America, with blood-dripping hands, heads, arms, and faces swathed in tattered towels and bundled rags often swept into the store, making a beeline to the pay phone. They dialed the police (infrequently), an ambulance (out of unequivocal necessity), or a loved one (most frequently) to come and help them out. I remember my cousin Raymond—the man who helped build our house in Little Africa—leaping over the counter on one occasion, tearing off his apron, tying it around the hemorrhaging arm of an improbably large brown man who seemed utterly astonished that someone had bested him in a brawl at Dixon's Tavern. Dixon's was a mile or so up the road from our store. Surely its owner's business world was as dramatically marked by violence as my family's.

Less bloody, but no less harrowing, were the stories of white violence that flew into the store on the lips of black men, women, and children who had journeyed outside into the white city. Being called "Nigger!" was common, as though such wounding hate speech was an acceptable way to treat human beings. Being bloodied by rocks and bottles hurled from the cars of whites, or roundly told to get their "nigger brats" out of the waiting rooms of General Hospital or Union Station were the tales blacks frequently recounted in Baker's Market. There were stories, as well, of deeply uncaring white absentee violence. As I turned the labels of canned goods to the front of shelves in the market, I often heard: "They cut off my phone, my lights, *and* my water . . . just because I missed one damn bill!" The reply in support: "I know what you mean, man . . . 'cause my wages done been garnished." And then with a sigh of weary resignation from another: "Just 'cause I couldn't pay that no-good bloodsucker his rent for February, he put us out! Damn!" Little Africa was plagued by the violence of American white supremacist economic uncaring. And it was not spare in its tales of the resulting wounds to the black body and spirit. It resonantly told its stories to my youth. In black gospel lore, the return upon such economic uncaring rings melodiously forth: "I'm a'gonna tell about how you treat me one of these days!" And I shall.

Misery, bloodshed, poverty, despair, and violence were staples of the Little Africa residents who frequented Baker's Market, and of the community as a whole. I did not learn to love black life under segregation in Louisville, Kentucky. No, I did not. I developed a bizarre and incurable form of black American agoraphobia, a deep and lasting anxiety and distrust of outside American spaces.

In addition to compounding the normal anxieties of childhood, my youth in Little Africa left me challenged with respect to the ethics and economics of inside and outside in America. "Home"—the house my grandfather and cousin Raymond built—was, like all the bleak territory that encased it, *inside*. But this home was always and ever in the midst of impoverished, bloody isolation caused, maintained, and condoned by the white Louisvillians *outside*. Louisville knowingly imprisoned and violently subjugated Little Africa. And the black elders of Little Africa knew that in the streets of the white city it was always open season on the black body.

The spatial disorientation and anxiety that resulted from my Little Africa days were, and remain, a twin discomfort. I developed acute claustrophobia. To this day I have a strong aversion to cramped spaces like those that nearly destroyed my youth. But I am even more terrified by the literal, material, open ground of white enemy territory. The lights of the global white city are never out; its killing fields and hypocritical apologias from white men and blacks seeking profit are of the most fearful wattage.

The irremediable, indelibly etched bleakness of Little African geographies is not, of course, the whole story. Against the anxiety, disorientation, violence, and isolation ordered and accepted by the white city, there were black counterforces. Later in life—during the powerfully racial, nationalistic days of the

Civil Rights and Black Power movements—I would learn to call such forces *black community*. Shorn of the militant posturing and extremist rhetoric that in recent decades has made the phrase "black community" party to charges of "romanticism," "nostalgia," "inept analysis," or simply "fantasy," the term "black community" for me still carries resonances of an underground, profoundly resistive current of black life. This current runs through collective assemblies of black America from 1619 to the present.

In Little Africa this current was amplified in rousing church moments; it swirled and eddied in conversations of the informal economies of makeshift black nail and hair salons and home-based black barbershops. It showed its economic savvy in the underground economy of goods that had somehow "fallen off of trucks." In sickness, it came forward as a conjuring doctor of homemade medicine, herbal remedies, and plain old prayer. I recall in my youth a tobacco-chewing wise man placing a wad of chaw on my fresh wasp sting. I knew no pain that evening. Vernacular healing. My parents thanked him with more than a loaf of Bond Bread. Just beyond the lights of the white city, in the vale of Little Africa, there flows a river of black community, resistance, and repudiation. I heard a tired black man who had spent a day laborer's sixteen hours on the outside declare to my parents in the store's soft glow at closing: "I would rather be a black fireplug in Little Africa, Mrs. Baker, than the white mayor of this whole damn town!"

Tapping into the spirit of black community self-help and informal economic networks of subsistence and resistance (witness Mr. Johnson's hogs) my parents were never absent with respect to black community. My mother was merchant, vendor, counselor, and scribe for customers who wanted to make contact with cousins in Detroit. She bought dresses, shirts, pants, blouses, underwear, and shoes from the white city and sold them at discounted prices to Little African patrons who shopped our store. ("I had to charge them something," she said to me in her later years, "or they wouldn't have taken them—they did not want charity.") She lent money to residents to take their children outside to the General Hospital or in search of employment. I have written elsewhere of a moment in which two of Little Africa's residents were on the steps of Baker's Market eating lunch. One of them said: " Praise God! He saw us through an awful winter!" His companion responded: "You mean praise Mrs. Baker. She's the one who brought me and my family through. She gave us *credit*." Even now, the phrase "she gave us credit" seems a stern black community rebuke to the comfortably well off, condescending black men and women who refuse to give the black majority any credit whatsoever. And here, because the phrase is a staple of the present book, I offer my definition of the "black majority."

By the black majority I intend to signal those populations of African, African American, Negro, and colored descent in the United States who inhabit the most wretched states, spaces, and places of our national geography. I mean those who live in census tracks where more than 40 percent of the population exists at or beneath the poverty line and unemployment is rampant. I call to mind and keep in the forefront of concern those black men, women, and children who have little hope of bettering their life chances through any simply (perhaps even "plausibly") available means, from laboring at jobs with inhumanely low minimum wage pay or bare subsistence day-to-day combat with what vestiges remain of an American security net. The black majority is the almost inevitably exposed, severely policed, desperately underresourced contingent of the African American population currently resident in the United States. The black majority is indubitably *the* majority of Afro-America at the present time. For we must also bring to the forefront as part of that majority, those black families of four who are considered by the census middle class when their annual, pretax income is as modest as fifty thousand dollars. This modest-income-defined black middle class, in fact, draws the interests of the black majority squarely into accord with American constituencies that are not of color. Which is to say, middle-class whites who once endorsed and actually were able to live the American dream have found themselves nearly completely abandoned—if not literally dispossessed—by the policies of the conservative federal plutocracy that has ruled the United States for the past three decades. Hence, the black middle class is—to paraphrase an observation by Richard Wright—"America's metaphor." Wright averred that as the black majority goes, so goes the nation. There is, therefore, much at stake in attending to the interests and committing oneself to the enablement of the black majority. In a sense, one can surely say those who fail the black majority at the present time are unequivocally in league with the ruling white elites who have destroyed not only the middle class but also so much more that is fundamental to the founding ideals of our nation.

What "community" means against the backdrop of the physical, mental, spatial, and emotional deprivation that marks black life in America is, I think, stark necessity, brilliant ingenuity, compelling imagination, unimaginable fortitude, and stern commitment to ideals forged in the fire of chattel slavery and Jim Crow's unforgivable inhumanity. My mother was my own first instructor in community. She was the model and exemplar. My father was but a hair's breadth behind.

As a businessman, my father naturally wanted to make a profit. The reason he thought he would fare better than the white owner from whom he purchased the store in Little Africa was that he was actually going to live (and persuade his wife and family to live) in the locale from which his profits derived. (A kind of *Lincoln Heights* precursor was he.) His first step was to have our family home built behind the store. No absenteeism would do for my father. Second, my father viewed Baker's Market as a critical resource for a black community blighted by neglect. He was an "uplift" disciple of Booker T. Washington's heroic Tuskegee dispensations, focused in his own way on black people farthest down. "Always speak to people," he instructed my older brother and me. "Everyone deserves your respect." And he was true to his teaching words. He brought some pretty bizarre and terribly inefficient black men and women into our family life in the name of race and respect. Like "Don," the self-styled down-on-his-luck black plumber who left Baker's Market flooded one cold weekend long ago. There were handymen who commenced repairs with less-than-substantial materials, disappeared for weeks on end, then miraculously reappeared to finish a job and collect their pay.

What I remember of my father's doctrines remains both practical and indelibly inscribed. One day as I made my way on foot to the black insurance company offices where he worked in Louisville, I encountered a shabbily dressed black man, holes in his shoes, reeking of alcohol. He caught my eye. "How are you?" I saluted his quizzical stare.

"Ain't you Mr. Baker's boy?"

I was surprised. What to do? I said nothing.

"You look just like him."

I fumbled about for what to say.

"Your father is one of the best people in this world. You spoke to me. You polite just like him. You got any spare change?"

I had a dime. I gave it to him with what I now consider filial responsibility.

To be known in the public world of the black majority as a "good man"— as my father was—can be a lifetime goal and calling. My father was, thus, important not only to me, but also to the flow of that resistive current of Little African community. Little Africa needed men like my father who knew how to secure money for and to build a health care facility like the "colored" Red Cross Hospital in Louisville, Kentucky. Red Cross Hospital was a credit to the black majority. I imagine my father always nodding "yes" to the query, "Mr. Baker, can you spare a dime?" I know my father as a race man. I know my mother as a race woman. Together they built and lived and worked among the black majority.

In black American life and culture a race man or race woman is one who dedicates his or her life and work to countering the lies, ideological evasions, and pretensions to "innocence" and "equal justice for all" that prop up America's deeply embedded, systemic, and institutionalized racism. Race men and race women (which I consolidate, and at the same time, I think, usefully expand to the term "race people") seek remedy for harms to the black body caused by the gospel and practice of white supremacy. Race people contest an ideologically inspired and profit-hungry white power structure that still maintains and reaps scandalous billions of dollars from a traffic in and enslavement of black bodies in the Americas. (Today's slavery is disguised as criminal justice in the form of a vast American private prison-industrial complex.) Race people model themselves as sharers of a culture, cause, and community held to be of African descent and labeled variously "African," "colored," "Negro," "black," "Afro-American," "African American." These are the selfsame people the precociously brilliant poet-essayist Amiri Baraka hailed as "blues people." Often patterning their labors after biblical prophets, race people commit themselves to a mobile, resounding, fierce redefinition of the state of race and the race in a troubled American nation. They do this in the very face of race's most brutal exclusions. When they are granted or when they secure public voice, they use their forum to advocate the interests of what they define as "their race" at its majority level.

Select black individuals may achieve fame—and a growing black middle class may work profitably at race-oriented and affirmative action–induced jobs. Elite blacks may even find themselves subjects for glossy, high-end magazines such as *Ebony*, *Sports Illustrated*, and *Essence*. But to state the unequivocal once again, the race reaps virtually no benefit from the bling of a black celebrity "elite" that is often more damning in its condemnation of the black American majority than white America at large. Where the majority is concerned, any real (consumable) public gains or advancement in America must provide nourishment for all; there must be a collective harvest. The life and legacy of Dr. Martin Luther King Jr. are rich in acknowledged commitment to the advance of the race as a whole, as well as to race as a valued and valuable category for the analysis of American life and history.

Little Africa and the incumbencies of my parents as race people thus open this book. This is autobiography, and I feel obliged to note that one advance reader of this manuscript asked, "What has Little Africa got to do with anything that follows in the book?" By way of answer I suggest that the most adept analytical traditions of black intellectual critique in America often privilege autobiography. Autobiography in black American intellectual traditions has always assumed a huge burden of evidence and carried a special explanatory power with respect to race and community. Autobiography has been a mainstay of black critical memory from time immemorial, manifesting a preservative reverence for verifiable historical facts as they have been filtered through the alembic of personal consciousness and conscience. In the black world, the self-story has served as self-defense against white supremacy's claims to know, statistically regulate, and police who precisely we are, and where we must live. It is this autobiographical tradition of memory, self-defense, and critique that I invoke with word of Little Africa. When I use the phrase "black majority," I refer to those globally ghettoized in Little Africas that are subservient always to interests of white power. Here is what the famous Kerner Commission, charged with investigating causes of urban rioting and black community disorder in the 1960s concluded: "What white Americans have never fully understood—but what the Negro can never forget—is that white society is deeply implicated in the ghetto. White institutions created it, white institutions maintain it, and white society condones it."[1] This statement of fact is a capsule account of what I have called an outside relentlessly pushing the black world into Little Africa. And I believe it is most effectively self-story—black autobiographical critique—that evidences and provides witness with respect to the subordinating effects of white supremacy in the creation, and condoning, of Little Africa. This is, in part, my answer to the query: What has Little Africa (by which I take my interlocutor to mean *autobiography*) got to do with anything that follows in the book?

Now certainly, autobiography in itself does not guarantee analytical adequacy. That is to say, it is always problematic to base one's claims of critical accuracy exclusively on the evidence of one's own life. Even the most intellectually astute partisans of the self-story have expressed reservations: "Autobiographies ... assume too much or too little: too much in assuming that one's own life has greatly influenced the world; too little in the reticences, repressions and distortions which come because men do not dare to be absolutely frank." W.E.B. Du Bois wrote these words. In *Dusk of Dawn: An Essay Toward an Autobiography of a Race Concept* he insists his life is not significant in itself, but only insofar as it is part of a "problem": the great global ignominy of the subordination of the "darker races of the world" by the lighter ones. Despite his autobiographical caveat, however, Du Bois resolutely situates his thoughts, speculations, analyses, reflections, and conclusions within a *personal* field of experience. In fairness, one must note that the sage of Great Barrington—as others were wont to label Du Bois—self-consciously refused to be reticent about men, events, ideas, theories, and crises that were decidedly outside his youthful ken. What most distinguishes Du Bois's autobiographical scholarly labors in many instances is his candid admission that only time, scholarly labor, and fortune brought him an awareness of who precisely he was as a personal self. In a sense, then, Du Bois acknowledges that the personal-autobiographical is always after the fact and *avant la lettre.* The alchemy and attraction of autobiography as a platform for critique, that is to say, consists not so much in claims for a special knowing that accrues to the writer simply from his living in the welter of the world. The real gold standard and most useful autobiographical critique, Du Bois seems to hold, results from the catalytic combination of personal recall and scholarly endeavor. The personal really only becomes effectively political or critical through disinterested study. Therefore, it does not make much sense from a Du Boisian perspective for a writer to assert, "I know it because I lived it." Living is not enough. We come fully to possess our rounded personal histories only through the play of the intellect and imagination over the wisdom and witness of the world.[2]

I summon Du Bois here because his analysis and demonstration of the virtues and liabilities of autobiographical critique are nonpareil. Hence, I take Du Bois's cautions seriously. I do not commence the present project with memories of Little Africa to claim some special existential knowledge based on personal experience alone. Rather, I invoke the world of my first personal memory as a metonym for certain registers of majority life whose significance it has taken me years to understand. World forces did in fact condition the bleakness of black life in the quarter of the "Negro" in Louisville, Kentucky. And I have spent almost half a century brooding over the men, theories, ideas, and events that, in effect, created *all* the Little Africas of the globe. I have indisputably learned that the significance of my life does not lie in some mythological ideal of rugged individualism or stout fantasy of self-reliance. No, the personal in my case is clearly a function of parents who seized the temper of a collective black American consciousness and instilled in their children allegiance not to self but to the interests of the black majority.

Only through time did I come to realize the global nature of that majority as it derived from a brutal trade in African bodies and a torturous course of white Western colonization across continents of the world. The horrors of the trade and colonization are difficult matters to think through, so burdensome in their genealogical weight and murderous implications that it is exceedingly difficult to understand how any informed intellect can suggest that such matters of horror and trauma can simply be swept out of memory, eradicated by court decisions, or transcended through chest-thumping scenarios of self-reliance. I hope that I have been successful during my years of study in correcting some of my inevitable (after-the-fact) blind spots. I hope, too, that I will in future always shy away from excessive praise of the black majority's creative, conservative Christian forbearance of white supremacy's heel in its face, while at the same time railing at the "abominations" of, say, rap music and gay marriage. Moreover, I believe it is baldly materialistic when so-called black public intellectuals such as John McWhorter and Shelby Steele titillate black and white middle-class audiences by fulminating against the badness of this same, sometimes-too-conservative black majority for its failures of group responsibility regarding youth illiteracy and teenage pregnancies. Attacking the abject of the earth is seedy business. In today's world it is an aberrant form of postmodern Mrs. Grundyism. Mrs. Grundy is, of course, the bluenose, priggish, conventional character in Thomas Morton's *Speed the Plough*. Her progeny are legion, having within recent days come to life in the person of comedian Bill Cosby and journalist Juan Williams, who both have viciously attacked the badness of the black majority while never uttering a mumblin' word against a morally indifferent white America that kills everyone randomly while softly hip-hopping to *our* songs. Cosby and Williams are neoconservative poseurs, willful in abetting the wounds and scars of Little Africa, seeking to make over its terror-filled past.[3]

Injunction number one of autobiographical critique, therefore, is asserting personal experience as factual verification for ideological preferences and profits always leaves the black majority in misery. One has to study and strive as rigorously as possible to provide accounts—beyond the personal—of social, economic, psychological, and historical fields of men, theories, and ideas that condition the abjection of the black majority before offering any critique whatsoever. Only then can one arrive at a conclusion about the vast, "colored," and subordinated populations of the world. The irony and horror of present-day America is that in the domain of the so-called black public intellectual, a comedian—whose EdD came out of a scandal-filled University of Massachusetts School of Education, literally selling doctorates—and his journalistic "Bundini Brown" are as likely to gain approval from the *New York Times* best seller list as real scholars.[4]

As I begin the present project devoted to the black public intellectual, I know that I am a black, southern-born scholar whose parents were fiercely black and middle class. They were decidedly respectable in their educational aspirations and attainments. And they were—as a result of their birth to working-class parents with little formal education—reared in compassion for and implicit alliance with the black majority. They never lost their natal bearing with respect to a black-majority mission. They were property and business owners (i.e., Baker's Market) among a too-large population of too-poor black people. However, the significant facts of what might be called "class" in Little Africa were not matters of rich and poor, privileged and deprived. Superseding such demarcations was the inescapable reality that we were all subordinates. We were segregated blacks who were segregated *because* we were black. We were restricted in our movements, rights, life expectancy, and choices—even in our choice of dreams and desires—by bedrock, all pervasive, Jim Crow segregation. We were not second-class citizens.

Separated and unequal, rejected and vilified by everything white and public outside the physical and psychological borders of Little Africa, my black parents were compelled to formulate economic strategies to keep us warm, fed, clothed. They had to strive creatively to keep us from acquiescing to degraded black caricatures of our humanity—the wide-mouthed minstrels, lascivious and lazy Sambos beloved by the white supremacy of Louisville's ruling class. In quiet hours of our parents' scenes of instruction, they worked to give us at least some semblance of a dream of empowered black citizenship that would carry all of Little Africa beyond dirt roads, drafty and nonelectrified houses, and uncertain incomes. Until such a future became a reality, we knew that we Bakers would share a state of blackness with those with whom we were deeply conjoined in the everyday life of Little Africa. Our destiny was a common one.

I came to sense in my growing up years—although it has taken me time and study and meditation and agony and reflection and theorizing to know it—that the terrorizing habitus of systemic, structural, racial segregation known as Little Africa was a pure function of enduring white supremacy. The reality that marked Little Africa's denigration has not disappeared. Today, it reveals itself as neoliberalism, globalization, structural adjustment, analytical nonracial cosmopolitanism, residential and social confinement of the black majority to unresourced zones of exclusion, and a booming private prison-industrial complex in the United States.

Only the texture of hopelessness, violence, fear, and despair occasioned by white supremacy can make comprehensible the confusion, anxiety, dread, and acute disdain for those who "bring the pain" characterizing the life and psyche of the black majority. A few years ago, I team-taught a law school course at the University of Pennsylvania. Arguably the most brilliant student among the twenty-five enrolled was a young woman who identified as African American. She concluded an essay on the fate white supremacy should meet in the consciousness of America: "I will never forgive them. They are unforgivable. I will never, never forgive them. I will never forgive what was done and continues to be done in the name of white supremacy. Such horror of violent subordination has not ended. It is ongoing, and it remains *unforgivable*. There is *nothing* they can do to persuade me to forgive them." In Little Africas of the globe, almost nothing prepares even the third and fourth generation's black majority to adopt a gospel of felt forgiveness.

I wanted out of Little Africa. And in my youthful imagination and despite my parents' ministrations there seemed no way out but death. After study and luck and serendipitous supportive scholarly collaborators and friends, I came to know that mine was an extensional fear (no, not an *existential* fear) that had causes. It was the impure result of the systemic, administrative, municipal, social, ideological, and legal commitments of Louisville's ruling white fathers to white supremacy. In its first terror, however, mine was a textured and disabling fear. It was, perhaps, party to the same affective intellectual economies of my law school student's response to white supremacy.

Only luck saved me—the good fortune to be born to strong-willed, able-bodied parents who coaxed and persuaded and guided me to study. I completely understand that my parents' survival and perseverance were due as much to fortune and luck as to any protocol of American rugged individualism and moralizing self-reliance. It was my parents who officially taught me that the only ethically responsible mantra to be recited by a black man in the face of black abjection in America is "There but for the grace of God go I."

My autobiographical "truth" is that Little Africa created in me the unshakable conviction that people in power will always employ their fullest arsenal to bring about the social debasement, and actual deaths, of those they consider inferior, uncivilized, barbaric, or simply nonusable. Further, I have, through study, realized that structural relations of lordship and bondage are always meant to produce and eternally reproduce paralyzing fear. This fear is overcome only at great cost to the human spirit. It requires a mighty summons from a mighty person or an uncannily diverse coalition to engender the courage to overcome fear. Only such courage can, in turn, forge exit signs from Little Africa and map the course toward a fully resourced black American citizenship. Dr. Martin Luther King Jr. has best exemplified such courage, coalition, and cartography in our time. If W. E. B. Du Bois laid down in his writings a program for autobiographical critique and informed talk for the liberation of Little Africa, then certainly it was Dr. Martin Luther King Jr. who, in harmony with the black majority, mapped the committed public intellectual walk to be marched beyond global black abjection. Dr. King's life and work offer a model of the black public intellectual that represents the best that has been thought, said, and accomplished in the black world. I believe many present-day, post–Civil Rights era black public intellectuals have betrayed Dr. King's legacy. But I do not proclaim this belief simply on the basis of personal experience or autobiographical anecdote. I first reexamine the life, labors, and accomplishments of Dr. King and then survey how succeeding generations of black public intellectuals have told their story with respect to the black majority. My hypothesis is that post–Civil Rights era black public intellectuals have been far more interested in serving as self-promoters than as thinkers committed to black majority interests. Much of what they have proclaimed, postulated, and published of their personal deliberations on the great problem of race, particularly race in the contemporary United States, has been profitably tailored to the tastes of conservative black and white audiences. But, of course, it does no good for me simply to state that in my opinion or based on what I have lived, this is the case. It is necessary to take matters fully and analytically in hand and make the case through autobiographical critique duly informed by study and close attention to the men, events, and proffered ideas of the past nearly half century of black intellectual endeavor and black majority interests in our land. The story I have to tell begins with a black man behind bars.

BULL CONNOR WAS IN a quandary. On Good
Friday, 1963, Dr. Martin Luther King Jr. planned
to get himself arrested.

As public safety commissioner, the last thing
Connor wanted was Easter drama. The Bull
had been hoping the Birmingham Civil Rights
campaign would soon dissipate. Project C, as it
was called (for "confrontation") was off to a slow
start, despite its aggressive name. But if Dr. King
were arrested tensions might quickly escalate.

Connor's hope for a quiet end to the campaign was not idle. Despite the fire and evangelical passion of Reverend Fred Shuttlesworth—
the pastor of Birmingham's Sixteenth Street
Baptist Church who had summoned King and
the Southern Christian Leadership Conference
to town—things were not going well for black
folks. A voter registration drive had limped
to a halt. Boycotts of white merchants had
achieved very limited success. Calls for marches
and demonstrations were barely heeded by the
city's black residents. (On one occasion Andrew
Young pleaded with a congregation for an hour
before securing seven volunteers to join a protest
at the downtown courthouse.) But the greatest
setback for the Birmingham campaign was that
there had been far too few public arrests.

Seven years earlier, and one hundred miles
south of Birmingham, a forty-two-year-old
seamstress named Rosa Parks unwittingly demonstrated the impact the public arrest of a black
person could carry. Refusing to give up her seat
in the white section of a Montgomery, Alabama,
bus, Mrs. Parks was taken to the county courthouse, fingerprinted, and jailed. As King would
later put it, the Zeitgeist had tracked her down.[1]
Rosa Parks's arrest galvanized black Montgom-

JAIL

SOUTHERN

DETENTION

TO GLOBAL

LIBERATION

I would rather be in jail ten years
than desert my people now. I have
begun the struggle, and I cant turn
back. I have reached the point of
no return.

MARTIN LUTHER KING JR.
1956

A prison sentence is usually regarded as a mark of shame. But
to Southern Negroes fighting for
freedom, going to jail is a badge
of honor. The State of Alabama is
planning to so honor me—for as
many years as it can. However, I do
not view my coming trial for "per-
jury" in any narrow, personal way. It
is clearly part of the total pattern of
Reaction—the result of a deliberate
plan to harass, destroy and eliminate *all* who strike out for freedom
with any degree of effectiveness.

MARTIN LUTHER KING JR.
April 24, 1960

ery, inspired a massive boycott, and gave birth to the Montgomery Improvement Association (MIA). Dr. Martin Luther King Jr., a handsome, academically trained young minister with a steely baritone, was chosen to lead both the boycott and the MIA. At the time, he was twenty-five years old.

When King and his family took up residence in Montgomery, he really only intended to continue the work of his soul as the new pastor of Dexter Avenue Baptist Church. As the black bourgeois son of four generations of respected Georgia Baptist ministers, he never imagined he would follow the course of Rosa Parks and soon find himself arrested and in jail.

But less than a year and a half after he arrived in Montgomery, King was arrested, allegedly for driving 30 in a 25 mph zone. Terrified that the cops were taking him to be lynched, King was actually relieved after a long, rambling ride to arrive at the Montgomery jail, where he was handcuffed, fingerprinted, booked, and delivered to a shoddy cell: "Men lying on hard wood slats, and others resting on cots with torn-up mattresses. The toilet was in one corner of the cell without semblance of an enclosure."[2] Police released King the same night when an angry crowd gathered outside the jailhouse.

Then, in February of that same year (1956), King was indicted along with eighty-eight other chiefs of the MIA for conspiracy to interfere with lawful businesses. The eighty-nine black men elected voluntarily to turn themselves in. Chaos erupted at the Montgomery Courthouse; the city had never witnessed such fearlessness and defiance from its black citizenry. Brilliantly, it was not an act of civil disobedience but this mass civil *obedience* that set the storm in motion in Alabama. As historian Stewart Burns put it, by freely submitting to arrest the MIA leaders showed "the world, not least their own children and grandchildren, that they were no longer terrified of the white man's jail. They were cleansing the forbidding gray courthouse of its corrosive evil ... discharging its demonic spirits, freeing its ghosts from suffering. Those who were there that day would never again see the courthouse, or themselves, in the same way."[3]

Following Rosa Parks's arrest and jailing, thousands of Montgomery blacks had turned out to hear their religious leaders pass judgment on the Jim Crow system that put Parks behind bars. So when the eighty-nine MIA leaders only two months later voluntarily submitted themselves to the authorities, Montgomery blacks were jubilant. They committed to boycott, pray, work, and walk for equality until *all* the city buses were desegregated and fairness and equal treatment under law were achieved.

With their minds set on freedom, blacks in Montgomery performed direct acts of civil disobedience in the name of justice. Getting arrested and taken to jail became itself a key part of the Civil Rights strategy. It was a shrewd, courageous, and dramatic tactic. Black men and women laying their bodies on the line for freedom—undoubtedly a newsworthy spectacle in the nascent TV age. Evening newscasts soon placed the Civil Rights movement at the epicenter of the tumultuous TV landscape, right alongside the Kennedy-Nixon debates and the peace movement against the war in Vietnam. The televised arrest and jailing of black people was the stuff of morality's best theater.

The spectacular image of black citizens being cuffed and thrown in the slammer was easy to read in moral, ethical, and religious ways. The drama was born from a cast of uniformed, club-wielding, gun-toting, jack-booted Jim Crow white supremacists brutally assaulting prayerful, nonviolent, neatly dressed black men and women offering little to no resistance. Merciless white evil was pitted against compassionate black good. And jail was the symbolic place of exclusion; it was owned and overseen by Jim Crow. *Jail* and *hell* folded into a single moral and political location. For many Americans, Jim Crow jails brought to mind the archetypal southern redneck sheriff and his domain: flaming cells of southern horror.

In all this, Martin Luther King Jr. quickly became a national celebrity. The countless arrests, the constant clashes between the white authorities and the emboldened black masses drew national and international media attention to the MIA and the Montgomery bus boycott. King was named *Time* magazine's Man of the Year in 1957. By the time he appeared on the cover, the Civil Rights Movement in the United States was an international emblem of morally grounded and religiously inspired resistance to oppression. The success of black citizens in Montgomery—and the recognition accorded to King—left the city's white leadership and public safety establishment looking precisely like the bigoted, inept, egotistical segregationists they were.

Just to the north, however Theophilus Eugene "Bull" Connor (his nickname was earned for his raucous sportscaster's voice and propensity for shooting the bull) learned a good lesson from the Civil Rights tactics employed in Montgomery. The Bull would be patient, shrewd, and polite (like Albany, Georgia's, sheriff Laurie Pritchett). Birmingham's law enforcement would not make Montgomery's mistake of open, dramatic, TV-worthy confrontation.

In Georgia, Sheriff Laurie Pritchett had responded to nonviolent, direct-action Civil Rights protests with southern charm—he would elaborately doff his hat and address black demonstrators in a genteel fashion. *Then* he'd arrest them. By acting civilly, Pritchett's police department provided few photo-ops and scant spectacle for TV. The cameras stayed away. And without national media attention, the Albany Civil Rights campaign couldn't gain any traction. Sheriff Pritchett headed on over to Birmingham to instruct Bull Connor.

The critical difference between Birmingham and Albany, however, was that Dr. King had settled into Birmingham for the long haul. (In Albany, King just swept through, rallied the troops to action, and moved on.) Still, during Easter week in Birmingham in 1963, King was mighty discouraged. Civil rights leaders were at each other's throats; internal politics and competition for the front seat were escalating; and, worst of all, no mass support seemed forthcoming from the black citizenry. It was a "movement" in name only.

Further complicating matters, key members of the Birmingham black community were strongly opposed to disturbing the status quo. Arthur G. Gaston, the city's only black millionaire, admitted he "didn't want to go against the good white folks in Birmingham."[4] Funds for the struggle were scarce, and black folks in general were terrified of the consequences of resistance. They knew all too well what racist whites in Alabama were capable of when it came to retribution. (Birmingham's nickname among blacks was "Bombingham.")

King soon realized that only a real crisis would motivate blacks in Birmingham. It would take something serious to stir the passions of the masses. And without that vital black energy and mass participation, the Birmingham campaign was doomed. The status quo would prevail. Bull would win the day.

So, on the evening of April 10, at the Saint James AME church, King spoke to a mass meeting: "We are not here to do something for you, but to do something with you. . . . Everyone in the movement must live a sacrificial life." King would lead a march to confront the Birmingham authorities. "I can't think of a better day than Good Friday for a move for freedom."[5] Bull Connor's cops had bugged the event and caught wind of King's plan. Immediately Connor sought and secured a temporary injunction banning any public demonstrations or marches in Birmingham.

Learning of the injunction the next day, King was not deterred. "I am prepared to go to jail and stay as long as necessary," he proclaimed.[6] This was pitch-perfect drama, and it finally caught the media's eye, landing the Birmingham Movement on the front page of the *New York Times*. Behind the scenes, however, SCLC's advisers pleaded with King not to defy the ban. They needed him as a fund-raiser and organizer, not a prisoner—they were running out of money and could not afford to post bail for any more protestors.

On this Good Friday the stakes were high. But Martin Luther King was resolved. The march was on.

And so, on Friday afternoon, a small group of marchers departed from Zion Hill Baptist Church. Ralph Abernathy and Martin Luther King Jr. were in the lead. The column of fifty or so walked past Kelly Ingram Park— the boundary between black and white Birmingham—and headed toward downtown. Connor was waiting with a blockade of cops and their paddy wagons. The column of marchers made an impromptu turn to avoid the roadblock, but police on motorcycles soon caught up with them. King and Abernathy fell on their knees to pray. Stewart Burns describes the frantic scene: "Burly cops grabbed each preacher by his shirt back and shoved them roughly into a paddy wagon. Police had trouble distinguishing protest-ers from onlookers, arresting a larger number than had marched out of the church."[7] By nightfall, King was in solitarily confinement, locked down in a filthy, pitch-dark cell without a mattress or linens. A crude, seatless toilet was its only accoutrement.

Almost seven years before this, King preached: "Whenever you take a stand for truth and justice, you are liable to scorn. Often you will be called an impractical idealist or a dangerous radical. Sometimes it might mean going to jail. If such is the case you must honorably grace the jail with your pres-ence."[8] Andrew Young of the SCLC would call King's arrest and jailing in Birmingham "the beginning of his true leadership."[9] But if we look back to King's Montgomery days, we might see this Birmingham arrest and jailing as simply another courageous extension of his hard-fought leadership dur-ing the better part of a decade. King's Birmingham moment was yet another astute articulation of resistance by a black public man whose commanding oratory had helped inspire tens of thousands to found and enact a new black gospel of compassionate Christian nonviolent resistance in the United States. In Montgomery, King demonstrated how "the Negro people can organize socially to initiate many forms of struggle which can drive their enemies back without resort to futile and harmful violence . . . the mass boycott, sit-down protests and strikes, sit-ins—refusal to pay fines and bail for unjust arrests—mass marches—mass meetings—prayer pilgrimages, etc." (*Testament*, 33). For King, the success of these new methods proved that while the arc of the moral universe might be long, it always bent toward justice.

With his southern minister's background and commanding oratory presence, King was seen by the black southern masses as a man who would never play them the fool—not so long as blood coursed in his veins. And he delivered his grandiose vision of moral righteousness and black liberation in majestic, sermonic ways black people understood, indeed felt in their bones. King further affirmed his vision by his own living example: his continuous self-sacrifice; his sharp and ceaseless chastisement of white authority; his sleepless nights of planning, strategy, and prayer. He was not making money off the struggle. He was not selling out his people and their culture and dignity in the offices of self-gratification. The black masses made and heralded King as their leader because they knew without a doubt he was willing to *die* confronting white authority of whatever stripe en route to actualizing his vision of black liberation.

Certainly by the time he arrived in Birmingham, King had already established his very real—indeed, prophetic—leadership role as a freedom fighter and spokesman for the black majority. The Nobel Peace Prize he was awarded in 1964 was the rest of the world's testimony to what black people in America already knew.

In the life and work of Martin Luther King Jr. the word "leadership" simply cannot be understood apart from the notion of a black public. "Black public" refers precisely to the life and institutions of the black majority—the zones in which they live, the churches where they worship, the places where they conduct their business; the music that energizes their souls, the modes of speaking that move them to action; the timeless agenda for freedom that has enabled them for centuries to make a way out of no-way, to "hit a straight lick with a crooked stick." "Black public" references the democratic places and spaces where the black people congregate, share their dreams, sing their songs, and dance their dances. Institutions that make up the black public sphere of life and energy include Baptist churches like Dexter Avenue and Sixteenth Street; barber and beauty shops; clubs and fraternal orders; jukes and pool halls; cafes and black radio stations in cities like Montgomery and Birmingham. In such black public spaces, people share a language, an idiom, a common allegiance, and mutual hopes and fears for the future. Black people in public spaces are allied in ways that make them members of a race, at least as King seems to have understood it. Martin Luther King Jr. was a man of race, a race man. Race, or the race, in fact, was the raison d'être of his leadership.

No white man anointed King to oversee the souls of black folk. He was not in the service or employ of any prestigious (white) universities, foundations, or institutes. He did not retreat to his study or library each morning, calm and financially comfortable, to churn out condemnatory essays about the self-destructive lifestyles of black folk. King did not curry white favor by criticizing the "excess," "immorality," "prodigality," or "criminality" of black folk. He did not make speeches suggesting that "race" was an outdated term no longer useful in social analysis. And he never once claimed that race was not precisely the locus of the struggle for all black men, women, and children seeking liberation in America. He knew America was deeply indebted to blacks for hundreds of years of brutal, unpaid labor, societal exclusion, and incarceration in one kind of jail or another, always with race as the rationale. He knew that white people in America had become enormously rich (and would continue to be fattened) through the workings of specifically racial dynamics and unjust legal renderings of race.

In 1963, therefore, King publicly endorsed Whitney Young and the National Urban League's projection of a "domestic Marshall Plan" to address the devastating and impoverishing effects of race as a category of American exclusion. King believed a specific plan was needed to begin to address and repair the monumental human misery and destruction that had been caused by white racism. And, as early as 1963, he vigorously endorsed what we have come to know as affirmative action, saying, "It is now only normal and moral to atone for past injustices to Negroes with a crash program of special treatment."[10] King issued these words the same year he was jailed in Birmingham.

The real leadership of Martin Luther King Jr. sprang from his remarkable ability to understand and boldly articulate the desires, deprivations, hopes and fears, and, most importantly, the needs of the black majority, a social configuration of American life unique in its historical and cultural bearings. The most immediate need for the black public—in its churches and songs, daily conversations, shops and businesses, habits of life, and frames of mind—was psychologically and physically to overcome its fear of the white man's jail. King demonstrated that centuries of racism, enslavement, segregation, exclusion, oppression, and abject black fear could be faced down in a single instant by faithful, unified, witnessing blacks en masse. They had only—civilly, honorably, disobediently, and in good conscience—to subject themselves to jail.

Early in the Montgomery struggle, black preachers realized the only way to unify their efforts was to follow King wherever he led them. If that was jail, then they must go too. This was the bold first step in the creation of a new regional space of black freedom, located precisely (and ironically) within the criminal justice system of the American South. The black community's jubilant reaction to the voluntary submission of eighty-nine MIA leaders in 1956 demonstrated the public-sphere potency of this new tactic. The slogan "jail, not bail!" was a thunderous expression of resistance—the new black declaration of independence, the cry of a black on-the-line revolt. Suddenly, the entire racial apparatus of the white south—the police violence, the surveillance and intimidation, abuse and jails—became a locus of power and publicity for the black liberation movement. *Jail* was no longer a southern terror but a space of assembly for blacks with their "minds set on freedom."

Jail, in fact, became a sort of public arena for strategies, songs, and black letters of freedom. In Rock Hill, South Carolina, black youth arrested at protests were given a choice between a hundred dollar fine and a sentence of hard labor. They chose the time. Jail actually provided key opportunities for communication and association among freedom fighters. Four members of the Student Nonviolent Coordinating Committee (SNCC) traveled to Rock Hill deliberately to be imprisoned with the nine men and women who had refused bail.[11] Being jailed for protest was a Civil Rights badge of courage.

And thus, at the very site of the southern jail, a new moment for the black public sphere was ushered in. As one historian described it, Rock Hill was "an unforgettable vicarious triumph for thousands of sit-in veterans . . . because the thirteen Rock Hill prisoners set a new standard of psychological commitment to be debated and matched. . . . As students began to think of any jail in any town as potentially their own, a new kind of fellowship took hold on the notion that the entire South was a common battlefield."[12]

The black public and its leaders fought and continue to fight on this common battlefield. The contours of the battlefield are defined by the workings of race and racism in this country. No one authentically engaged in the struggle—then, or now—would suggest otherwise. Certainly not Dr. King.

Neither would any Civil Rights leader or worker cavalierly dismiss race as a useless, unscientific term to be tossed with quickness into the dustbin of history. Freedom songs were born in racial struggle and refined in southern jails—as in the case of the Albany, Georgia, activist and musician Bernice Johnson Reagon. Race leaders transformed southern jails into independent black studios for writing and singing the terrible workings of race in America. Bob Marley captures the effect and consequences of such creativity in the lyrics of his song "Could You Be Loved?"—"In the darkness there must come out the light!"

There are Christian scriptures black people hold dear that make it clear that "righteousness held captive" will ultimately speak a lyrical and public truth for all to hear. "In the darkness there must come out the light!" And, surely enough, out of the Birmingham city jail came one of the most eloquent and enlightening meditations on "law and injustice since Henry David Thoreau's . . . 'Civil Disobedience.'"[13] Out of the darkness came Martin Luther King Jr.'s "Letter from a Birmingham Jail."

"Letter from a Birmingham Jail" was King's response to an open letter, signed by eight white Alabama clergymen, calling on King and his allies to abandon their nonviolent direct action Birmingham campaign. The Alabama clergy suggested King should allow matters of justice and rights to be handled by the courts. They called King's Civil Rights campaign "untimely" and incendiary, and characterized the activists gathered in Birmingham as outside agitators who would best serve the laws of God and man by leaving Birmingham altogether. (The letter from the Alabama clergy resonates with a hapless desire for the oppressed to accept their abjection out of sight, in darkness, just go away—the same desire Bull Connor had when he attempted to imitate the strategies of Laurie Pritchett.)

The clergy intimated that recent events had demonstrated that justice could and would be achieved through judicial and legislative processes. After all, hadn't the U.S. Supreme Court decreed in its famous *Brown v. Board of Education* decision (1954) that "separate but equal" in matters of public schooling was "inherently unequal"? And hadn't the white clergymen themselves made it clear that they opposed defiance of the court ruling by fervid segregationists like Governor George Wallace? The clergy viewed themselves as moderate and reasonable men who believed in law and order. For them, since justice would amend all wrongs in the fullness of time, King and his allies just needed to be patient and wait.

In his immortal response, King wrote: "For years now I have heard the word 'Wait!' It rings in the ear of every Negro with a piercing familiarity. This 'Wait' has almost always meant 'Never.' It has been a tranquilizing thalidomide, relieving the emotional stress for a moment, only to give birth to an ill-formed infant of frustration. . . . We have waited for more than 340 years for our constitutional and God-given rights" (*Testament*, 292). King defiantly lays it out for the Alabama clergymen (and all who might take their side): "When you are forever fighting a degenerating sense of 'nobodiness'; then you will understand why we find it difficult to wait. There comes a time when the cup of endurance runs over, and men are no longer willing to be plunged into an abyss of injustice where they experience the blackness of corroding despair. I hope, sirs, you can understand our legitimate and unavoidable impatience" (293).

Pulsing with determination to continue the Birmingham campaign and the larger national struggle for black freedom, King's "Letter" is a brilliant defense and exposition of the Civil Rights movement's motivation and tactics. The "Letter" can, of course, be compared to Thoreau's "Civil Disobedience," but I believe it also belongs in the company of Plato's *Apology*. In that dialogue, Socrates (who has been condemned to death for trespassing the laws of his society) explains and justifies his life and acts in the name of truth, justice, and reason—which transcend the mere letter of society's law. King writes: "Just as Socrates felt that it was necessary to create a tension in the mind so that individuals could rise from the bondage of myths and half-truths to the unfettered realm of creative analysis and objective appraisal, we must see the need of having nonviolent gadflies to create the kind of tension in society that will help men to rise from the dark depths of prejudice and racism to the majestic heights of understanding and brotherhood" (*Testament*, 291).

"Letter from a Birmingham Jail" is a profound apologia, a defense of the Civil Rights movement in the name of racial, social, distributive—and Christian—justice. Chastised by white clergy for breaking the law, King patiently explains the distinction between *just* and *unjust* law. Quoting Saint Augustine and Thomas Aquinas, he expresses the conviction that "an unjust law is a code that is out of harmony with the moral law . . . an unjust law is a human law that is not rooted in eternal and natural law. . . . Any law that uplifts human personality is just. Any law that degrades human personality is unjust" (*Testament*, 293). Laws mandating segregation are unjust because they "distort the soul" and damage human personality. Therefore it is morally right and justifiable in the courts of heaven conscientiously to disobey, seek change, and challenge through nonviolent, direct-action measures all manifestly unjust laws that run counter to the discernable human moral conscience.

Ultimately, civil disobedience may result in arrest and jail or worse. Fortunately, some of our most passionate and eloquent defenses of conscientious objection and moral resistance have flown from the putrid interiors of jail cells. Some of these testimonies have proven as soul stirring and invigorating for the larger moral good as the scriptures themselves. In "Letter from a Birmingham Jail," King does not just answer his critics. He utterly condemns them—their misguided intentions, their inaction, and their culpable complicity with the status quo. And he does so in rousing figurative language that sets feet to patting and voices to crying out, Amen! "I have almost reached the regrettable conclusion that the Negro's greatest stumbling block in the stride toward freedom is not the White Citizen's Councilors or the Ku Klux Klanner, but the white moderate who is more devoted to 'order' than to justice, who prefers a negative peace which is the absence of tension to a positive peace which is the presence of justice" (*Testament*, 295).

King proceeds to blast the church and its clergy in general for a near absolute failure to stand up and declare that segregation is against God's moral law. "We will have to repent in this generation not merely for the vitriolic words and actions of the bad people, but for the appalling silence of the good people" (*Testament*, 296). "White ministers, priests, and rabbis of the South," says King, "have been more cautious than courageous and have remained silent behind the anesthetizing security of the stained-glass windows" (299). Demonstrations, boycotts, arrests, and jailing must continue not only because blacks have reached a breaking point with respect to Jim Crow, but also because the vast majority of the "good" and "moderate" white people in America are silent on the issues, absent from the cause of justice. When the real heroes of the South are counted, some future day, King knows they will be predominantly the black men and women who could not and did not "wait."

"Letter from a Birmingham Jail," King represents, is the product of a man "alone for days in the dull monotony of a narrow jail cell"—a man with no option but to "write long letters, think strange thoughts, and pray long prayers" (*Testament*, 302). Poetically true, this description fits the ultimate purpose of King's letter of explanation and defense. But the historical truth is that a white reporter from the *New York Times Magazine* proposed to King months earlier that he, like Saint Paul, should write a letter from prison. Moreover, King's lawyers helped him immensely, providing paper and transporting handwritten drafts to Reverend Wyatt T. Walker, who deciphered and edited King's prose.

Though aided by his compatriots in the composition of the famous "Letter," one of King's own confessional passages provides the best insight into why "Letter from a Birmingham Jail" is so eloquent, such a masterful display of the richly figurative language so important to the black public sphere in which King worked. "I love the church; I love her sacred walls. How could I do otherwise? I am in the rather unique position of being the son, the grandson and the great-grandson of preachers." King's religion is not "completely otherworldly" (*Testament*, 299). He makes no distinction between the body and the soul, the sacred and the secular.

Who else but King could provide as graphic an image of the work of black liberation as this:

> We who engage in nonviolent direct action are not the creators of tension. We merely bring to the surface the hidden tension that is already alive. . . . Like a boil that can never be cured as long as it is covered up but must be opened with all its pus-flowing ugliness to the natural medicines of air and light, injustice must likewise be exposed, with all of the tension its exposing creates, to the light of human conscience and the air of national opinion before it can be cured.
>
> (*Testament*, 295)

The heroic and the common, the abstract and the concrete come together in King's style of public speaking and writing. This holistic style makes the universe seem alive with King's passion. Secular and sacred—body and soul—move fluidly across common boundaries. King's passion for justice and liberation finds flexible and effective companions in both the earthly and the higher realm. As easily as King captures the tone of day-to-day secular struggles he shifts to biblical registers: "Like so many experiences of the past we were confronted with blasted hopes, and the dark shadow of a deep disappointment settled upon us. So we had no alternative except that of preparing for direct action, whereby we would present our very bodies as a means of laying our case before the conscience of the local and national community" (*Testament*, 291). This is King James syntax stitched into the quilt of a seemingly ordinary expression of black desperation.

Martin Luther King Jr. possessed far more than his learning from Plato, Augustine, and Aquinas, biblical prophets and Christian scripture to contemporary theologians like Martin Buber and Paul Tillich. King possessed a gift for transformation. He was able to shape his words and learning into a public voice of leadership.

King's voice became a potent figurative accompaniment to redemption songs such as "We Shall Not Be Moved," which played a crucial inspirational role in the black liberation struggle. Like the powerful oration King delivered to thousands in Montgomery during the first days of the boycott, his public sermons are testaments to his ability to rouse a mass black audience. From the pulpit he declared, "We are determined here in Montgomery to work and fight until justice runs down like water, and righteousness like a mighty stream."[14] King's source was the biblical Amos, and his deft integration of those words into a scene of concrete racial crisis transformed them into a living truth and a call to defiance. "Letter from a Birmingham Jail" is the document that most profoundly displays King's intellectual talents and revolutionary resolve to chastise white folks when they needed it. His passion for justice, even at the cost of life itself, rings through the epistle. It is "Letter from a Birmingham Jail," moreover, that absolutely showcases King's figurative abilities. King had a way about him that was indubitably black, eminently public, and clearly recognized and loved by the masses he was dedicated to serving.

Martin Luther King Jr. suggested terms for his own eulogy. In a sermon delivered shortly before his death, he asked his audience to remember him not as a Nobel laureate, not as the recipient of more than three hundred other prizes and awards. King wanted to be remembered as a Christian practitioner who fed the hungry, clothed the naked, and refreshed the thirsty. These terms of memory would show the harmony between his life's work and the New Testament preachments of Christ, specifically those in Matthew 25:35–45. King's metaphor for this harmony was striking: he asked to be remembered and celebrated as a "drum major for justice."

A drum major leads a marching band of followers, usually with a disciplined but unique and figurative style. If we call to mind the high-stepping, smoothly coordinated Florida A&M marching band of the 1960s, we might rightly say a distinctive black cultural style. In the tradition of Marcus Garvey's remarkable drill teams of the 1920s in Harlem, the Florida A&M marching band brought together the flair of black fraternity step shows, the choreography of black postfuneral gyrations in New Orleans, and taps-sparking military drill discipline. The result of the Florida band's performances was at the very least a revolution in halftime entertainment.

Florida A&M's drum major fronted and guided a dazzling display of black talent with his baton-wielding, deep-bowing, downright magical grace. Dr. King's own black public leadership as a drum major for justice demonstrates just such grace. It is the product of glorious black rhythm and energy.

Biographers and historians typically view King's talent as a drum major for justice as an inheritance from the generations of preachers from which he came. King, of course, knew well the language of the church in its full emotional resonance. Yet to say he inherited his gift is wrong. King's figurative language and the effectiveness of his Civil Rights leadership point to a specific habit of mind, a unique, cultivated ability that was his, and his alone.

This habit of mind enabled King in an instant to envision and express a living universe where unmerited suffering was always redemptive; where moral justice might be long in coming, but would never fail ultimately to reign exultant; where jail was the awful conduit and channel to a black freedom of body and mind. King's gift was the ability to offer up in figurative magnificence a world of living concepts, breathing ethical notions that manifested themselves as the prophetic revelations of a God who would never desert the black race in its righteous crusade for justice. With ringing and sonorous passion King converted the complex lines and images of race in the United States into a brilliantly expressed program for social reform.

A graduate of Morehouse University, a historically black institution in the Deep South, King shared a heritage of black collective energy and language almost inconceivable in the fragmentation and rubble of today's black America. Today, the secular realm almost exclusively occupies the mind of the black minority and majority alike in virtually all matters of day-to-day existence. But to be a drum major for justice, one has first to be spiritual, to be touched by the frenzy of a holy existence. W.E.B. Du Bois describes this revelatory experience: "Finally, the Frenzy or 'Shouting,' when the Spirit of the Lord passed by, and, seizing the devotee, made him mad with supernatural joy, was the last essential of Negro religion and the one more devoutly believed in than all the rest."[15]

King's drum major leadership during his journey from Montgomery to Memphis proved that he fully appreciated what Du Bois had described. Before one could be a successful leader in the black public sphere, one must first be "instructed in the spirit." Surrounded by a multitude of competing interests, opinions, and agendas for reform, King was compelled to speak as passionately and convincingly to Rosa Parks and her generation of black adult wage earners as he spoke to the young avant-garde of college sit-in participants. He had to make as much sense to the well-heeled James Lawson of Vanderbilt University as he did to homeboy Reverend Ralph Abernathy of SCLC. He had to convince the black millionaire A. G. Gaston that it was in his best economic interest to provide the capital to bail out those arrested and jailed in Birmingham.[16] King rose to the challenge. He adjusted and keyed his voice and vision to the music of the black sphere and was awarded a premiere leadership role. King's constituency included not only those farthest down, but also those at the top: celebrities like Harry Belafonte and Lena Horne. Once, on a "peace tour" through the most economically depressed sector of black Birmingham, Abernathy and King entered a black pool hall. "Do you know who our leader is?" demanded Abernathy. "King!" was the strong reply. Abernathy then asked: "Are you willing to do whatever Martin Luther King tells you to do?" "YES!" was the thunderous, Saturday night response.[17]

In his "Letter," King took stock of the Alabama clergy's demand that he "negotiate" rather than "agitate": "You are exactly right in your call for negotiation. . . . Nonviolent direct action seeks to create such a crisis and establish such creative tension that a community that has constantly refused to negotiate is forced to confront the issue. It seeks so to dramatize the issue that it can no longer be ignored" (*Testament*, 291).

King's dramatic Birmingham arrest and imprisonment—and the ensuing federal intervention that resulted when Robert F. Kennedy empowered the Justice Department to monitor Bull Connor's treatment of his prisoner—did indeed create a crisis. Still, it failed to garner extensive media coverage and motivate serious negotiation between Birmingham blacks and whites. King and Abernathy posted bail within a week and were released. King's "Letter" was not published until weeks later and did not gain canonical status among Civil Rights documents for years.

The charismatic SNCC leader James Bevel engineered the crisis that really rocked Birmingham. Bevel gained King's sanction and approval, and ultimately received the nod from all the Birmingham interests working for a racial change from Jim Crow darkness to Civil Rights light.

James Bevel appealed to young blacks from the ages of six to twenty. He whipped up their energy and commitment to fever pitch. Within weeks of his arrival in Birmingham, Bevel had organized demonstrations, comprised mainly of young people, numbering in the thousands. When Bull Connor finally responded with violence—canine squads and full-bore streams from fire hoses (so intense as to rip the clothes off protesters)—the national media put Birmingham on the evening news and on front pages from Sunday's *New York Times* to the *International Herald Tribune*.

White folks suddenly were ready to negotiate. Perhaps their timing was a bit disingenuous, but they had come to feel it was time to lance the boil! The tide had turned, decisively. Birmingham was the key victory and heralded exemplar of the black public sphere's energy and creative fearlessness—its literal and figurative ability to pronounce the death sentence of Jim Crow.

James Baldwin surely was correct when he suggested the most popular image of black religion in the white American imagination is Uncle Tom (the title character of Harriet Beecher Stowe's 1852 novel, *Uncle Tom's Cabin*): "Uncle Tom is jet-black, wooly-haired, illiterate; and he is phenomenally forbearing. He has to be; he is black; only through this forbearance can he survive or triumph . . . [and] his triumph is metaphysical, unearthly." Baldwin claims Uncle Tom is not really a person, but a category white America has substituted for black humanity and personality. Why did Stowe create and market such a category? Because she was one in the congregation of an American "theology of terror," Baldwin says—an imagined white American religious belief that "blackness" and "evil" are one and the same; that only by clothing blackness in white robes of salvation can the nation be redeemed.[18]

But for Baldwin the result of this black soul draped in white is not a *saved* black Christian soul, a full and righteous black human personality, but a "thing" called Uncle Tom. Uncle Tom becomes, in Stowe's theology and in the American imagination, the black one who will always wait. He is ordained by the letter of the white Christian law, but never allowed to manifest or preach its spirit. He is, in fact, the black devil and the sinful "other" who is not saved, but imprisoned by the white missionary robes thrown round him. He cries out to be washed in scarlet—crucified—in order that his soul (in the exclusive view of his captors and Jim Crow abusers) may become whiter than snow. While whites reap enormous secular profits from Uncle Tom's waiting, Uncle Tom himself buys into the "bull" of white robes in the hereafter. Baldwin's terrifying and excruciatingly brilliant version of white American Christianity vis-à-vis black America is precisely the image King dedicated his intellectual energies and masterful figurative conceits to eradicating. King was the anti–Uncle Tom of a nonviolent (yet militant) gospel he knew would rock the foundations of white American injustice.

The genius of King's campaign was its transformation of black religion from a soothing palliative (represented by Mrs. Stowe's dark, medieval martyr Uncle Tom) into a radical, Christian revolution. King's defiant courage, strong intellect, and unappeasable thirst for freedom helped shape a new national religious and legal scene. He gave birth to a black religion that was sharp and irresistible in its representation of and commitment to creative tension and moral crises, as well as their ultimate result: the interracial negotiations that would end racial injustice. "I am [here]," King declared in his famous letter from jail, "because injustice is here" (*Testament*, 290).

King understood he had to walk and talk in the ways of a southern, rural, black community that transmitted its wisdom as often by oral traditions of story and song as by means of the written book. He also realized he had to carry the black church and its congregation out of its comfortable complicity with Jim Crow (marked by his own father's cautious Republican ministry in Atlanta). "Forbearance" and "death," which serve to make Stowe's Uncle Tom a quiet casualty of theology, were converted by King's leadership into moral weapons to be gainfully employed in the fight for the public good.

In King's theology, weapons were necessities. He knew from his first engagement at Montgomery that he had entered the fight of his life, and he intended (with God's help) to win. "Don't be afraid," he intoned during one memorable speech. "Don't even be afraid to die. . . . For I submit to you tonight that no man is free, if he fears death. But the moment you conquer this fear, you are free." For King, the ability to face death without fear, in the knowledge that you have confronted the beauty and rights of your own humanity is a mighty weapon indeed.

Using intellectual and imaginative gifts gleaned from the black public sphere, Dr. King transformed mortality, forbearance, and white America's theology of terror into weapons and led his followers in bringing down Jim Crow walls. Despite the bull and evasion, the clerical hypocrisy, black apostasy, and black adult fear, Birmingham came a' tumblin' down.

In August 1963, hundreds of thousands, with their minds set on freedom, made their way to the nation's capitol for a march on Washington dedicated to securing jobs and freedom for the dispossessed. The famous Civil Rights Act of 1964 was almost a direct outcome of the moral and ethical southern crisis and confrontation (remember, the Birmingham campaign was dubbed Project C) in which King's Joshua-like prophetic leadership played a critical part.

In the spring following his imprisonment and the monumental "negotiated" victory in Birmingham, King took account of the effects of the struggle on America. "Within a few months, more than one thousand American cities and towns were shaken by street demonstrations, and more than twenty thousand nonviolent resisters went to jail. Nothing in the Negro's history, save the era of Reconstruction, equals in intensity, breadth and power this matchless upheaval." The shift in the Civil Rights agenda signaled by Birmingham amounted to the elevation of "jobs and other economic issues to the summit, where earlier it had placed discrimination and suffrage. It thereby forged episodic social protest into the hammer of social revolution." A movement had been converted by Birmingham into a revolutionary "hammer" for change, affixing itself, according to King, to the spirit of a global era in which the formerly colonized, enslaved, and oppressed of Asia, Africa, Latin America, and the Caribbean were "fissuring" existing oppressive social structures and "pressing in from the past to enter modern society" (*Testament*, 169).

King's interpretation of the meaning and importance of the Birmingham moment indicates he knew quite well that a new order of black public thinking, organizing, leadership, and action was required to deal with the new focus (on jobs and other economic issues) and requirements of the quickly evolving revolutionary energies of the black majority. After all, it was James Bevel of SNCC and the young people of Birmingham who had carried the day. And younger black generations were far less patient and tolerant with respect to the black elders and chiefs of SCLC (like Abernathy and King) than even the conservative, Civil Rights–phobic black entrepreneurs and bourgeois accommodationists.

Entrepreneurial, status quo blacks had, in effect, never wanted to depart from the *Plessy v. Ferguson* days of yore. An evolving younger generation saw that such caution would not help the cause, nor help lead to what really was in order: a wide-scale economic and political restructuring and resourcing of black majority life in America. In the forefront of black American nationalism were Elijah Muhammad's Nation of Islam and its fearless, gifted, and charismatic spokesperson Malcolm X. Riots began in Harlem in 1964, and within a year had spread across the country to Los Angeles. The devastating Watts Riot of 1965 produced the mantra of urban insurrection, "Burn, baby, burn!" If moderate whites and blacks had considered King's nonviolent agitation untimely, they looked upon the rhetoric, strategies, and urban insurrection of black nationalism as otherworldly. What in the world had gone wrong with "the Negro"?

The suddenness and ferocity of the black urban rebellions that spread from New Jersey to Michigan, Missouri, Oklahoma, and California made it unequivocally clear that the nonviolent, direct-action protest agenda of King was dead in the water. The revolutionary impulse signified by black urban rioting was aptly described as Black Power. The phrase had existed in the social and political vocabularies of black America since time immemorial. But it took on its modern significance in 1966 during the March Against Fear organized by James Meredith and continued by Stokely Carmichael and other Civil Rights activists after Meredith was shot.

In Greenwood, Mississippi, on a sweltering summer's night, Carmichael demanded of the weary marchers: "What do you want?" The overwhelming response was "Black Power!" Dr. King had accepted an invitation to participate in the march, even though he believed that black nationalism, at its worst, was a no-win gospel. In "Letter from a Birmingham Jail," he characterized the followers of Elijah Muhammad as "people who have lost faith in America, who have absolutely repudiated Christianity, and who have concluded that the white man is an incurable 'devil'" (*Testament*, 296–297). Black nationalists represented a force of bitterness and hatred and came "perilously close" to advocating violence against American society. Yet King recognized that there was violent insurrection everywhere in urban black America, even if he chose to interpret it as "unplanned, uncontrollable temper tantrums brought on by long-neglected black poverty, humiliation, oppression and exploitation" (55).

King was astute enough to realize that Malcolm X, Stokely Carmichael, H. "Rap" Brown, and other nationalists (like Huey Newton and Bobby Seale of the newly minted Black Panther Party) commanded respect, drew huge audiences, and were granted entirely safe passage in the labyrinthine back alleys and rotting tenements of the urban, black public sphere. Carmichael and Malcolm X, moreover, had captured the American media spotlight. And Carmichael had even managed to transport (or import) the rebellious Black Power spirit into King's formerly exclusive domain of southern nonviolent leadership. The immensely influential book *Black Power*, written by Carmichael and the black political scientist Charles Hamilton, is not an account of liberation work in America's urban ghettos, but a description of voter registration efforts by SNCC in Lowndes County, Mississippi. Things had changed in the world of black liberation, and King's inclinations toward the goals of Black Power reflected once again a commitment he frequently expressed when he quipped, "I am a leader; let me hurry now and catch up with my people."

The appeal of Black Power was generational as much as regional. If one watches carefully the videos of the black sanitation workers strike in Mem-

phis, Tennessee (which was King's last engagement), one sees young, southern black men brandishing clubs in the camera's eye and shouting "Black
Power!" When the youth corps begins to drum a different cadence, what
choice does the drum major have but to rethink his work? Although King
was enveloped in the imagery of the black South at his death—his funeral
cortege was led by a mule-drawn wagon—he had committed himself by
1964–65 to a gospel of global economic justice, anti-imperialism, and urban
confrontation of white forces of American injustice. He went global and
revolutionary. He eloquently opposed the war in Vietnam, and had easy conversations with Carmichael and other black nationalist leaders. He was on
the path of Black Power.

In the South, the scene had changed for black folks forever. The region
had grudgingly and violently excavated itself from the slough of segregated
medieval morality; it had reluctantly committed to a legally civil, twentieth-
century premodernity. Blacks could vote in Lowndes County, Mississippi,
by 1965, eat at the Woolworth lunch counter in Greensboro, North Carolina, and ride a Greyhound bus from Durham to Birmingham without being
murdered. The South had crawled, kicking and screaming, out of the muck
and mire of a violent white feudalism. But the real stakes for what King describes as the entry of blacks into the "modern world" were in the ethnically
divided cities of the North and West. Here, there were jobs, economic security, gleaming cars, and sturdy homes as realities and symbols to be gained in
token of the American dream.

In cities of the North and West, young, black urban dwellers were confronting the forces and effects of white racism with combative, black nationalist, and sometimes paramilitary rhetoric and insurrection. The North, West,
and Midwest were not progressive regions where race did not matter. "By
1965, as Chicago's black population approached one million and accounted
for almost a third of the city's residents, more blacks lived there than in the
entire state of Mississippi."[19] Certainly, a faith-driven and committed Dr.
King, whose principal constituency was always the black majority, realized
that the scene of black modernity—if it was to be meaningful—had to be
staged where most black Americans lived.

Richard Wright is helpful in understanding why King's own notions of
black modernism are firmly connected to Chicago. Wright's most famous
novel, *Native Son* (1945), is set in Chicago. Chicago was the scene of modernism for blacks who migrated there at the urging of the black newspaper the

Chicago Defender (edited and overseen by Louis Abbott). Chicago was touted as a northern space where a "Bigger" (the name Wright gives his black hero in *Native Son*) black consciousness was to find redemption. Instead, Wright's Bigger (like the black immigrant majority he is intended to represent) finds himself caught in a nightmare of acquisitive white real estate owners, callous labor leaders, corrupt political officials, and morally blind social welfare adherents.

Wright's hero ends up murdering his employer's (white) daughter and bashing in the head of his black girlfriend, Bessie. His pathology is a result of his vicious exclusion, racial stereotyping, and oppression in white Chicago. Mobs bring Bigger to the ground, quickly arrest and jail him, and finally send him to the electric chair. Wright's black man-child in the promised land tells his attorney that he has lived all his life with the conviction that in Chicago he would never reach the age of twenty-one. King realized that the story of the urban ghetto in the United States (a story Wright had prefigured for Chicago and a black immigrant majority) demanded new tasks for black activists in the mid-1960s.

Where his own leadership role was concerned, King realized he would have to formulate a new conceit for black modernism. Isolated; spatially confined; abandoned by industry; challenged by crumbling schools and dangerous, abandoned lots; plagued by wretched housing worse than the cabins of slavery, black urban ghettos (as Wright knew) were jails. They were horrific, unique, and carefully monitored white configurations of life designed for the black American majority. America's urban ghettos were apartheid writ large.

The blight of urban ghettos has been disingenuously justified by an American myth of immigration. This myth tells of white Irishmen and European Jews who sought asylum, coming heroically to America, scratching their way out of poverty and ghetto confinement into spheres of independence and political and economic power. If white immigrants could achieve such results, then surely the path is open for anyone, right?

Since black people remain marooned in urban ghettos, it must be their own fault. They must have some problem or deficiency. Perhaps an intellectual inferiority, dread of hard work, or a congenital lack of ambition. If blacks *want* to work hard and get out of the ghetto, surely there is nothing preventing them from doing so. They simply need to pull themselves up by the bootstraps and join the real (white) world. (Anyone who has not heard this tale of "failed" black immigration has lived a sheltered life, indeed.)

King knew better than to lend credibility to this racist immigration myth. He had dedicated his life and work to making the true condition of the black American majority known to the world. He would have agreed with James Ralph that "throughout much of American history blacks were exploited, beaten, and oppressed while most Americans and people around the world went about their daily affairs barely aware of the situation. Indeed, racial segregation and oppression isolated blacks from the American mainstream, making their wretched conditions invisible."[20] King fought to bring the immiseration of black folks into the light. In the forefront of the Civil Rights Movement, he carried the liberation struggle of the black majority from invisibility to legal Civil Rights enactments.

But these enactments (and the War on Poverty) were but minute installments on a colossal debt America owed. White America liked its blacks enslaved, segregated, underpaid, stereotypical, undereducated, and imprisoned. King radically suggested that the immemorial conditions of black life in America should be addressed not only with "all deliberate speed," but also with "special treatment" and massive sums of American capital.

America's black urban ghettos were no longer willing to wait, and even though King knew the urgencies of his moment of leadership in the mid-1960s, he had difficulty understanding the magnitude of the unleashed violence and insurrection of those long hot summers of black rioting and looting. After surveying the destruction of the Watts riots, King was shocked to hear community residents claiming victory. How could they think they had won in the face of the monumental wreckage of their own territory? They answered: "We won because we made them pay attention to us."[21]

Civil rights and voting rights enactments were almost a joke in the face of such raw anger and fierce destruction. King declared: "I am appalled that some people feel that the Civil Rights struggle is over because we have a . . . Civil Rights bill with ten titles and a voting rights bill. Over and over again people ask, What else do you want? They feel that everything is all right. Well, let them look around at our big cities."[22]

There was a much, much larger debt to be paid to black folks by America than the country had legislatively and moderately begun to address. King knew that the voice of Black Power was, in fact, the chorus of the black American majority, the dissonant sound of dark bill collectors—men, women, and children of color to whom the nation had passed a bad check. It had been returned to the black community stamped "insufficient funds."

King felt he had no choice but to endorse, as he always had, the agenda of the black majority. He worked to tune his drum major leadership and his voice to the rough harmonies of Black Power. In his final book, *Where Do We Go from Here: Chaos or Community?* King wrote: "Most people are totally unaware of the darkness of the cave in which the Negro is forced to live. A few individuals can break out, but the vast majority remains its prisoners. Our cities have constructed elaborate expressways and elevated skyways, and white Americans speed from suburb to inner city through vast pockets of black deprivation without ever getting a glimpse of the suffering and misery in their midst" (111).

But to say King accepted the main lines of Black Power is not to say he ever sanctioned violence or gave a nod of approval to urban ghetto riots as the best strategy for black liberation in America. In fact, he believed the gains achieved from the riots were farcically minor: "something like improving the food in a prison while the people remain securely incarcerated behind bars. Nowhere have the riots won any concrete improvement such as have the organized protest demonstrations" (*Where Do We Go?* 58). Yet insofar as Black Power meant economic, social, educational, and political empowerment for the black majority, King accepted its goals and attempted to build alliances to formulate strategies to bring about such empowerment. The Poor People's Campaign and King's eager attention to unions and the labor movement in relation to blacks testify to King's new directions and changed emphases.

A Black Power agenda accompanied Dr. King through the final years of his life and work. It was a necessary complement to his determination to face the future head on and with the most useful analyses and strategies possible for the black majority. To better understand and ally with the urban ghetto majority, King took up residence with his family in the public housing projects of Chicago and launched a Chicago liberation campaign designed to empower black tenants in their urban community. The bitter and immeasurably violent white response to this campaign shocked and appalled King. He said that he had never seen white mobs in Alabama or Mississippi as vicious as those he encountered in Chicago. Chicago whites had no desire whatsoever to attend to black "suffering and misery in their midst." Coalition, community, and collaboration with the forces of empowered white America came to appear to King like cooperation with the offices of global imperialism and economically irresponsible militarism (such as the Vietnam war).

Black Power led to the establishment of black studies programs in American colleges and universities and gave birth to nationwide initiatives designed to foster black business and economic development. It led to the emergence of a new black theology circulating in economically independent and popularly based black churches across the land. Its stern advocacy and, yes, threats, aided and abetted the exponential increase in new and well-heeled black middle-class professionals in the American workplace. It fostered an energetic black arts movement on the American creative scene. To these achievements might be added the growth of separatist professional groups such as the National Bar Association, the African Heritage Studies Association, and the National Medical Association.

Black Power led the way and established guidelines for the upsurge in marginal constituency politics and black professional institutionalization that occurred during the past forty years in the United States. Black Power decisively broke (sometimes in problematic ways, to be sure) the lock on national definitions of America and American that had been held for centuries by wealthy, academically and socially privileged white men. The possibilities for a new and structurally significant black American visibility became an oft-borrowed and empowering model for initiatives led by women, gays and lesbians, Chicano and Chicanas, Native Americans, Asian Americans, and other so-called minority Americans.

A catalog of Black Power's accomplishments should not occlude the fact that the movement encountered vehement and sometimes brutal opposition from blacks and whites alike. Conservative black intellectuals such as Jay Saunders Redding and comfortably situated civil rights leaders like the NAACP's Roy Wilkins adamantly opposed in print and from podiums black nationalism and Black Power agendas in the arts, politics, religion, and the general social life of black America. Federal officials such as J. Edgar Hoover, as well as local police officials across the land, instituted widespread covert surveillance of Black Power leaders and constituents, while declaring open paramilitary war on ghetto communities whenever the new black militancy seemed to be getting out of hand. Hoover labeled the Black Panthers the most dangerous threat to law and order in the United States. Faced with the "threat" from such Black Power organizations, police forces were upgraded through federal funding to armed combat status in equipment and strategies. The war of U.S. policing against Black Power resulted in numerous confrontations in cities such as Chicago and Los Angeles, where concentrated black populations seemed quickly moved to endorse the mantra "arm yourself or harm yourself!" Repression—swift, brutal, and massive—of such sentiments and their accompanying black urban rebellion came in law enforcement waves in the East, Midwest, and West. The militaristic violence of this urban repression struck with a tsunami violence that made Bull Connor's Birmingham campaign seem like a minor firefight.

Within the ranks of Black Power organizations in myriad walks of life, from the arts to community patrols of the ghetto streets to free breakfasts for poor black children, there were multiple instances of dissension—and always theatricals of black machismo militaristic posturing and leadership rivalry. Black male bravado and blatant misogyny were ugly realities of more than one Black Power occasion. The bold ideals of national empowerment of the black masses proclaimed by Ron Karenga's US and Black Panther leaders in Los Angeles were more honored in the breach than the observance when the groups' respective leaders came into open, armed conflict. Their rivalry led to black-on-black gunfire in the ghetto and resulted in the deaths of Black Panther leaders John Huggins and Bunchy Carter at a black studies organizational meeting on the UCLA campus. Black Power was not without impediments, opposition, and enemies—including vicious internal organizational failures—as it moved to articulate and accomplish new designs for the liberation struggle.

In focus and goals the later leadership of Martin Luther King was entirely commensurate with the best model and modal energies of the Black Power movement. Only a colossal act of historical amnesia or nostalgia allows us to envision the Martin Luther King Jr. of Memphis, 1968, as anything other than a black political radical of the first order. He had been jailed for his conscience and conscientious stand against injustice more than fifteen times. He was devoted to black majority interests wherever they led. He wanted always to be in the vanguard of those seeking to destroy injustice and bring just compensation and reconciliation to the American blacks who had suffered oppression's worst deprivation and blows.

And King knew that America had not come close to living up to the visionary color-blindness and glad camaraderie across racial lines that he himself gestured at in his famous "I Have a Dream" speech in front of the Lincoln Memorial. He wrote in 1967 that "being a Negro in America means not only living with the consequences of a past of slavery and family disorganization, but facing this very day the pangs of 'color shock.' Because the society, with unmitigated cruelty, has made the Negro's color anathema, every Negro child suffers a traumatic emotional burden when he encounters the reality of his black skin. . . . If . . . one is rejected because of his color, he must face the anguishing fact that he is being rejected because of something in himself that cannot be changed" (*Where Do We Go?* 109–10).

At the time of his death (in a still fiercely racist and economically exploitative South), King was indisputably a global, black, public intellectual recognized and revered from Atlanta to Angola, from Birmingham to Bengal. He knew that he would never be judged on the content of his character—no matter how forbearing he might be—until Black Power, in its most reparative and just dimensions, had become the order of the American day.

Black Power was dedicated to a prisoners' rights revolution. It wanted men and women who had been incarcerated by unjust white laws and inequitable arrangements of power in the United States to be set free. Black Power knew that many thousands of blacks had perished in one American jail or another simply because of the color of their skin. It foresaw the burgeoning of what today is a vast American archipelago of incarceration known as the prison-industrial complex. Black Power was "disappeared" under the economic, political, police, and prison forces of what might be called the Ronald Reagan/George Herbert Walker Bush compromise. The seemingly new Reconstruction marked by Civil Rights' victories was utterly obliterated by a white Republican code of deregulation, wealth transfer upward, and dismantling of American jobs and industries, as well as of affirmative action and professional and educational gains for the black majority. Our own century finds more black men in prison than in college and the construction of more new prisons than schools or universities. The black urban scene of places like Chicago is a thousand times more destructive of black life than in Wright's or King's glory years, bereft now of all opportunity and impossible to emigrate from unless the destination is the prison-industrial complex. There has been an apocalyptic failure vis-à-vis justice, the repair of past black injuries, even of the manifest Civil Rights for people of color in the early years of the century following King.

In the face of our century's indisputably color-based inequity, Dr. King would be appalled if anyone asked him to wait for justice or attempted to assure him that it is the "content of the character" of people of color—an absence, that is to say, of resolve, common decency, ability, or intellect—that keeps the colored majority locked down in urban ghettos or prisons.

King never had as an adult the black bourgeois luxury of a peaceful life. He died from a single shot fired from a high-powered rifle owned by Byron De La Beckwith, a white southern racist of the first order, on April 4, 1968 in Memphis, Tennessee. His life unfolded as both the occasion for and within the rough seas of crisis. The white American violence against him and his fellow participants in the Civil Rights Movement was legendary.

The white southern majority's response to a black call for "Freedom now!" was bombings, sexual assault, police brutality, canine squad mayhem, murder, and countless other unspeakable attacks on the black majority. King knew such violence firsthand, from the stink of its dark putrid jails to the sickening hatred spewed by white New Orleans mothers on the heads of black children wanting no more than what the Supreme Court had ordered for them—a decent education in America. From the first days of his leadership in Montgomery when his home was bombed, death threats against King were constant. His initial instinctive response was an armed counteroffensive. When Bayard Rustin arrived in Montgomery in 1955 to aid the boycott efforts, black guards armed with shotguns patrolled the perimeter of King's property. Inside his house, loaded revolvers were at hand. King applied for (and was denied) a permit to carry a handgun in his car. As King came to see the hypocrisy of advocating nonviolence while living in an armed compound, he gave up the armaments. But he never doubted just how violently many whites in America—North and South—were likely to act in the face of black demands for equal rights and just acknowledgment of their citizenship. As the ghettos exploded in summer rioting and armed National Guardsmen with personnel carriers and high-powered weapons stormed black areas to restore "law and order," King was further reminded that white America's first response to forceful, frustrated, and sometimes bellicose calls by the black majority for justice and empowering resources in America had been (and today remains) violence.

KING DID NOT LIVE a peaceful life. Any portrait or history, scholarly account, or religiously motivated biography that presents King's existence as quiet, Christian, coalitional, morally unimpeachable, and nonracial is false and incomplete. The best example of such false accounting is the manner in which the country has decided to distill the entirety of King's life—a life in the violent whirlwind of social change and reform—into a single instant: his "I Have a Dream" speech.

The Washington Monument, Lincoln Memorial, and the capitol were radiant in their burnished whiteness of stone and their implicit monumental promises of an American dream that all might possess. Indeed promise beamed on that excellent summer afternoon in 1963. The popular historical imagination marks that August day as a moment of national race relations grandeur. "King the dreamer" is quintessential to such history. For, King the dreamer harmonizes with the shining national monuments of Washington, D.C. But like the monuments, King the dreamer is a deceptive and hypocritical construct assembled by empowered whites. Beyond the shining surfaces of those monuments on the National Mall there unfolds a complex and sometimes extraordinarily dark history of the "real" American enterprise. Inside the sepulchers, we hear and read stories of colonization, extirpation of native peoples, chattel slavery, imperialism, and the violent exclusion of nonwhite, nonwealthy, nonmale inhabitants of the United States. From the early colonization and founding of the Americas, people of color have been shut out and off from all national processes, posts, and institutions bearing on policy, property, and profit. Similarly, behind the facade and frozen instant called King the dreamer, there unfolds a complicated and violent, courageous and depressing, bold and tragic history of a real man named Martin Luther King Jr., a black freedom fighter who did not have a peaceful life and never found evidence enough to suggest that America had any firm commitment to founding a genuinely good life for the black majority. Originally, the March on Washington was conceived as a nonviolent, direct-action protest—a civil interruption commensurate with activist, black, public southern civil disobedience like that which had rocked Birmingham in the springtime. But federal and local authorities in the District of Columbia threatened to withdraw all police protection from the city if the march followed its original design. More than two hundred thousand orderly people converged slowly and peacefully on the Mall for what turned out to be more of a faith watch than an effective disturbance of the white racist peace of the United States.

King suited his delivery—his dream speech—to the eviscerated aims and the calm "go slow" consensus of the day. He gave a sermon (much of it drawn from set pieces that had entered his repertoire of conceits during real battle and struggle), offering up a vision of interracial harmony predicated only on the evidence of things hoped for (jobs), the substance of something yet to be seen for the black majority in the United States (freedom). Then he returned to the South as a drum major for justice who knew he could not wait.

IN THE BRIGHT WAKE of the recounting of King's revolutionary legacy, I call to mind the historical, social, and political developments in the United States that paralleled the Civil Rights and Black Power movements. Chroniclers of our liberation struggle—their eyes resolutely focused only on the prize of victory—have sometimes read Civil Rights as the only game in town. They have analyzed the movement as unparalleled—a commanding solo performance on the nation's social and political stages. Notions of a nonpareil black Civil Rights activism emphasize the movement's primacy in network and broadcast news, as well as the forging by blacks of radically new media and publication histories. The movement's "stars" are defined as unparalleled heralds and singular agents of new light and enlightening additions to America's ethical repertoire. Such accounts are stirring dramas of blacks going it alone, to the exclusion of any commandingly significant opposition or relevantly coextensive tracks of national actions and ideas. But it takes only a few bars of the great jazz artist Nina Simone singing the "Backlash Blues" to turn our attention away from contentions that we were alone in our liberation struggles. Nina, of course, set Langston Hughes to music when she insisted that it was Mister Backlash who had raised her taxes, frozen her wages, and sent her son to Vietnam.

Nina's raw, boisterous, gritty jazz invocation of backlash is more than adequate to remind us that those in black liberation struggle were never alone, nor left alone. The epigraph above clearly reveals that the great leader understood the dynamics of white resistance marked by Mister Backlash's existence in the Americas.

FRIENDS LIKE THESE

RACE AND NEO-CONSERVATISM

Loose and easy language about equality, resonant resolutions about brotherhood fall pleasantly on the ear, but for the Negro there is a credibility gap he cannot overlook. He remembers that with each modest advance the white population promptly raises the argument that the Negro has come far enough. Each step forward accents an ever-present tendency to backlash.

MARTIN LUTHER KING JR.
Where Do We Go from Here: Chaos or Community?

Certainly, we remember, and find inscribed in the dark chronicles of American social injustice, the horrors of snarling police dogs, tree bark–splitting fire hoses, electric cattle prods, Sunday morning bombs, assassins' bullets, and rabid southern mobs spewing racist venom while bringing brickbats down on the heads of nonviolent protesters. Civil Rights and Black Power— from Montgomery to Selma, Newark to Watts, and beyond—never occupied the social stage in triumphant solo performance. There was always violent, combative, physical white opposition. When "We Shall Overcome" issued forth, Mister Backlash was always within earshot.

It is not, however, the terror, devastation, murder, hurled bombs, and physical assaults against the black body that I wish most to call attention to here. Rather, I want to foreground parallel operations of opposition to Civil Rights and Black Power that are generally less well known, and certainly less amenable to stirring visual media memory, than bus burnings and police brutality. I want to bring to the fore, to coin a phrase, "Mister Backlash's ideological driving wheel." Focusing on the less often seen, I want to analyze one deeply influential set of white American ideational machinations and affective turns of the heart that has played itself out in intriguing ways from the thirties to the fraught days of our new millennial struggles to forward the interests of the black majority.

Black spokesmen and -women during the fifties and sixties usually offered a uniform response to cautions that their actions would occasion white backlash. They denied there was any such thing in the Americas as reactive white violence; white violence was always proactive—it was frontal and direct, frequently ahead (in slaveholder protocols) of any discerned wrong on the part of the slave. White violence, that is to say, was as American as cherry pie. The most savvy of those to respond to notions of white backlash was none other than Dr. King. In addition to discounting threats of such backlash as a reason to curtail black liberation struggles, Dr. King knew there were unseen orders of violence far more difficult to overcome than bombs, bullets, and skull-crushing bats.

Unequivocally stated or implied in all of Dr. King's writing and oratory was his cogent recognition that white physical violence was but an objective correlative of embedded white ideas. This white ideational world of things unseen, according to King, has always been the bedrock ideological foundation of a violent white supremacy. King believed that, in the long view, *ideas* were vastly more dangerous to the interests of the black majority than Louisville Sluggers or Birmingham bombs.

Ralph Ellison records an autobiographical episode in one of his essays that reinforces in brilliant ways the sagacity of Dr. King's notion of the significance of ideas. In 1937 during the Great Depression, Ellison and a companion went quail hunting in the country outside Dayton, Ohio. On a bright winter day, they had just flushed a covey of quail from a hedgerow when there emerged "from a clump of trees across the field, a large, red-faced, mackinawed farmer." He runs toward the two young men "shouting and brandishing a rifle." Shotguns at their hips, the young men are paralyzed with fear. Ellison writes: "I felt as exposed as a Black Muslim caught at a meeting of the K.K.K." Turns out the white farmer only intended to warn Ellison and his companion off of land that was not even his, but belonged to the foster father of the companion. "He [the warning white man] stood there between the two shotguns pointing short-range at his middle, his face quite drained of color now by the realization of how close to death he'd come, sputtering indignantly that we'd interpreted his rifle, which wasn't loaded, in a manner other than he'd intended. He truly did not realize that situations could be more loaded than guns and gestures more eloquent than words. . . . Fortunately, words are not rifles."[1]

The story so eloquently recounted by Ellison reveals precisely how "load-ed" ideas can be. The "largest, loudest, most aggressive-sounding white man" Ellison had ever seen simply assumed he could "come up" on two young, armed black men and assert a fierce monitory power over them. Why? His actions were grounded on bedrock ideas buttressing his sense of white au-thority and supremacy. He was plugged in, one might say, on that winter's day to the ideological channels of white supremacy in America. He was indeed fortunate that there was a "smoking fury of cursing" rather than the smoking barrels of shotguns. The Ohio winter hunting encounter was a revelatory and terrifying American racial moment for Ellison. It affirmed for him that the most formal racial violence in our land is a function not of guns, but of white ideas. And between the ideas of white supremacy haunting lower frequencies of the American mind and the violent realities of U.S. racism that mark black majority everyday life, there is hardly ever an intervening "shadow." The poet Michael Harper suggests that all of American history—where race and the responses of whites are concerned—can be reduced to "the sound of a rifle cocking." Ideology in America precedes marksmanship.

For Ellison, as for Dr. King, ideas are "the thing" in which we catch the formal consciousness of white frontlash and its preemptive American vio-lence against the black body. An undeniably ascendant body of white ideas

was preeminent in the destruction of the global revolutionary dream articulated by Dr. King. The body of ideas was derisively named "neoconservatism"
in the seventies, though its genealogy can be traced back to the thirties. But
the lineage did not become uber-influential with respect to U.S. politics, policy, and poverty until the administration of President Ronald Reagan.

The genealogy of American neoconservatism is distinguished by at least
one pointed moment of black/white alliance. For a brief time, some adherents
seemed committed to the ideals and struggles of the Civil Rights Movement.
In that moment, some allied neoconservatives did not have their ideological
firearms trained on the ideas and bodies of young black women and men.
There was a time when some of those who were to become fierce opponents
of the second American Revolution were (or so we thought) friendly to interests of the black majority. What, though, of friends and the ideological
effects of neoconservatism on the best hopes and material redress fostered
by the Civil Rights Movement in the United States? What significant bearing did neoconservatism have on the resources and resonances of post–Civil
Rights era black public intellectual life and work?

In the summer of 1966, when Stokely Carmichael (later, Kwame Toure)
declared in Greenwood, Mississippi, that the new goal of the black liberation
struggle in America was Black Power, and that blacks must always, always,
always be wary of so-called white allies and take control of their own liberation, the high dudgeon and resentful outrage of white liberals, white religious
leaders (not unlike those who chastised Dr. King in Birmingham), mainstream white funding agencies, and many other "helping hands" resounded
like a heavyweight's body blows to the torso of the freedom movement's
vulnerable body. White ressentiment became the order of the day, and liberals peeled out of formation like missing-man formations at an air show. Liberals, Communists, bearded youths, and white feminists seemed pointedly
aggrieved that Stokely had said: "It's OK, white people, we are going to build
our own fire!" Why such storm and stress? Because, one has to assume, whites
realized that their titular privilege in the black liberation struggle could no
longer include the designation "leader," "boss," "massa."

At the precise moment of Kwame's declaration of Black Power and African American independence, legions and whole think tanks of white historians, social scientists, and evangelicals began statistically (rabbinically and
mathematically) to issue their own Wittenberg theses. Like Martin Luther in
the sixteenth century, they climbed the stairs of their white racist resentment
and posted their ninety-five reasons for being righteous "player haters" of the

black liberation movement. Erstwhile white liberal "allies" manufactured and highlighted the "internal failings" of the Civil Rights Movement, while ignoring completely the climate of violence, subversion, murder, duplicity, bad faith, and outgoing government hostility against black liberation. Everything bad that was happening was, in their view, the fault of the black majority. Martin Luther King. Jr. remarked on the turning of the liberal tide:

> Over the last few years many Negroes have felt that their most troublesome adversary was not the obvious bigot of the Ku Klux Klan or the John Birch Society, but the white liberal who is more devoted to "order" than to justice, who prefers tranquility to equality. . . .
>
> The white liberal must rid himself of the notion that there can be a tensionless transition from the old order of injustice to the new order of justice.
>
> (*Where Do We Go?* 88, 90)

When things began to go murderously wrong in America (e.g., with the murders of King, Black Panthers, and ordinary black citizens attempting lawfully to walk American streets), the white American historical, sociological, evangelical, philanthropic, and rabbinic communities at large said that such mayhem was the result of internal failures of leadership in the Civil Rights community. They also implied that people of color might well have an innate propensity for criminality.[2] All of this had to do with the decision of black Americans to build their own fires. The young and militant among them, such as Stokely Carmichael, John Lewis, H. Rap Brown, Malcolm X, Ron Karenga, Huey Newton, Angela Davis, Bobby Seale, Erika Huggins, Elaine Brown, and many others, decided, at whatever cost, utterly and committedly to repudiate what the French call their *faux amis*—those false white friends masquerading as liberal, dedicated fellow travelers. In a poetical rebuttal to the self-aggrandizement of former white allies and their ressentiment, Amiri Baraka writes:

ALL YOUR HEROES ARE DYING. J. EDGAR HOOVER WILL SOON BE DEAD.
    YOUR MOTHER WILL DIE. LYNDON JOHNSON,
these are natural
things. No one is
threatening anybody
that's just the way life
is,
boss.[3]

During the era in which the poem was published, the word "boss" meant "co-pasetic," "fine as wine," "truly dope." To build your own black fire was "boss."

White about-faceism illustrates a general American pathology in motion. This national pathology and its polity are most aptly called the "forty acres and a mule syndrome" (FAMS). When the invaluable *Diagnostic and Statistical Manual of Mental Disorders* (DSM) expands to include national contagions, FAMS will clearly receive a prominent place under the heading "American Disorders." What is this syndrome?

Several months before the famished, disillusioned, and tattered Army of Northern Virginia surrendered at Appomattox Court House, the Union general William Tecumseh Sherman issued a famous field order. Field Order 15 promised forty acres of "abandoned" Confederate land to each newly freed and ably qualified southern black man. The general even suggested that Union army mules might be supplied to work those forty acres. Promptly enacted, enforced, and perpetuated, Sherman's field order would have served to place a black population in the millions on a firm economic footing in America.

In the rage and racism characterizing the "politics of restoration" (meaning, President Andrew Johnson's giving back, wholesale, lands and resources to traitorous white aristocrats of the former Confederacy), the promise of forty acres and a mule became nothing but sounding brass and a tinkling cymbal. Blacks—through tenant farming, black codes, white mob violence, and bogus "wage contracts"—were virtually returned to slavery. Treasonous southern whites were granted pardon, immunity, debt forgiveness, and reclaimed lands that were to have been distributed to blacks. Mules were nowhere in sight. Freed blacks were abandoned without any economic means whatsoever. "In 1863 the Negro was given abstract freedom expressed in luminous rhetoric. But in an agrarian economy he was given no land to make liberation concrete. After the war the government granted white settlers, without cost, millions of acres of land in the West, thus providing America's new white peasants from Europe with an economic floor. But at the same time its oldest peasantry, the Negro, was denied anything but a legal status he could not use, could not consolidate, could not even defend" (*Where Do We Go?* 79).

And the consequences of such rank abandonment? "While hardly an economic panacea, land distribution would have had profound consequences for Southern society, weakening the land-based economic and political power of the old ruling class, offering blacks a measure of choice as to whether, when, and under what circumstances to enter the labor market, and affecting the former slaves' conception of themselves."[4] Which is to say, if blacks and whites had reached a distinctly material (read, real) alliance in which freed slaves had actually received land and means and federally enforced protection to work that land for profit the very notion "welfare blacks" would not today exist in the United States lexicon. Of course, such American integrity of postwar racial arrangements and alliance never occurred. A white southern President, Andrew Johnson—the first American President, in fact, to be impeached—offered the spoils of war not to the supposed black beneficiaries, but to what might be thought of as the Kudzu Benedict Arnolds.

In a 1984 preface to his brilliant collection of essays titled *Notes of a Native Son*, James Baldwin offers a retrospective on his erstwhile white allies of the 1940s and 1950s. He writes: "In those years, I was told, when I became terrified, vehement, or lachrymose: '*It takes time, Jimmy. It takes time.*' I agree: I still agree: though it certainly didn't take much time for some of the people I knew then—in the Fifties—to turn tail, to decide to make it, and drape themselves in the American flag. A wretched and despicable band of cowards, whom I once trusted with my life—*friends like these!*"[5]

Friends like these! Indeed, Baldwin's is certainly the only appropriate cry of the heart from any black person, black audience, or black movement in response to the forty acres and a mule syndrome. It is a desperate, lonely, and unavoidable outcry that carries in its resonances the sick catalog of an immemorial, white, radical betrayal of the best offices of American democracy. It is an exclamation that befits the endless American betrayals of the interests— time, and time, and time again—of the black majority. From the founding fathers' white-male-privilege hypocrisy to the stuttering and nearly shame-faced stammering of Senator John Kerry's presidential debate response to a question about his position on affirmative action in 2004, that wisdom has proved dramatically sound. They—the supposedly allied, leftist, liberal, revolutionary whites who claim to support blacks in their never-ending struggles for American liberation—must be warily viewed. *Friends like these!* They are, and have ever been, but a shave and a haircut away from the establishment.

It is important to take a candid look at the failures and abandonment of black America by all manner of white so-called allies—leftist, liberals, Communists, weather people, hippies—to provide a *context* for understanding the workings and real import of what has come to be known in the United States as "neoconservatism." The term circulates in present day conversation as though it describes a discrete ideology, or a group of entirely like-minded men and women who have recently come to the world of American politics and power. It is sometimes invoked as a catchall category for social scientific, fiscally astute managers of right-oriented journals, think tanks, political causes, and moral punditry. Neoconservatives, at times, are seen as concerned more with big picture issues of global politics and heady numerical analyses than with race and its vexed history in the United States. A Hayes-Tilden Compromise or the abandonment of millions of blacks to southern violence after the Civil War seem bothersome, perhaps even tawdry, matters of national racial politics that neoconservatism has somehow escaped, or, transcended. And what could neoconservatives possibly have to do with Civil Rights, the slaughter of tens of thousands of American young people in Vietnam, homophobia, or a private prison-industrial complex that currently locks down more national citizens than any other prison system in the world except China?[6] And how can neoconservatism be automatically condemned or discounted as racist, since an increasing number of black Americans have joined its ranks in recent years? In truth, neoconservatism in the United States is an example par excellence of the very worst and most duplicitous order of the forty acres and a mule pathology. It is as ethically bankrupt an emergence in our national life as any calculatedly immoral pyramid scheme. The neoconservative mantra might well have served as the source of the most famous line in the film *Jerry Maguire*: "Show me the money!" Their numbers are legion, and one wonders if Baldwin, were he alive today, might label them "a wretched and despicable band of cowards" with respect to the well being of the black majority. And who among black men would trust them with his life?!

The dress code for the "happy few" who made the commute from faraway Brooklyn to City College at the tail end of the Depression was dramatically different from the neo-African fashion of the Black Power years. Savvy adolescents like Irving Kristol—the godfather of neoconservatism—donned the best raiment they could muster in what Kristol himself calls the "slums or near-slums" from which his cohort hailed. These first-college-generation immigrant children of the 1930s decked themselves out in bargain basement jackets, slacks, vests, shirts, and ties to make their journey uptown. Already striving to look like the establishment that had them in "quota-lockdown," they were thankful for City College (CCNY), a working-class school.[7] In the absence of an institution without racial quotas, they would have had no American access whatsoever to higher educational opportunities. Elite private colleges and universities liked their student bodies to be what the novelist Ralph Ellison calls "optic white." Quotas pushed the happy few from their cramped ghetto environs to the heady heights of Harlem, and the college on a hill.

They were prodigies, breaking free of the stultifying immigrant existence of their working-class parents and grandparents who, often, had arrived on American shores without a dollar to their names. As Kristol and those like him hurtled through the dark underbelly of Manhattan, they could sometimes be seen clutching wrinkled bags holding hard-boiled egg, peanut butter, and cream cheese sandwiches—their sole fortification for the day.[8] If they were matriculating at City College, they were students of an institution that had earned its title as the "Harvard of the proletariat."[9]

Kristol recalls that in his day: "City College was known ... as a 'radical' institution, and in an era when most college students identified themselves as Republicans [and WASP] the ascription was not incorrect." In such a radical environment, Kristol eagerly allied himself with the Young People's Socialist League—the campus Trotskyists. He seems to have been predisposed, early on, to identify far more enthusiastically with a "general intellectual," suit-and-tie cadre than with an ethnically specific campus cohort and its interests. (For there was, to be sure, at the CCNY of the time, a "Jewish alcove.") Trotskyists claimed as their campus space Alcove 1 of the CCNY lunchroom (made famous by the documentary film *Arguing the World*, which focuses on Kristol and members of his cohort at the college and by Kristol's own reminiscences). The Trotskyists, in fact, gathered each day to "argue the world" and, as Kristol tells it, to exchange sandwiches and play ping-pong.[10]

The CCNY Trotskyists of Kristol's day were not short on utopian dreams of a world in which economic equality, racial harmony, and international accord would be standard fare. Their agenda was both local to Alcove 1 and actively social and in the streets. Kristol writes: "Shortly after I was graduated from City College, I was assigned to attend meetings of a 'branch' of young Trotskyites in Bensonhurst, in Brooklyn, at the opposite end of the borough where I lived. I dutifully attended the meetings, which were quite farcical since we were trying to recruit young blacks in the neighborhood who were sensible enough not to take us seriously."[11]

In search of a more expansive field of intellectual and associational commerce (one in which he would be "permitted" to read Max Faber), Kristol abandoned his recruitment of blacks altogether. And, as far as one can surmise he has never given hint of a desire to return to it. He departed the Trotsky-ists entirely (and without regret) before his twenty-second birthday—the first in a long line of Irving Kristol's loving and capital-accruing volte-faces. Abandoning Trotsky along with the Negro, Kristol was on his way to the intellectual, journalistic, collaborative, political, academic, and business alli-ances that, during the next four decades, would bring wealth, prestige, power, fame—and the title godfather of neoconservatism.

The path that Irving Kristol pioneered through the thickets of Cold War polemics, journalistic feuds, political skullduggery, corporatist sycophancy, think-tank blueprinting, and misogynistic, racist, and homophobic hate mongering today forms the neoconservative highway of a thousand points of "lesser lights." Many have chosen to walk in his acrimonious and loose-fitting ideological shoes. He remains, however, nonpareil in his brilliantly choreographed, quixotic, whimsical, none-too-scrupulous shifts and turns of allegiance. These ideological twists and turns have set him up for life—inside the Beltway. He is feted and celebrated with presidential medals, honorary degrees, distinguished lectures, and oodles of ready conservative foundation cash, banked next to his political insider cultural capital.

Before surveying the covert rest stops along the Kristol Memorial High-way, however, it is perhaps wise to pause and reflect on the historical back-ground of neoconservatism:

> The original neocons were a small group of mostly Jewish liberal intellectuals who, in the 1960s and 70s, grew disenchanted with what they saw as the American left's social excesses and reluctance to spend adequately on defense. Many of these neocons worked in the 1970s for Democratic Senator Henry "Scoop" Jackson, a staunch anti-communist [and a principal inquisitor in the Army-McCarthy tele-vised investigations of 1954, and an early advocate for American military interven-tion in Southeast Asia, and known as the "senator from Boeing"]. By the 1980s, most neocons had become Republicans, finding in President Reagan an avenue for their aggressive approach of confronting the Soviet Union with bold rhetoric and steep hikes in military spending. After the Soviet Union's fall, the neocons decried what they saw as American complacency. In the 1990s, they warned of the dangers of reducing both America's defense spending and its role in the world.[12]

Tracing the full formation of neoconservatism to the sixties and seven-ties makes sense if one thinks primarily of their multiplication and growing national influence. In effect, however, the basis of neoconservatism's influence was established in the muck and mire of post–World War II, American anti-Communist politics. Standard histories tell us that in the postwar era, the globe was divided ideologically and geopolitically between the Soviet Stalinist East and the Truman Democratic West. The Iron Curtain and the Berlin Wall became both rhetorical shorthand and dread reality for a new standoff of world powers. Many who are now inscribed in neoconservative rolls of honor first made their reputations as men and women distinctively to the right of what they deemed a soft American liberalism that endorsed appeasement as a policy for dealing with a menacing Soviet communism.

These early inductees to the neoconservative honor rolls complained that a soft liberalism publicly and relentlessly set itself in opposition to the persecutions and witch hunting of Senator Joseph McCarthy and the House Un-American Activities Committee but never brought enough wrath to bear on the real enemies of the United States—domestic, internal subversives like Julius Rosenberg. The overriding enemy was, in fact, Communism. Ferreting out its internal agents—by whatever means necessary—was a matter of moral, military, and political expediency.

Michael Harrington recognized in the 1970s that a faction of former Democratic coworkers in the kingdom of equitable politics had shifted their allegiance distinctly to the right. To describe these shape-shifters, Harrington coined the term "neoconservative." And at the moment of the term's coinage, a death knell rang to the post–World War II liberal consensus concerning American global policies, domestic goals, and agendas. Neoconservatives (whether they liked the label or not) were well on their way to membership and colossal influence in the Republican Party. At first the New Right resisted the designation "neocon." They were still, at least according to their own lights, simply the right wing of the Democratic Party's left. They hoped to bring Democrats into line with their ideological leanings. But it did not take more than a decade for neoconservatives to embrace the label.

Noting the reluctance of neocons initially to accept the label applied to them by Michael Harrington, Robert Westbrook writes:

> At the outset, these intellectuals insisted that they were still *liberals*, and, with the notable exception of Irving Kristol, they were slow to embrace the "new conservative" or "neoconservative" label with which their critics sought to stamp them. They remained dedicated to what they took to be the fundamentals of postwar American liberalism—a commitment to a modest welfare state, racial

integration, and the containment of communism—fundamentals they saw threatened by the accommodations that other liberals were making with the New Left and the counterculture.[13]

"Counterculture" and "New Left" return us, in a sense, to Black Power, the white youth–led antiwar movement, college and university free speech rallies—in short to the American revolutionary "dancing in the streets" that defined national life during the sixties and seventies. It was a time of the Great Society, demonstration cities, and black community empowerment: "make love, not war" . . . "turn on, tune in, drop out" . . . and young people's refusal to trust anyone over thirty.

It was a time of domestic turmoil and new activist formations—especially in Democratic politics. Television network news broadcasts had expanded from fifteen to thirty minutes. The small screen brought into living rooms across the land the raucous, freewheeling, anarchic demonstrations of black, student, and bearded youth. It also revealed—up close and personally—proud, radical women burning bras and demanding freedom now. Television presented us with horrific, gothic images of body bags holding corpses of what would eventually total fifty-five thousand American casualties. We witnessed jungles and children burning. We refused to use Dow Chemical coverings to wrap our leftovers because Dow was, indisputably, the manufacturer of Agent Orange, meant to eradicate those jungles. (It was when he witnessed photographs of napalm-burned children in Vietnam that Dr. King knew he had no moral choice but to become an antiwar partisan.)

Network television news guaranteed that the ubiquitous revolutionaries of the counterculture and the New Left were never unseen or alone on the national scene. All of us caught up in the revolutionary fervor were attentive to the local, state, national, and global unfoldings of our times. We were suddenly "unprovincialized" and were attempting to redefine our global selves in humanitarian and revolutionary terms that were prophetic, evangelical, and imminently concerned with social and distributive justice at a world level. We were young, and we did not strive for assimilation into WASP dinner parties. We were hoping for a new world order that would actually feed the hungry, give drink to the thirsty, and treat our world neighbors as we hoped to be treated. A flower in a gun barrel was our signature gesture; we were serious about redistribution of the world's wealth. Who opposed our every outreach toward utopian futures? Neoconservatives.

What surely might be thought of as a second American Revolution—in values, goals, desires, politics, philosophy, economics, epistemology, curricular revision, cultural definition, ethical standards—was launched by the counterculture and the New Left. Revolution II spoke in the name of "we"—the black, feminist, gay, lesbian, multicultural people. This national eruption might justifiably be traced to the social movement that prompted Dr. King's resolution to endure the very real danger of a Birmingham city jail. The movement was intended to bring about an equitable, resourced, and inclusive way of American life for those farthest down.

Given neoconservatives' stated, reiterated, polemically attested, and journalistically asserted rhetoric concerning distributive and social justice in the best of all possible democracies, does it not seem natural that they might have welcomed a revolution for equality? Can we not imagine neoconservatives, who avowed allegiance to the best liberal strivings of the modern democratic state, wanting (to borrow a phrase from Langston Hughes) "America to be America again"? Ah, but here precisely is the rub. Neoconservatives are not at all what they profess, aver, or promise to be. They oppose precisely the types of social and distributive justice that have been the ends of such not-so-distant initiatives as the Great Society, the War on Poverty, demonstration cities, and, of course, affirmative action. Hence, when we speak of democracy's best advocates and defenders we clearly cannot mean *friends like these!*

Neocons have never been concerned with fulfilling the best intentions and implicit promises of the Declaration of Independence or even their own best selves. They have *always* salivated for insider status vis-à-vis the American WASP establishment. Both Kristol and Norman Podhoretz have been autobiographically forthright about their hunger for establishment perquisites. Suits-and-ties, shaves and haircuts ... neocons have desperately longed for stature and standing in the corporate, conservative, journalistic sectors of our nation's elite. If any group of partisans ever fiercely yearned unreservedly to be genuinely *white* in America, it was—always and always—neoconservatives! They took up and abandoned theories and programs at the merest temptation. Their theme song of desire might well resemble the zippy tune by the Calloway band, the singer insisting he wants one thing only: a very, very great deal of money![14] One is reminded of a *New Yorker* cartoon of some years back where one Puritan on shipboard explains to another: "Religious freedom is my immediate goal, but my long-range plan is to go into real estate."[15] The American ways of neoconservatism are not without precedent in our land's vexed history.

Norman Podhoretz offers a dazzling case in point. In 1962, he became affiliated with the millionaire Huntington Hartford's arts periodical *Show*. Hartford hosted a writers conference at his Paradise Island estate, just off the coast of Nassau in the Bahamas. Finding himself in the soft, tropical lap of luxury, surrounded by celebrities of power and influence, Podhoretz executed the critical neocon volte-face of his career. "This," he enthused, "was what success looked like, all its various components brought together in one dazzling display."[16] From the "buzz" he got from sybaritic Caribbean sunsets and a proximity to wealth, Podhoretz contracted a sharp and incurable case of FAMS. A viral overload. He wanted money, power, and kudos. He quickly let it be known that he no longer considered himself an alienated leftist. He turned on the counterculture and the New Left with vengeful, well-financed, ad hominem venom. *Commentary*, under the plutocratic afterglow and images of his Paradise Island sojourn, became a bully pulpit stream of print relentlessly attacking American Revolution II. Irving Kristol, Norman Podhoretz, Nathan Glazer, Charles Murray, Midge Decter, Daniel Patrick Moynihan, Jeane Kirkpatrick, Michael Novak, and James Q. Wilson were all dedicated, corporately financed, academy and think tank–housed warriors against the second American Revolution.

Such neocons were (and remained) fierce counter-counterculturalists. Over time, they have cast their vigorous aspersions on impoverished blacks, homosexuals, the "new class" of American intellectuals and professionals, feminists, campus activists, doves in the realm of defense strategy and spending, and, always and forever, Communists. On occasion it is possible to look from Stalinist rhetoric and propaganda to the neoconservatives, and back again, and not be able to tell the difference. (The so-called culture wars of the 1980s witnessed uniquely vicious ad hominem rhetoric from neoconservatives.) And under the never-sleeping eyes of the neoconservatives still willfully laying claim to aboriginal allegiance to American democratic ideals and a compassionate conservatism, prospects of the good life for the average American have plummeted farther and farther down the economic grid. The bluesman Otis Taylor satirically describes the survival strategy of many and many an average American family in these neocon times when he sings of families "eating dog food on a plastic spoon."

Moreover, neocons have tacitly supported construction of the gulag of privately financed prisons and internment camps for illegal immigrants that now bears the stamp and issues the stock of Wackenhut and Corrections

Corporation of America. There are more black men in prison or under the surveillance of the criminal justice system in the United States than are enrolled in the nation's colleges and universities. Neocons think of this disgrace to national ideals as the appropriate outcome of the rule of law and order. It is the old smoke-and-fire primitive thought of the quarter-educated. If there is more crime in black neighborhoods than elsewhere in society, it is because such neighborhoods simply house more innate criminals. Where there's smoke, there's fire. If there are more black and brown men incarcerated in the United States, it is because they are more prone—"volitionally," is the presumption—to criminality. The number of men and women who make such structurally unwarranted, but statistically massaged, assumptions about criminality (and much else to do with race in America) has increased dramatically in recent years. Their influence captured the Republican Party during Ronald Reagan's presidency. They are legion, these neoconservative spokespeople.[17] Their campaign and assault against the New Left and the counterculture might be captured by formulations of the poet Sterling Brown. In his powerful poem "Old Lem," Brown's black speaker describes the terrorism faced by blacks in a violent Jim Crow South. In a dry monotone, Brown's speaker catalogs the stacked deck of southern justice that places all of the law's apparatus in the hands and offices of whites. The result for blacks is that they get lynch law justice in the end when violent whites "come by tens." Many a counterculturalist, feminist, and black militant got the "justice in the end," and the neocons who got them "came by tens."[18]

Far from embracing what the writer Lawrence Ferlinghetti called a "re-birth of [American democratic] wonder," neocons went to war against American Revolution II.[19] They attacked on all fronts: economic, academic, welfare, criminal justice, political, journalistic, and—in particular and most especially—personal. They were all masters of the very type of hammer-fisted ad hominem invective appreciated by Uncle Joe Stalin. Their covert sympathizing with the worst of our country's imperialism, intelligence shenanigans, denials of equal rights, and flat out corporatist greed segued easily for them into an overt campaign against the best American revolutionary energies of the counterculture and the New Left. Neocons drew on all of their accumulated cultural and financial capital and performed the ultimate volte-face. They (literally in some instances) married themselves to business, religious fundamentalism, and world imperialism. Mean-spirited self-interest was wedded in their minds to something called the American way and the national interest. (*Friends like these!*) Here is Michael Bérubé's assessment of Irving Kristol:

> In 1980, Kristol's IEA [Institute for Educational Affairs] started funding a new brand of aggressively conservative campus magazines, dedicated to the revival of traditional conservative values such as racism, misogyny, red-baiting and gay-bashing. In 1982, Hilton Kramer's *New Criterion* was founded with the help of office space and funding provided by the Olin [Foundation]; in 1990–91 the journal received $205,000 from the Olin (whereas Kristol himself received a mere $124,000).[20]

The neoconservatives were masters of the journalistic enterprise. They established such influential periodicals as the *Public Interest*, the *National Interest*, the *New Criterion*, the *American Enterprise*, the *New Leader*, and others. They had access to op-ed columns in all the major American dailies. They transformed the historic commentary into a bully pulpit against such progressive programs as affirmative action. Why did Podhoretz as editor of *Commentary* oppose affirmative action? His explanation was because affirmative action had nothing to offer "for the Jews."[21] The neocons "control or substantially influence numerous corporate-funded policy centers, including the Institute for the Study of Economic Culture, the Institute for Contemporary Studies, the Institute on Religion and Public Life, the Manhattan Institute, the American Enterprise Institute . . . and the Center for Security Policy."[22] Irving Kristol once wrote: "We had to tell businessmen that they needed us. . . . Business understands the need for intellectuals much more than trade unionists understand it, but not enough. . . . Basically, it [business] wants intellectuals to go out and justify profits and explain to people why corporations make lots of money."[23]

Hey! If you'll take money from the CIA, then why not every enterprise? Here were former Marxists cozying up to corporate interests and greed in a manner Anthony Trollope called a "sneaking kindness for a Lord." Mere toadies for lots of money. Attendant lords to the rich and famous. Sycophants of WASP capitalism.

Kristol became a corporately financed professor at New York University while disingenuously attacking a new class (a holdover term from the Russian revolution of 1917 that saw the bureaucratization of the state at the hands of a "new class") of academic intellectuals. Kristol railed against preferential treatment for liberal causes in the media and elsewhere while his neocon

movement accepted prodigal sums from the Olin Foundation.[24] Kristol re-
sorted to rank "I'm just a victim here" lamentations that conservatives on
university campuses were subjected to political correctness, while he himself
provided the funding for some of the most viciously ad hominem campus
periodicals ever put into print.[25]

What was the yield of Kristol's forty acres and a mule sickness that led
to the death of the liberal in him? "The benefits of Kristol's money shaking
did not fall only on others. In 1985, the Olin Foundation gave him $600,000
to start a magazine, *The National Interest*, and made payments on his John
M. Olin Distinguished Professorship at New York University. . . . [He] became an Olin Fellow at the American Enterprise Institute in 1988 and collected $376,000 from the Olin Foundation that year alone."[26] One might
well concur with the sardonic conclusion of Gary North that "anyone who is
planning to write a book on [the] rise of neoconservatism" should heed "the
advice of Deep Throat to Woodward and Bernstein: 'Follow the money.'" He
also notes: "The neoconservatives have always been insiders. . . . They have
always had bases of operations that have served as entry points into the ranks
of the power brokers. . . . The difference between neoconservatism and conservatism [in America] has been the difference between the greased skid and
the bootstrap."[27]

One could go on elaborating and reviewing the rise and spread of neoconservatism in the United States. But, in truth, there is an ample bibliog-
raphy and Internet archive for anyone who wishes further elaboration. Here,
it seems critical to look specifically at race as neoconservatism has cast its
reactionary shadow over that ever-vexed domain of American life. And I
draw now on the endeavors of a university research assistant, Eden Osucha
of Duke University, who provided help for the following discussion of race
and neoconservatism.

Much of the contemporary scholarship on neoconservative thought suggests that, in addition to Vietnam and the radicalism of the New Left, a
major backdrop for the neocon ideological consensus and their alliance with
conservatives proper has always been the politics of race. Race, in fact, eclips-
es or subtends all other issues, and it persists into the present-day popularity
of a neoconservative temperament in America. A significant early document
in the archive of neoconservative attention to race matters is Daniel Patrick
Moynihan's *The Negro Family: The Case for National Action* (1965). Moynihan
locates responsibility for the black majority's social and economic marginal-

ization in what he calls the "pathological" culture of the black family. Seeming blind to the history of the violent exploitation and brutalization of black males in American society, Moynihan surprises himself by discovering a matriarchal black family. Lo and behold, the black family seems devoid of strong black male presence. (The rules of Aid for Dependent Children at the time Moynihan compiled his study forbade the permanent, residential presence of a "man in the house.") Black breadwinner husbands were in desperately short supply. Moynihan's recommendations included enlisting black men in the armed services, so that they could rediscover their masculinity, return to the ghetto, discipline their families, clean up their communities, and presumably attend church regularly. (The dramatic influence of Moynihan's study reveals itself in even the prescriptions for black community of Dr. King, who writes that blacks cannot ignore the fact that the ultimate way to diminish social problems of the ghetto "will have to be found through a government program to help the frustrated Negro male find his true masculinity by placing him on his own two economic feet" [*Where Do We Go?* 125]). Moynihan's formulations and recommendations invoke what came to be known as the "feminization of poverty." Blacks were poor because black women (mostly on welfare and AFDC) had no breadwinner men around to support the infra- and economic structure of what Moynihan considered a normal, healthy family. Moreover, there was no law and order in ghetto streets, not because the police refused to service such streets, but because there were, presumably, no black ex-marines to patrol against black crime. The George Herbert Walker Bush presidential campaign of 1988 deployed Willie Horton as an example of what happens when no righteous, family-oriented "deacons of defense" are around to take down black criminals. Horton was on prison release when he committed sexual assault and murder in Maryland. The Bush campaign created the famous revolving door advertisement that showed convicts being continuously released from correctional facilities and back onto the streets of "civilized society." Clearly something had to be done about the "criminal" black male, and it seemed that in the aggregate, there were no other kind of front-and-center black men. Moynihan and Bush . . . *Friends like these!* While black women were tarred with the label "welfare queen" in some measure as a result of Moynihan's efforts, black men were scandalized almost beyond recognition as responsible human beings by the Bush campaign. Then there was affirmative action to be dealt with in the racial politics of neoconservatism.

Without exception, historical accounts of neoconservatism identify the advent of affirmative action programs in the private and public sectors as a pivotal moment in a narrative of unabashed political realignment in the United States—what I have called the volte-face politics of men like Kristol and Podhoretz. Most of the neoconservative cadre were firm supporters of Civil Rights in its early phases of religiosity, nonviolent direct action, and sometimes co-black-and-white-leadership. But they almost all—to a man and woman—backed away from the black liberation struggle when it transmuted into the offices and demands and strategies of Black Power and the coextensive establishment of affirmative action. (President Lyndon Johnson's 1965 Executive Order 11246 required federal contractors to "take affirmative action to ensure that applicants are employed and that employees are treated during employment, without regard to their race, creed, color, or national origin.")

Why did the neocons flee like startled deer from the aura of two simple, two-word phrases: Black Power and affirmative action? Their argument for abandonment was that though blacks deserved equality in American society, especially in the workforce, affirmative action as it evolved insisted not on a meritoriously achieved "equality of opportunity," but a nefarious "equality of results." Any attempt at equality based merely on skin color would scarcely rectify centuries of discrimination and exclusion against blacks in America. Skin-color-employment quotas were, in fact "discrimination in reverse," assaults upon the average white man's opportunities for a new deal, a fair chance to work. (And then came the urban legend of the angry white male as a neoconservative icon of ressentiment.)

To make a case for an American color adjustment—from black exclusion to black inclusion—on the very, very specifically American-constructed basis of skin color was rejected by neoconservatives across the land. It was against the American way of equality.

Echoing their critique of affirmative action, neocons concerned with the politics of race claimed that the public assistance programs that had originated under the aegis of President Lyndon Johnson's Great Society were grossly out of practical and ideological step with their New Deal precursors. Black women were "lording it up" on the welfare dole, while new class social services administrators and minions siphoned off dollars that could be used for guns, not butter. Black men were becoming virtual Mafioso brokers of community empowerment programs sponsored by the Great Society. (Were these the same supposedly absentee or "criminal" black men whom Moyni-han believed could barely lift their heads above water when drowning?) In short, the protoreparations character of the Great Society and War on Poverty funding that had been intended, as the president himself made clear, to correct in some measure years of chattel slavery and bottom-end labor by blacks, was held to be the wrong way to address poverty. For the neocons, the only freedom from poverty lay in the free market. What was required of blacks was good old-fashioned individualistic effort—creativity, desire, and mobility of the black body at work!

If the aim of the social philosophy called "utilitarianism" is "the greatest happiness of the greatest number," then the neoconservative slogan runs directly contrary to utilitarianism. For, the neocons have always desired the greatest happiness for the smallest elite of the fittest members of American society. "Fit" here, within an American politics of race, means that those who should be most rewarded by supply-side, free market, capitalistic polity are educated, even intellectual, savvy, white men with a knack for seizing the main chance. "Fit" implies most of all an explicit form of societal-ethnic cleansing in the endeavors, think tanks, corporatism, and racial politics of American neoconservatism.

"Wash me in scarlet," enjoins one traditional American Negro spiritual, and "I shall be whiter, yay whiter than snow!" Those who made the commute from Brooklyn to the heights of Harlem to attend the "Harvard of the proletariat" were bent all along on eradicating the ghetto-mandated difference between themselves and those who look out over the Caribbean from Paradise Island estates. One of the most convincing ways to show loyalty to such luxurious pure whiteness is, of course, to join forces against black majority interests in the United States. To stop, as it were, recruiting black boys to any worthwhile venture or course on which your own forward march toward cleansing is set. Blackness must be abandoned in the offices of cultural capital and financial gain. Besides, if one expends and spends capital on the plight and remedies of domestic black impoverishment, there will be insufficient funds for a Pax Americana military to sally forth and intervene in other country's domestic affairs—bringing them, of course, democracy. Blackness is not only criminally dangerous, but a too severe drain on the national resource pool to be sustained.

Such neoconservative ethnic protocols are not new. Such thinking represents the undergirding ethos of white unity (indeed, optic white supremacy) in America, which has never been equally your land and my land. Aphorism number one in the slave economies of the Americas: "Aught's an aught / Zero is a figger / All for the white man / And none for the nigger." The saying forms part of the rich folk archive of Afro-American culture. If we look back to the mid-sixties, we can find a perfect, intriguing, and engaging example of the exclusionary politics of race that has immemorially conditioned neoconservative thought in America.

James Baldwin's brilliant autobiographical essay on American race relations, *The Fire Next Time*, appeared to rave reviews in 1963. In the same year, Norman Podhoretz published in the February issue of *Commentary* his marvelously provocative essay "My Negro Problem—and Ours." Baldwin's guiding thesis is that only through offices of a historically informed bonding in love can blacks and whites achieve perfect accord and beloved community in America. Such an accord would be difficult to reach, says Baldwin, not because blacks are ill informed about whites. Blacks are repeatedly subjected to white racist assaults like that of the policeman who shouts at the young Baldwin: "Why don't you people stay uptown where you belong?"[28] Nor are they unwilling to join in equitable communion with whites. Baldwin suggests, however, that most black Americans understand that white animosity proceeds from a sense of superiority that whites can only cling to if they refuse—at all costs—to look at their own morally bankrupt history of hating, violating, lynching, and exploiting their black fellow men. Rather than face this horror at the abyss of a fundamental white-American selfhood, whites in the United States have constructed and maintained a system of reality that prevents their breaking through to the epiphany that would make them, as it were, *real*. Out of the bubble of their myopic and protective vision, there occasionally come gestures of what whites deem goodwill or even ethical reform in matters of race. The famous *Brown v. Board of Education* school desegregation decision of the fifties was one such gesture.

But, writes Baldwin: "The sloppy and fatuous nature of American good will can never be relied upon to deal with hard problems. These [hard problems] have been dealt with, when they have been dealt with at all, out of necessity—and in political terms, anyway, necessity means concessions made in order to stay on top."[29] In the main, where matters of American race relations are concerned, there is no white goodwill nor pretense to an equality of status. This is because whites continuously—from time immemorial—have projected their own darkest fears, fantasies, libidinous desires, and outlaw inclinations onto the body and soul of "the Negro." (Herman Melville's archetypically American novella *Benito Cereno* about a slave ship rebellion ends with the question from the cheerful New England ship's captain to the Old World Don Benito at the close of the incident: "We are saved, Don Benito. What has cast such a pall over thee?" Don Benito's prototypical New World response is: "the negro.")

And that is just it, says Baldwin; "bad blacks" in America are but shadows created out of necessity by whites to staunch the bloodletting of their guilt, melancholia, and ethically shameful pretenses to innocence in the face of a murderous history from which their legacy wealth and cultural capital have exponentially and obscenely arisen and continuously multiplied. Baldwin offers this prescription:

> The only way [white America] can be released from the Negro's tyrannical power over him is to consent, in effect, to become black himself, to become a part of that suffering and dancing country [a rich African American cultural heritage that has made possible survival] that he now watches wistfully from the heights of his lonely power and, armed with spiritual traveller's checks, visits surreptitiously after dark. How can one respect, let alone adopt, the values of a people who do not, on any level whatever, live the way they say they do, or the way they say they should? I cannot accept the proposition that the four-hundred-year travail of the American Negro should result merely in his attainment of the present level of the American civilization.[30]

Unless, whites are born again into blackness, there is no hope for any ending of the American enterprise save Armageddon and apocalypse: "God gave Noah the rainbow sign / No more water, the fire next time."[31] Black people are simply long past tired of awaiting the rebirth into blackness of white wanderers in the wilderness of American racism.

Baldwin is profoundly aware of the evasion, volte-face, and "fatuous good will" of whites that masquerade as "liberalism," "democratic largesse," "alliance in the black liberation struggle." And the irony of Norman Podhoretz's 1963 essay "My Negro Problem—and Ours" is that it validates (in psychology, social doctrine, personal ressentiment, and prescribed neoconservative remedy) Baldwin's analysis. Briefly, Podhoretz turns the tables of racial accusation against black America. Growing up in the Brooklyn ghetto like his cotraveler Irving Kristol, Podhoretz found himself the victim of racial animosity and violence. Black guys beat him and his youthful cohort up with a fine glee, swinging baseball bats to white heads. They brutally robbed them of all notions that they were brave, adventurous, or wrapped in the joys of life. The black guys skipped school whenever they liked and answered to no orthodox authority at home. Hence, Podhoretz defines himself as a "prisoner" in his own skin and a victim of black violence as a result of that skin. He is no naive denizen of what Baldwin defines as a covering and protective "system of reality." He is an actual, suffering, impaired, traumatized victim of outgoing black violence. He observes: "To me, at the age of twelve, it seemed very clear that Negroes were better off than Jews—indeed than *all* whites. . . . The Negroes were tougher than we were, more ruthless, and on the whole they were better athletes. What could it mean, then, to say that they were badly off and that we were more fortunate? . . . I was . . . afraid of Negroes. And I . . . hated them with all my heart."[32]

Podhoretz develops this line of "white trauma speak" through the following stations:

1   Black Americans have it good because they are enviably graceful on the dance floor and spectacular on the playing field;

2   Black Americans probably could not, with any satisfaction, take their rightful place in a generally pluralistic society, because, unlike the Jews and other "real" American ethnics, blacks have a past that is only "a stigma . . . [and his] vision of the future [that] is the hope of erasing the stigma by making color irrelevant";

3   as long as they exist on the planet with them, whites—traumatized by the "unfair" distribution of graceful choreography and athletic skills and the "black violence" perpetrated against them—will "hate" Negroes.[33]

The irony is that while he is setting forth such mistily racist nonsense, Podhoretz is citing *The Fire Next Time* and believes he is making a convincing case against the black author's prescriptions of love. Podhoretz, ironically, misinterprets Baldwin as saying that blacks do *not* love the "singing, dancing" resilient "country" of their formation and tradition. Podhoretz also implicitly believes Baldwin is suggesting that blacks take no pride in their color and "want to be white." The precise opposite is true.

Baldwin says unequivocally that it is whites who substitute sentiment and goodwill for love, incapable as they are of escaping their own self-hatred and masquerades of historical innocence. "You must be born again, Norman," is what Baldwin would say to Podhoretz. And Podhoretz would not get it. Why? Because he is in the mode of his own white-ethnic celebration and cleansing as he moves toward a world that may land him on Paradise Island in the homes of the rich and famous.

What then is to be done with, by, about, for, to "the Negro"? Rather than the white man being born into blackness, it is essential, according to Podhoretz, for the black man to lose his color—make it "irrelevant, by making it disappear as a fact of consciousness." And this in a time when black consciousness was coming into being as the dominant African American thought in the United States—fruitfully into being in a new independence that mirrored the decolonization efforts of the new nations of Africa! At precisely this moment, Podhoretz writes that he "shares" the hope that color *will* disappear "but I cannot see how it will ever be realized unless color does *in fact* disappear: and that means not integration, it means assimilation, it means—let the brutal word come out—miscegenation." [34] Was there ever a more "twisted" (Podhoretz's own words for his thinking) version and proof-by-error of the Baldwinian gospel than "My Negro Problem—and Ours"?

It is possible that even in those early days of black consciousness and an imminent Black Power movement that Podhoretz earnestly believed he was being purgative and confessional with respect to the politics of race. Of course, savvy Baldwinians who perused the neoconservative's essay knew he was merely revealing himself and his proclivities as dangerous to all the best interests of the black majority. As one Caribbean reggae has it, he was like a "walking razor." He *was* dangerous. For, Podhoretz makes it abundantly clear that even in its embryonic phases, neoconservatism—with its notions of individual achievement and WASP-like conformity to capitalism's most belligerently warlike and racist tendencies—was a forty acres and a mule syndrome of the first order.

The only material items explicitly missing from neoconservatism's monuments to insider, ethnically cleansed egos were signs on their think tank office doors reading: "No unassimilated Negroes welcome here!" In a general assessment of neoconservatives' effect upon the national polity, Dorrien writes:

> Neoconservatism cut the heart out of populism. . . . Neoconservatives gave a free ride to the business and financial elites who controlled America's investment process. They justified the corporate class's leverage buy-outs and greenmail, and defended the managerial prerogatives of technocratic elites no longer bound to community, cultural, or even national loyalties. They rationalized America's regressive

tax code and its worsening maldistribution of wealth. They deflected responsibility for America's social and economic decay onto America's cultural elites.[35]

Such a litany evokes once again Baldwin's reprise applied to the interests of our nation at large: *friends like these!* And this exclamation turns, finally, inward to the African American intellectual community itself, as it is structured today. For one paradox is that the rhetoric, numbers, beliefs, and volte-face of a general neoconservatism have been enhanced in recent years by a vocal and influential (at least upon the white world) black neoconservatism that is stunning in its alliance with what Haki Madhubuti in "A Poem to Compliment Other Poems" famously called "the real enemy."

I analyze the productions of black neoconservatives in later chapters of this book. For the moment, however, I can say that if black neoconservatives such as Shelby Steele and Stephen Carter have not exactly assimilated and lost their stigmatizing color in ways desired by Podhoretz, they have at least plumped down squarely on behalf of a tricky doctrine of colorblindness, black individualism, and demonstrated merit that rings many familiar changes on the historic unfolding of neoconservatism through its American decades. Of course, from Booker T. Washington's Tuskegee prescriptions for Negro life to be led in abject, apolitical, merit-based subservience to white interests to George Schuyler's condemnations of the Civil Rights Movement and paeans to the bountiful goodness of life for Negroes in America, there has long been a black conservative tradition of thought. But, somehow, in these darkest hours of African American need, one has wanted to see such rhetorical and institutional flourishes as those of Washington and Schuyler as exceptions to the rule of an ongoing and assertive tradition of black liberation struggle in the United States. Who among us would join the party of Schuyler—which is terribly similar to the party of Booker T. Washington—when he writes in *Black and Conservative*:

> My feeling ... is ... that Negroes have the best chance here in the United States if they will avail themselves of the numerous opportunities they have. ... In the United States ... it is easier than anywhere else I know for him to get the best schooling, the best living conditions, the best economic advantages, the best security, the greatest mobility and the best health. ... Once we accept the fact that there is, and will always be, a color caste system in the United States, and stop crying about it, we can concentrate on how best to survive and prosper within that system.[36]

This is the equivalent of "cast down your buckets where you are!"—the famous injunction from Booker T. Washington to blacks to stay in the viciously Jim Crow South and be deprived of rights, while making bricks and doing anachronistic craftsman labor for low wages.

Alas, Schuyler and Washington cannot be considered anomalies or passing blips on the black radical radar. The world of post–Civil Rights era black public intellectuals has been far more akin in many of its manifestations to their injunctions than to the indignant radicalism of the King and Malcolm decades of black liberation struggle. The next chapter describes how a first wave of black intellectuals responded to and performed the changes wrought in America by Civil Rights. *Friends like these!*

FOR CENTURIES, BLACK MEN and women have placed race at the forefront of their labors. Often, they have had no choice. The categorical imperatives of race (its structures of dominant white and subordinate black operations) are still everywhere apparent in the United States, from the deep apartheid of residential housing to the starkly racialized gulag of the nation's private prison-industrial complex. Where initiatives on behalf of the black majority are concerned, race people are as essential today as they were on that Good Friday when Dr. Martin Luther King Jr. was locked behind bars in Birmingham. There are always dread incumbencies of race to be addressed by race people in the United States. This will be so as long as the most universal condition of black people across the globe is that of Little Africa. I state again what was set down in the introduction: "In black American life and culture a race man or race woman is one who dedicates his or her life and work to countering the lies, ideological evasions, and pretensions to 'innocence' and 'equal justice for all' that prop up America's deeply embedded, systemic, and institutional racism. Race men and race women seek remedy for harms to the black body caused by the gospel and practice of white supremacy." Martin Luther King Jr. was not only the most exemplary race man ever born in the United States, but also the greatest black public intellectual leader of the liberation struggle our world has ever known.

In recent years, however, there has been a strong inclination to discount Dr. King's devotion to the ideals of race people. His close affiliation with the black majority has been disregarded, and his undeniable endorsement of

AFTER

CIVIL RIGHTS

THE RISE OF

BLACK PUBLIC

INTELLECTUALS

race as perhaps the single most important lens and analytical category for reading (and changing for the better) the dynamics of our national history has been dishonestly buried under a mountain of universalist, neoconservative platitudes. Some of the oratory and tactics King deployed so effectively from Montgomery to Selma have been relegated to the dustbin of history. America seems far more comfortable genuflecting to a fantastically nostalgic notion of Dr. King as a saintly Christian martyr who transcended race than honestly and comprehensively assessing King's role and efficacy as a race man in furious battle always against global white supremacist economic, militaristic, and political domination. King had his bearing and being in the violence, exclusion, glory, and achievements of that battle.

Currently in America, it is fashionable to decry any felt, perceived, or stated need for a leader or leaders for the black community. In our post–Civil Rights era, blacks are held to be diverse, resourced, handily individualistic, and ruggedly capable of going it either alone or cheerfully and multiculturally in coalition with assorted new brethren. *Every black tub must stand on its own black bottom!* Here, of course, is the seductive purr of that deep-pocketed, libertarian, think tank engine that has driven U.S. polity and policy for the past four decades. White neoconservatism's ascendance and influence has provided ideological horsepower for affluent whites to become entirely comfortable with phantasmagoric social panoramas of leaderless black Teletubbies bleeping across the screen of national consciousness. These imaginary colored grotesques are, of course, in the neoconservative imagination, animatedly oblivious to race.

Certainly there are a great many neoconservatism-zapped whites that believe the Civil Rights Movement of the fifties and sixties repaired and remediated the harms wrought by white supremacy. They earnestly feel that Civil Rights remediation brought a decisive end to American racism. They are convinced that Dr. King and crew were faithful and efficient black custodians, successfully mopping up white racism for all time. Only the shining corridors of opportunity should now occupy the time, talent, and treasure of black Americans at large. This is a naive triumphalism, marketed by white neoconservatism with the same lusty pioneering spirit of those frontier conmen who peddled fool's gold. Interestingly, the reasons for the new disposition of whites—and blacks—who buy such unreliable neoconservative wares are largely economic.

The most published and publicized blacks on the American public scene today are well-dressed, comfortably educated, sagaciously articulate, avowedly new age, and resolutely middle class. Such black Americans are, in their own designation, men and women of color who have often just said "no" to race. The evolution of their relationship to the black majority during the past three decades can be summed up in a single word: good-bye! A number of them have bought into a white neoconservative genealogy (rather than a true history) of America, and feel deeply proud of their antiblack majority bona fides. These "new Negroes" are resonant and prolific but often utterly useless to the most fundamental interests of the black majority. They have both half perceived and half created an immensely capitalized black public sphere of athletics, arts, and entertainment whose salaries and other rewards are as astronomical as any public spaces blacks have inhabited in U.S. history. This present-day public sphere is peopled by members of the new black middle class and fueled by the relentless demand of the American public—indeed one might say a global public—for entertainment from dawn to dusk and beyond, twenty-four hours a day 365 days a year. The new black public sphere (with some notable exceptions) is less amenable to black dissent than to black caricature, more receptive of neoliberal black economics and black neoconservative adventurism than to black social justice.

For an exemplary instance of the extravagantly successful new black life as entertainment rather than leadership, we might trace the ascendance of basketball legend Michael Jordan from North Carolina high school neophyte to the most recognized athletic face on the planet. For a time, everybody wanted to "be like Mike." Mike, however, only wanted to be liked by Nike. The corporation's big cash dollars, and Jordan's own amiable race-transcendent smile, gave him the freedom to do as he pleased. Yes, indeed, no one was more talented on the court than Mike—but what about those exploited, starving, Indonesian children who pieceworked Nike's Air Jordans into overpriced commodities that became motivations to black-on-black homicide in America? What about that? Mike drew a bye in that tournament of real life misery and joined Nike in a frail start-up called Swoosh to aid inner-city kids. And although he never claimed to be a race leader, he never shied away from the corporate profits to be gained by allowing whites to pass him off as a leading black—a race-aversive role model. William C. Rhoden has recently provided the gospel on such calculated talent-for-money economics as Jordan's; his book is titled *Forty-Million-Dollar Slaves*.

In journalism, pulp fiction (called by the in-crowd "urban realism"), media representation, academic tenure-track posts, and so many other professional venues of American life, black men and women came to public light and life in the immediate post–Civil Rights era. Certainly, most were far from green-lighters, but at least they were part of the "there" of opportunities that were in effect actually "there." To invoke the poetic oeuvre of Elizabeth Alexander, one can say that when we went "in search of color" in the post–Civil Rights Era, we could find it almost everywhere! But to what effect, with respect to the black majority?

By way of historical example, one might inquire how the public labors of recent decades stack up against the example of, say, Paul Robeson—a black athletic, oratorical, thespian, political genius of a man. The contrast between, let us say, a likable Mike and a vigorous Robeson could not be starker. Robeson was tireless in his commitment to the interests of the down-and-out globally. As a consequence of this commitment, he was poorly resourced, had his titles and records stripped from the walls of Rutgers University, and was roundly and cowardly denounced before the House Un-American Activities Committee by none other than Jackie Robinson. Robeson was not globally recognized for a race-transcendent and deleteriously corporatist likeability. Those men and women with whom he shared comradeship in courageous and outspoken activism were dedicated, like Dr. King, to redistributing the world's wealth, enhancing the life and health of all those considered restless refuge of society, and ending militarism as the first resort of competing ideologies of power. Like Dr. King, Robeson might well be our touchstone for a definition of the black public intellectual by what he articulated, defended, and advocated in the black public spheres he chose to work in and to some extent created.

Alas, among so-called black public intellectuals of the eighties and nineties, there were not many who remotely resembled Dr. King or Paul Robeson. For the eighties and nineties were characterized by that signal farewell-to-the-black-majority. Rich athletes, affluent writers, and newly middle-class black Americans had but one word for their racially affiliated brothers and sisters: sayonara! The exception may be the domain of black American hip-hop, where black university graduates took off suits and ties, donned Kangol caps and Adidas sneakers, and filled immense auditoriums with sometimes-problematic backbeats and audacious lyrics. Preeminently, though, a new black middle class that received its natal blessings with passage of the Civil Rights Act (1964) and the Voting Rights Act (1965) was most obsessively dedicated to moving on up and away.

Title VII of the Civil Rights Act made "discrimination in employment based on race" a crime.[1] It also mandated the national establishment of an

Equal Employment Opportunity Commission to enforce and oversee the new laws. In actual percentage of the black population, the growth of the new black middle class was quite dramatic. Based on a median household income of $25,050 in 1997, about 40 percent of black households were deemed middle class. This was a proportion almost double that of 1960. In state, local, and federal government employment, blacks have held a higher percentage of available jobs in recent years than at any other time in the United States. The opening of traditionally all-white university and graduate school admissions to black students has been measurably successful in increasing the ranks of black professionals. Of course, black America still suffers mightily in a comparison of its occupational status and wealth with American whites. Some argue, in fact, that the difference between being black and poor and black middle class is one paycheck. Most black capital exists not in stocks, bonds, or mutual funds, but in tangible and nonsustainable assets such as cars and houses.[2] "At midcentury [in the United States], only ten percent of all black workers held middle-class jobs, compared to forty percent of white workers." Therefore, members of what the writer Bart Landry calls "the new black middle class" of the sixties were, in the main, descendants of lower-class "garbage collectors, assembly line workers, domestics, waiters, taxicab drivers, and farmers." New sons and daughters of the old class were, with few exceptions, first-generation black Horatio Alger success stories.[3]

With the law on their side and in the midst of great national economic prosperity, these rags-to-riches babies moved into more salaried white-collar jobs, professional posts, government positions, affirmative-action-financed entrepreneurial start-ups, affirmative-action-motivated managerial slots, and white-fear corporate sector placements than at any time in American history. Life chances of black Americans were—in response to the black activist and revolutionary noise of the sixties—ascendant (as were salaries and publicity for successful blacks). The dream of better days ahead seemed to translate in the post–Civil Rights era in distinctively economic terms. It simply could not rationally (or statistically) be said that things were "as bad" as they had been in the past for black Americans. The way, therefore, was prepared for black economic expansion and the enhancement of life chances. These new phenomena came, perhaps indubitably, to be defined—especially by neoconservatives in America as "freedom." Economics was the enabler of the dream: we were free at last! Even though we had scarcely any sustainable wealth to manage, fall back upon, or pass on to succeeding generations. Many of the best middle-class denizens of the black world today are only "colored rich."

Black folks—separated for centuries from the full resources of the American good life on the basis of race and race alone—were now supposed to occupy a level playing field of psychological good health and potential economic well-being. The Civil Rights Movement and ensuing legislation were regarded—especially by white American neoconservatives—to be the most significant grants to American public life black America had ever enjoyed. By that Freedom Summer of 1964 (when hundreds of young black and white men and women made their way to Mississippi to teach and bring the news of modernity and voter registration to the black majority) the concept of representative government seemed—for the very first time in American history—to be a truly accessible reality for black America.

Penned one year after the end of the Civil War, our Constitution's Fifteenth Amendment seemed ready (finally, in the sixties and thereafter) to become a genuinely operational public reality. The amendment read: "The right of citizens of the United States to vote shall not be denied or abridged by the United States or by any state on account of race, color, or previous condition of servitude." This was the law of the land in 1865. Yet, it required another hundred years and the violent upheavals of the 1950s and 1960s, in combination with brutal attacks on hundreds of Civil Rights workers to secure passage of the Voting Rights Act of 1965. Dr. King himself, while acknowledging voting as a good thing, averred in 1967 that much more than constitutional changes, federal mandates, and legislative enactments were required to provide genuine, tangible resources to achieve black American dignity and empowerment in the United States. A new sense of somebody-ness in formerly exclusively white public spheres of ownership and greenlighting would have to be complemented—this was King's declaration and goal—by enormous cultural and capital resources.

> The Constitution assured the right to vote, but there is no such assurance of the right to adequate housing, or the right to an adequate income. And yet, in a nation which has a gross national product of $750 billion a year, it is morally right to insist that every person have a decent house, an adequate education and enough money to provide basic necessities for one's family. Achievement of these goals will be a lot more difficult and require much more discipline, understanding, organization and sacrifice.
>
> (*Where Do We Go?* 130)

The implicit goal of Dr. King's black public leadership doctrines was a Marshall Plan for the global relief of poverty, militarism, and the U.S. imperialism of a Pax Americana. King's doctrines were in almost every way directly contrary to the expostulations and cynical selfishness of white neoconservatism. And without question it was his vibrant ability to draw world opinion and the black masses to his side that, at least in part, brought about his assassination. Calling for a "true revolution of value" that would "soon look uneasily on the glaring contrast of poverty and wealth," Dr. King was at the time of his death preparing to lead a poor people's campaign to Washington, D.C.—a mass movement that he hoped would culminate in the "adequacy" of life's resources that he knew were beyond the legislative injunctions of mere constitutional amendments (*Where Do We Go?* 188, 130).

"True compassion," he said, "is more than flinging a coin to a beggar; it understands that an edifice which produces beggars needs restructuring" (*Where Do We Go?* 187–188). President Lyndon Johnson concurred with Dr. King. He knew our nation could not fulfill its democratic ideals if it was a nation divided—one half abjectly poor, the other fabulously affluent. Johnson thus declared a war on poverty and secured congressional approval to fund that war. Extraordinary resources were suddenly available in the public sphere to provide jobs, adequate housing, business start-ups, urban renewal, and countless other initiatives designed to bring about a revolution of values and real life chances for black America. With President Johnson's Executive Order 11246, issued in 1965, our national government gave birth to the phrase and injunction "affirmative action." The Fifteenth Amendment seemed to have been retrieved—put back on the active lists of American law.

What I am, of course, attempting to re-create here is the battle of darkness and light that has been the disquieting competition of ideologies of economics, government, culture, law, and day-to-day life in the United States during the post–Civil Rights era. Properly reading this cultural conflict is complicated. Our national imperialistic adventurism abroad, our media's 24/7 embedded regime of corporate-team-player journalists, our corporately financed congressional representatives playing not for or in the national interest but for the corporate big bucks—these standard features of everyday American life make it extremely difficult for truth to be aired. For example, how long has it taken for a national consensus to arise that our imperialistic, transparently corporatist invasion of Iraq is an illegitimate, murderous, and unjust war? How long has it taken to get beyond bromides like "no child left behind" and realize that our national educational system is an unabashed disaster, attract-ing fewer foreign students and retaining fewer U.S. students to graduation than at any time during the past half century? We live in a world of scholas-tically and popularly approved and confidently bantered disconnections—a world where neoconservative ideology and high corporatist enterprises sell the myth of the American dream as a reality fully and freely achieved by none other than black America at large. What, though, is the truth of this matter?

Today, black politicians do occupy key posts—from municipal mayors to a black secretary of state. Black entrepreneurs and small business owners are legion. Black CEOs and CFOs are officers of global enterprises. Some, like Cathy Hughes and Earl Graves, are CEOs of their own multimillion-dollar projects. Median income of the new black, post–Civil Rights era middle class is nearly on par with that of its white counterpart. Black middle-class edu-cational attainment has moved steadily toward equality with white degree accomplishments. Black and white life expectancy and other health measures in the United States have moved closer than ever. As Orlando Patterson said in 1995:

> There is no denying the fact that, in absolute terms, African Americans, on av-erage, are better off now than at any other time in their history. . . . The black presence in American life and thought is today pervasive. A mere 13 percent of the population, they dominate the nation's popular culture: its music, its dance, its talk, its sports, its youths' fashion; and they are a powerful force in its popular and elite literature. . . . These are without doubt the best of times for middle-class African Americans, who own more businesses and control a greater share of the national wealth that at any other period.[4]

But before we pop a cork and sing "Auld Lang Syne" to the passing of race and white supremacy, we might reflect on Dr. King's estimate of the sig-nificance of well-heeled blacks entering the public sphere and the relevance of his estimate for our era. In *Where Do We Go from Here?* King eloquently noted: "There are already structured forces in the Negro community that can serve as the basis for building a powerful united front—the Negro church, the Negro press, the Negro fraternities and sororities, and Negro professional associations" (124). Encouraging, indeed, this notion of a black institutional base, at the ready.

In truth, however, the end of legal segregation and (re)birth of legal black access not only to worlds of education and business, but also to media and popular culture, found what might be called our "black structures of possible enhancement" all too eagerly rolling out of the hood and into ideological condominiums and hungry-for-profit corporate and think-tank arms of the elite white American managerial and ownership classes. Of arms and the Man they sang! They sensed gold in them thar high rises. Gladly, they went forth into a strange land to sing a new song and eradicate from consciousness the bleak urbanscape and deep malaise of the ghetto. "Adios, former amigos! Adios, au revoir, adieu!"

Among those whose profiles and voices were elevated to new and resonantly articulate status in American life during the nineties was a group of black men and women who wanted to set matters straight with respect to race and the race in the United States. This group consisted of several young (fortyish) black beneficiaries of Civil Rights, affirmative action, and access to elite (formerly all-white) universities, first as students, then as academic mentors and professors. Unlike their black intellectual predecessors—the "father of the black American intelligentsia," W. E. B. Du Bois, and his fellow travelers like Anna Julia Cooper, Carter G.. Woodson, Charles Johnson, Ida Wells Barnett, and others—many among the young black intelligentsia of the nineties were *not* circumscribed or limited in their endeavors to a predominantly black audience. They were welcomed at CNN, C-SPAN, the *New York Times*, the *New Yorker*, *Atlantic Monthly*, *Harper's*, and the *Nation*. In short, during the nineties a new black intelligentsia became an American expansion team much on the order of those blacks who flooded professional sports, independent filmmaking, electoral politics, and popular culture. The emergent black intelligentsia's members materialized as fresh faces in the big leagues of American public opinion. Unlike their forebears, they were not simply participants in a Negro league of their own. Here is how Michael Bérubé describes their habitus:

> Thirty years after Du Bois gave up on America and renounced his citizenship [and went into exile in Ghana], African Americans have emphatically taken the lead in the national conversation about "the Negro problem." Indeed, what's distinctive about this generation of African-American intellectuals is that their work has become a fixture of mall bookstores, talk shows, élite universities, and black popular culture. Plainly, they have consolidated the gains of the civil-rights and Black Power movements in at least this regard: they have the ability and the resources to represent themselves in public on their own terms.[5]

The new group was quite appropriately designated "black public intellectu-als." Their "own terms" were decidedly and unashamedly corporative and eco-nomic ones. They were embraced by virtue of their race transcendent ideology by the same intellectual arena that extended its arms and money to their white and Jewish predecessors of the post–World War II generation. They were the "new New York intellectuals" in blackface. Lionel Trilling, Philip Rahv, Clem-ent Greenberg, Irving Howe, and others were—through a sort of bizarre sim-plification of tradition and the ethnic individual talent—pronounced direct intellectual ancestors of Cornel West, Michael Eric Dyson, Derrick Bell, Henry Louis Gates Jr., and other young blacks gracing the public sphere.

Certainly the ubiquity of such black intellectuals as Cornel West and Henry Louis Gates Jr. (both of whom could be witnessed in churches, on television, in national news media, at political conventions, and on the glitzy flatscreens of dance clubs in Spain during the nineties) suggests a compari-son with their culturally pervasive New York brethren. A comparison is also suggested by the accessibility of black public intellectual writings, speeches, proclamations, self-advertisements, essays, media pronouncements, and per-formances that were sometimes inexcusably intellectually shallow and un-mannerly. Alas, to be heard, endorsed, read, and supported by a general pub-lic, one must speak in generalities. The waters of your public wisdom must be wide, but never analytically or theoretically deep. *Demos*—the people— will scarcely ever stand for heavy analytical anchors or evidentiary and sup-portive footnotes. Articles, essays, and even books that are designed not to tax the general reader's imagination become the welcome manuscripts of the mass media.

George Gissing, the nineteenth-century English satirical novelist, under-stood the correlation between ideology, accessibility, and public intellectual credibility better than most. In *New Grub Street*, he designated the target au-dience for the yellow journalism of his era as the "quarter educated." Where race and its dynamics in the United States are concerned, the ranks of the quarter educated are extensive—ironically among both blacks and whites that should know and read more than they actually do. And black public intellectuals often seemed eagerly self-tailored and willing to say or do any-thing to meet this quarter-educated audience's desire for scintillating race talk. Writings such as *Race Matters* by Cornel West and *I May Not Get There with You* and other works by Michael Eric Dyson, are akin to what might be deemed pamphlet literature.

To speak of such race writing of West and Dyson as carrying the weight of pamphlet publication is simply, I think, to read them in company with the host of present-day American commentary on all aspects of our national life. There are myriad accessible and, at most, "two sitting" effusions devoted to everything from the conflict in Iraq to flimsy and caustic celebrity hagiography (Juan Williams's canonization of Saint Bill Cosby in *Enough*). These tracts are more copious than the competitors in Jonathan Swift's battle of the books. They march out of profit-hungry trade divisions of monopolistic publishing firms. Their authors are intent on getting attention, and seemingly they will do anything to ensure guaranteed shelf space in the corporate bookstores of the world. A recent piece in the *New York Times Book Review* titled "The New Pamphleteers" (July 11, 2004) surveyed some thirteen or fourteen tomes, all of which fell under the generic heading "pamphlet." Alan Wolfe described all the works as "general," often deeply uninformed, and uniformly ponderously acerbic in tone. They were, nonetheless, infused with a breathless enthusiasm. Wolfe writes: "Judge our contemporary culture warriors by the standards of books, and they disappoint: logic, evidence and reason are conspicuously absent. Judge them by the standards of pamphleteering, and they may be doing democracy a favor, reminding our apathetic public why politics matter."[6] Substitute "race matters" and there is the tangible allegiance between some emergent black public intellectuals and the world of the pamphlet.

"Pamphlets," which were of monumental significance as resonantly informed incitements to social and political action, even revolution, during the early days of our nation's formation, have now degenerated into poorly researched and sometimes silly polemics. However, the race works of West and Dyson, in my opinion, are less acerbically polemical than all-too-general and surface-oriented in cast. Both West and Dyson are ordained ministers. Both are, understandably, for good and against evil. Nevertheless, their works—for all the moral credit we can yield to them—are structurally and intellectually pamphlets. They display a conspicuous absence of research, few carefully weighed projections of rational plans of action, and scant humility in the face of the racial complexities bestowed on society by evil. Finally, their race works seem astoundingly smug (as when West suggests he believes in the allegiance of Jewish intellectuals to causes he supports) and self-satisfied (as when Dyson reveals the black committee's championship of his qualifications to be sent to college)—as though they as authors and everyday black thinkers are somehow unequivocally smart, good, and entitled to the reader's praise. Booker T. Washington, in his pronouncements on the black ministry of his day, spoke of the wretchedly poor educational attainments of black ministers, but certainly that has nothing to do with the impeccable bona fides of Professors West and Dyson. I think, however, that it was not educational *lack* that most concerned Washington. I believe it was, in fact, the proliferation of such putative black ministers, masquerading as knowledgeable race leaders, that perturbed him. He denounced their unctuous, self-aggrandizing, windy, deluded notions that the barest commonsense observations somehow translated as wisdom on, by, or for the race. It is difficult for me to avoid thinking of Washington's critique as I read the race writings of Professors West and Dyson. For I hypothesize that it is the faux ministerial and pamphleteering cast of these two intellectuals that lends them credence and acclaim. They are trying to fill the void created by the assassination of Dr. King and seize an opportunity created by the black, public, middle-class American sphere that is hungry for explanations of race.

In Cornel West's best-selling *Race Matters* (1993), we learn that black America is in "crisis." But the crisis is not so much one of oppression or deprivation as of the mind or the soul, depending upon whether one wishes to look at race matters psychologically or religiously. His amateur psychology prompts him to talk (without any reference to psychological studies or to statistical accounts) of a "profound sense of psychological depression, personal worthlessness, and social despair so widespread in black America."[7] Black America, he declares, suffers from "collective clinical depression" (*Race*, 27). His tone is half biblical prophet, half storefront preacher. West in the black religious bully pulpit is really quite something in *Race Matters*; he reprises Baldwin's Temple of the Fire Baptized from the novel *Go Tell It on the Mountain*. Professor West's conclusion is that the greatest threat to black America at the present time is a suffusion of "nihilism" overwhelming us all as a result of market forces and market moralities. Everyone—by whom he means the black majority—has given him or herself over to pleasure and a "hedonistically driven present" (*Race*, 26). But West's mountaintop generalities are not analysis. They are scarcely more than what one might call Reverend West's Sunday morning exhortations, meant for Borders' bookshelves and big revenues.

Professor West is constructed and promoted by American media as a race prophet for all sections of U.S. life, especially the politics and policies

of race. Yet he offers nothing even vaguely reminiscent of a policy recommendation for rational social programming. He provides no clues on how
to break through a putative nihilism to begin a rational social dialogue. Instead, he invokes the good old red, white, and blue that knows no division.
(I allude to the stale myth of united racial states in a boldly single union so
eloquently applauded by Senator Barack Obama at the 2004 Democratic
National Convention.) West calls for a "politics of conversion," by which
he means a change of heart—an endorsement of what Baldwin might have
called a "theology of light"—by former black nihilists. What would facilitate
such an affective paradigm shift? "Nihilism is not overcome by arguments or
analyses; it is tamed by love and care. Any disease of the soul must be conquered by a turning of one's soul. . . . A love ethic must be at the center of a
politics of conversion" (*Race*, 29).

Though West excoriates leaders, intellectuals, market forces, politicians,
homophobes, and other maleficent examples of present-day evil, he does so
strictly in pamphleteer mode. His work is full of earnestness, ethical polemic,
flimsy evidence, and a faux sense of urgency. Professor West asserts that to
"be a serious black leader is to be a race-transcending prophet who critiques
the powers that be (including the black component of the establishment)
and who puts forward a vision of fundamental social change for all who suffer from socially induced misery" (*Race*, 70).

Another example of pamphleteering is Michael Eric Dyson's *Between God
and Gangsta Rap: Bearing Witness to Black Culture*. And I must admit that
on reading Professor Dyson's book, his words in their rapid-fire allusiveness
fooled me, caught me out enough in my quick enthusiasm and my hope for
the black intellectual future to produce a supportive blurb invoking comparison of Dyson with geniuses of times past. I, thus, made a grievous mistake as
a blurb writer. Sometimes he has astounded me.

After a more careful reading of *Between God and Gangsta Rap*, I find no
logical consistency or happiness of style (unlike *Race Matters*, which possesses a logical consistency and, at times, a religiopopulist stylistic efficacy).
To wit: "As rap expands its vision and influence, its unfavorable origins and
its relentless quest to represent black youth are both a consolation and challenge to hip-hoppers. They remind rappers that history is not merely the
stuff of imperial dreams from above. It isn't just sanitizing myths of those
with political power. Representing history is within reach of those who seize
the opportunity to speak for themselves, to represent their own interests at

all costs." Does this mean that gangsta rap is on par with a true and complete history of black ghetto plague years that commenced with the postindustrial American 1970s? Not exactly. A few paragraphs later, Dyson writes: "Gangsta rap is no less legitimate because many 'gangstas' turn out to be middle-class blacks faking homeboy roots. This fact simply focuses attention on the genre's essential constructedness, its literal artifice. Much of gangsta rap makes voyeuristic whites and naïve blacks think they're getting a slice of authentic ghetto life [social history?] when in reality they're being served colorful exaggerations."[8]

Furthermore, in his essay "Gangsta Rap and American Culture," Dyson does not offer sharp analyses or grounded artistic and ethical evaluations of gangsta rap. He simply and off-handedly presents what I call "pamphleteer apologetics." He does so in response to conservative attacks on the genre by opponents such as Bob Dole, C. Delores Tucker, and William Bennett. He seldom speaks in evidentiary or aesthetically knowledgeable ways about the degrees of problematic creative license assumed and zealously defended by gangsta rappers themselves. He never flat-out says that grown black men who, in their popular cultural eminence and rich celebrity, call black women "bitches" and "hos" are scarcely unambiguously reliable cultural historians. Dyson's black public intellectual mode is a Sugar Ray Robinson–style duck and cover strategy. It intermixes metaphors, and dodges and skips evasively away with the light drama of nonce formulations. There are no intellectual knockouts. Further, there is virtually no irony whatsoever. Dyson labels the essay I have just critiqued his "most succinct statement of the ambitions and contradictions of gangsta rap."[9] Finally, though, there is no escape from or justifiable apology for gangsta rap's patriarchal, viciously brutal acts and urgings toward the "snuffing" of black women. Dyson's *love* of black women is, alas, more than a day late in its succinctness. What, then, must a critic of pamphleteer-style black public intellectualism do? I suggest that it is incumbent upon a critique to further explore Dyson's exposition as a representative example of what transpired for race writing in the post–Civil Rights era domain of black popular and race matters critique in the United States. Such an engagement must begin, I believe, with the energetic black expressive cultural world of hip-hop. While rap is essential to Dyson's intellectual project, it is important to note that not all rap is equal in ideology, form, content, or effect. Casual use of the word "rap" can obscure, for example, the distinction between what might be called "hip-hop formational rap" and the more recently emergent "gangsta rap." Dyson often elides distinctions and speaks as though rap's demographics, major distribution and publicity venues, and performance repertoires constitute a unified field. About the manifold offerings of rap, there can be no doubt that Dyson is as learned as any *academic* critic one might call to mind. But his general reading audience—adult, middle-class blacks and whites—is unlikely to be as well informed. The same is quite possibly true of my own readers, so it makes sense here to provide a brief account of two primary subgenres of rap. I do so in the office of a keener critique of Dyson's public intellectual project than might be possible without some idea of the variances within the larger genre. Moreover, I want with as much candor as possible to outline my own critical intellectual relationship to rap.

Tricia Rose has provided one of the most captivating analyses of hip-hop formational rap in her influential book *Black Noise*. Professor Rose astutely demonstrates that the originating form of rap was the product of a specific urban, postindustrial, internationally inflected order of blackness on the world stage. She notes that America's bleak zones of black urban confinement—scantly resourced territories marked by the absence of economic and social services and pocked by violence and blight—became virtual Bantustans of youth unemployment and desolation when the United States ceased being a major manufacturing nation. The new, high technology services economy that replaced manufacturing required little unskilled labor. Meanwhile, American jobs were being exported en masse. Globalization fostered new trade agreements and made deregulation the order of the day. Neoconservative movers and shakers were what Aristotle would have called "efficient causes" of outsourcing. No longer a source of surplus value or a necessary pool of cheap and exploitable manual labor, the black youth of urban America became a virtually redundant demographic. They came to be viewed as a menace to society. The nation decided such inner-city urban youth were in need of strict policing. They were, in effect, imprisoned under stringent new urban surveillance and new police and judicial mandates. Simultaneously, they were technologically impoverished by the refusal of municipal or private suppliers to string television cable lines or later to offer affordable Internet access. Isolated communities in the Bronx had no choice but to cultivate resources and influences in the neighborhood. Young black men and women in the 'hood, thus gave birth to a new genre of entertainment and instruction: "hip-hop formational rap."[10]

This new form was characterized from the outset by innovative elements from the United States, Africa, and the Caribbean. This combination of transatlantic elements has been persuasively elaborated by important works in hip-hop studies such as David Toop's classic *Rap Attack: African Jive to New York Hip Hop* and Mark Anthony Neal's comprehensive anthology *That's the Joint: The Hip-Hop Studies Reader*. Hip hop's improvisational resourcefulness was not out of keeping with a black expressive cultural tradition that has always "made a way out of no way." Denied the traditional materials of their everyday life and creativity, deported Africans in the New World converted their bodies into the "hambone" drum; their feet patted "juba." Their voices created shouts, hollers, and a cappella sorrow songs. In the evolution of black American expressive culture, many a bluesman's first guitar consisted of a broom handle, cigar box, and what wire could be found for stringing. Black folk tales and sacred bush arbor songs were modes of knowing and worshiping that required only the human voice and a temporarily safe haven for communal exchange: "a way out of no way."

In such postindustrial black urban enclaves as Brooklyn and the Bronx, there occurred a commingling of B-boy styles (most adeptly analyzed by the writer Nelson George) with West Indian reggae and Dub. Graffiti tags, break dance kinesthetics, skillful DJing, and brilliantly creative and sometimes freestyle rhyming were all "found" elements (the bricolage, as it were) of hip-hop formational rap. Artists such as KRS-1, Public Enemy, LL Cool Jay, Curtis Blow, Afrika Bambaataa, Kool Herc, and others elaborated hip-hop formational rap's codes of dress, performance, and style. A global youth audience almost immediately endorsed their efforts. A hybrid and international black creativity moved to the economic and entertainment forefront of international youth culture. All at once there were rappers everywhere, "sampling," "beatboxing," drawing "hooks" and inspiration from a host of extant musical traditions of Europe, Africa, Latin America, India, and the Caribbean, as well as homegrown U.S. popular music, rock, blues, and jazz.

In fundamental ways, the initial artists and offerings of hip-hop formational rap not only birthed a popular new youth cultural form, but also declared their work to be resistive, oppositional, and age specific. "If it's too loud (too rapid to understand, too vernacular and allusive to grasp)," its practitioners shouted, "then you're too old!" As rap evolved and became increasingly profitable, performers grew more financially and artistically empowered. They became wealthy, independent producers and joined forces with large distributors. In the process, they amassed a critical cultural capital that enabled them to shape rap in ideologically instructive ways. Public Enemy's most vocal advocate for resistance, Chuck D, famously proclaimed that rap was the CNN of the black world. Educators internationally began to devise innovative pedagogies incorporating rap. Media networks that had ignored or resisted the form began accommodating and promoting rap.

During the evolution of hip-hop formational rap there were, of course, pundits, parents, teachers, and preachers who objected to the new generational sound. There was also, of course, a familiar grumbling among music "professionals" that rap was not music, only noise. It was during the germinal phases of hip-hop formational rap that I wrote *Black Studies, Rap, and the Academy* in which I saluted and endorsed the achievements, instructional ideology, and energy of the form. Rap seemed to me commensurate with longstanding black expressive cultural traditions. One thinks here of the improvisation and internationalism of James Reese Europe's jazz and its celebration by the French at the end of World War I. When I wrote my book, black studies also seemed to me creatively improvisatory and international in its work, producing significant shifts in global canons of knowledge, traditional demographics, and standard pedagogies of the academy. In *Black Studies, Rap, and the Academy*, I did take issue with the misogyny that marked rap lyrics, as well as the form's hypermale claims to exclusive occupancy of the stage and profits of the industry. I rigorously condemned this misogyny at one of its most publicized and distributed sites, namely the productions of the *2 Live Crew*, for which Henry Louis Gates Jr. was a key witness, a "star" for the defense of the groups' misogynistic beats.

Even after allowing for its sometimes-awful gender-specific failings, it still seemed to me that the ever-increasing public denunciations of rap from politicians and publicity hounds alike were more egotistical bids for media attention and capitalistic profit than real critiques. (Although, I will not deny that there were many serious-minded parents, teachers, and scholars who were moved principally in their critique by heartfelt concerns for child welfare and social sobriety.) Many media denunciations seemed simply the usual clichéd adult/generational responses to any new and influential expressive cultural production. The genuinely healthy, educational, politically resistant energies of Public Enemy and KRS-1 did not become apparent to many initial detractors of rap until a new and powerful generic variation brought a vastly different noise to hip-hop.

This new variation assumed the name "gangsta rap." It burst most decisively onto the popular cultural scene with the release of the compact disc
Straight Outta Compton (1988) produced by the group NWA (Niggaz with
Attitude). Exploding with reverberant, confrontational, deep bass beats and
bodacious lyrics, *Straight Outta Compton* altered the ground rules and transformed the vocabularies and intentions of hip-hop formational rap. Gangsta rap was full-barreled, sawed-off, verbal representation of the pent-up
rage of black urban America. Replete with bold contempt for all authority
and agencies of oppression, it blasted the hypocrisy and violence of those
who wished to hold black America in lockdown. At its origin, gangsta rap
was a distinctly West Coast sound, and it frightened much of "respectable"
America (black and white). Pundits who had fired moral warm-ups at hip-
hop formational rap were incensed by gangsta rap. They labeled it crude, in-
artistic, violent, anarchic, misogynistic—a danger to itself and others. Mor-
alists considered its young, black producers, performers, and distributors a
disgrace to their race.

Performers like NWA, Ice-T, Dr. Dre, Ice Cube, and others asserted that
their productions were reality reports, sonic "black papers," as it were, on the
condition of urban ghetto life in America. Their work was a wake-up call to
a nation that had abandoned the black majority to rodent-infested public
housing and starkly reduced social services. Moreover, black urban America
had been abandoned to the ravages of crime. The concluding lines of the
film *Boyz in the Hood* stated the response of the country at large to the terrible structural realities of the ghetto: "Either they don't know, don't show, or
don't care." NWA's rap titled "Fuck tha Police" was gangsta rap's own CNN
newsflash announcement of the roiling discontent of black urban America to
such indifference on the part of the country at large. Gangsta rappers were
decidedly mad as hell, and they loudly announced that their communities
weren't going to take it anymore. Genteel decorum of bootstrap uplift, Civil
Rights nonviolence, and juridical "all deliberate speed" were, in the vision of
gangsta rap, old school. There was a Franz Fanonian intonation to the form's
implicit assumption that only black violence could bring liberation from or
amelioration of the white condoned violence represented by the living conditions of the black majority.

While I was decidedly too old for the Snoop Dogg era—with its hyper-
masculinist sexuality and semiautomatic gunplay—I have to admit to lik-
ing a good deal of gangsta rap's vocal genius and antiauthoritarian truth-

to-power delivery. By and large, though, gangsta rap quickly became too materialistic and self-consciously melodramatic, too repetitious and profit hungry, too clichéd for me. Gangsta rap as a genre fairly quickly began to seem more interested in playing the filthy-rich, misogynistic black thug than in creatively molding a genuinely oppositional sonics, or a sound politics of black resistance.

But Michael Eric Dyson is younger than I, and his first enunciations as a black public intellectual were coextensive with the emergence of gangsta rap. I think gangsta rap's forms, performers, economics, and styles were Dyson's models for his own public address. They marked his entrée into the field of black public intellectualism. Thus he is wont to invoke gangsta rap—in its iconoclastic, economically profitable, and hybrid energies—as a synecdoche for black majority youth culture as a whole. In his use of the word "rap," Dyson usually means not hip-hop formational black poetics but gangsta modalities like those of NWA. His generational-conditioned proclivity for the urban grittiness of gangsta rap is significant and intriguing in its implications for his work as a public intellectual.

For example, in his book *I May Not Get There with You: The True Martin Luther King, Jr.* (2000), Dyson announces his project as a revisionist account of the "true" Dr. King. He wishes to "rescue" the great black Civil Rights leader from maudlin canonization and heroic martyrdom. Correcting the Civil Rights record is not incommensurate in its stated ends from my own purpose. But Dyson's scholarly approach to this goal is immeasurably different. Dyson wants candidly to reveal King's warts rather than his stigmata. He wants to show King in all his failings. Why?

> Having a more balanced view of King may help us appreciate the value of black youth who are often dismissed for their moral flaws, especially by older, middle-class blacks who defend King. Of course, we do not have to deny the huge differences between King and many contemporary black youth, but both have good and bad things in common: how they view women, how they borrow and piece together intellectual sources, how they view sex, and how they confront the evils of racism and ghetto oppression.[11]

Dyson seems here to suggest that if he can persuade us that the effusions and public behaviors of gangsta rap are synonymous with the labors of the true Dr. King, such rap and its practitioners should immediately be handed a get-out-of-jail-free card.

Dyson highlights Dr. King's bad public and private behavior (his revealed failings) as the true King in order to forge a comparison between the great Civil Rights leader's American performance and that of gangsta rappers. What are those failings of King that Dyson has in mind? They are now well-documented and much discussed shortcomings. Dr. King, as Dyson documents, was legendary in his adulterous sexual excess; he plagiarized freely in the composition of his doctoral dissertation. He borrowed liberally from high classical and low vernacular expressive sources to forge his quite brilliant oratory. Dyson suggests that the Civil Rights leader is a predecessor par excellence to the misogynistic, boisterous, materialistic, self-regarding economies of gangsta rap. Simply realizing that the gangsta rapper's signal goal is to get paid by any means necessary is, in itself, enough to distinguish him from the economically sacrificial labors of Dr. King, who never amassed wealth or labored exclusively for money during his leadership years.

But Dyson's comparative sleight-of-hand would have us believe that his attention to the "bad" Dr. King and to "bad" rappers offers revelatory, thoughtful black public intellectual discourse, especially for a middle-class black audience. "How," Dyson seems to ask, "can you [respectable middle-class citizens] venerate Dr. King in his 'badness,' and yet condemn gangsta rappers, the young expressive cultural artists whom I admire?" One has to admit Dyson's is an audacious gambit. It is, of course, in keeping with the frequently skewed logic, manly boasts, and the "what you gonna do?" interrogations of gangsta rap.

Dyson suggests that the essence of King's leadership is located in his personal failings, which, presumably, are to be compared to the criminality, gun-toting commerciality, and substance abuse of gangsta rappers such as Tupac Shakur. In scholarly correspondence with me, one of my brilliant students Alexis Gumbs asked: "[Does] it really make any sense to base a program for the future [of black America] on the weakest moments in the life of a leader"? Ms. Gumbs went on to point out that the "youth" whom Dyson claims to want to defend scarcely make an appearance in *I May Not Get There with You*. She is correct. Such youth certainly are not the intended audience for his book. What actually is at work in Dyson's text—especially when he devotes lavish textual space to his own public appearance on *Meet the Press*—is authorial self-promotion. Black youth are simply Dyson's alibi. They are, finally, only the screens from behind which Dyson works (in commercially savvy syllables) to mesmerize a black middle-class audience. He titillates them with tales of intellectual dishonesty and sin found in the life of one of their great-est leaders. He tells them of sinful new saviors of the race. This is the stuff of tabloid journalism. It is not worthy work for a true black public intellectual.

The middle-class reader bias signaled by *I May Not Get There with You* con-tinues in Dyson's other works: *Is Bill Cosby Right? Or Has the Black Middle-Class Lost Its Mind?* and *Come Hell or High Water: Hurricane Katrina and the Color of Disaster. Is Bill Cosby Right?* is Dyson's response to a series of public attacks launched by the millionaire comedian on the black poor. Cosby's at-tacks began in his presentation at a celebration of the fiftieth anniversary of *Brown v. Board of Education.* Dyson believes that Cosby's assaults on the beleaguered black poor (which is, of course, to say the black majority) are not, finally, those of someone who has "lost his mind." Cosby's venomous out-bursts against the black poor, in Dyson's account, are articulated outcomes of a black middle-class elitism of values. He divides the black world into the binary categories: privileged and poor, ghetto and seditty. These categories are implicitly God ordained as in "the poor we have always with us." What is required of the black middle class is compassionate understanding of their ghetto brothers and sisters. Dyson implies that Rodney King's famous ques-tion is the crux of his own analysis: "Can't we all just get along?" In Dyson's view, Cosby and the black middle class need to get their values straight and be more charitably Christian. Further, he posits that they need to recognize that it is precisely out of the ghetto that such forceful expressive cultural forms as gangsta rap emerge to entertain and instruct.

But where in all this is Dyson's serious address to the economic, material-ist, and textual analyses that would reveal Bill Cosby and his well-heeled and viciously condemnatory ilk as assimilationists, performing the same deni-grating work their kind have performed since time immemorial? Namely, promoting the values of the white middle and upper classes—indeed getting paid by those classes to emulate and almost live the same life as they. Assimi-lationists promote always-white values to "the desperate class"—the name James Weldon Johnson bestows on the black majority in *The Autobiography of an Ex-Colored Man.* The assimilationist's message is always the same: "If I have pulled myself up in the dread racial economies of white America by my own bootstraps, if indeed the most hard-pressed of immigrants can do the same, why can't you (the black majority) get a handle on things? Why do you (the black majority) have to be so irresponsible, disreputable, so lasciviously, criminally, and illiterately *black?*" (This is my paraphrase of the *assimilados'* familiar injunction to those of his race who are most desperate.) The idea is that if the desperate class would just get some *values* alternative to those irresponsible behavioral codes that embarrass their middle-class counterparts, they would (in that signal word from a poem by Maya Angelou) *rise!*

What is completely missing from Dyson's vernacular writing of the Bill Cosby assaults on impoverished blacks is precisely the type of economic, materialist, and textual analyses of proposed structural determinants of poverty and problematic values that cause the poor to be "always with us." There is a talismanic saying in black everyday life that goes something like this: "I thank God that I woke up this morning in my right mind."

Now, who, in his right mind, would posit that the black majority has been resourced, educated, and structurally situated in a socially equitable distribution of national wealth and resources and set to its own devices on a level playing field? A field where that majority can let its children safely play on urban sidewalks, feel secure against violence, have no traffic whatsoever with drugs, earn a living wage, and stroll down to any corner of South Central, East Durham, or East Palo Alto, pick up a novel at the local bookshop, and have a cup of java at a gleaming Starbucks? I am talking here about those black majority spaces where anyone in his right mind would hesitate to stroll about after dark. Where, then, is the level playing field for the black majority: the field of dreams? Who would posit such a field?

In the manifest presence of a black urban bleakness that has been structurally created, socially and politically tolerated, textually defended, and jurisdictionally policed into spatial stasis by our national polity, how can anyone give utterance to the assimilationist manifesto as though it contained a shred of social justice or compassionate logic? Further, who would claim that *Brown v. Board of Education* actually created the kind of field of dreams so touted by the Cosby Show of new black American assimilators? So many of its implicit and utopian promises have been utterly defeated in time's passage. Finally, why would anyone suggest that such a field of dreams is a reality of everyday black majority life? If it were, in fact so, why would that majority reject it and willfully opt for illiteracy, single-parent households, and criminality? "They are legally free as birds," charges the assimilator, "but they simply do not choose to fly."

Dyson—who has told us he grew up working class, and found himself a teenage father and welfare beneficiary—*knows* that the current Cosbyettes and their denunciations of the black poor repeatedly prove they are off base.

Even in their philanthropy (always a last refuge for robber barons of capital-istic societies), they seek no duly analytical or potentially coalitional line with the black majority. And Dyson merely feigns disgust with and rejection of such assaulters of the poor. For, in the end, he is completely unwilling to risk his own achieved class privilege and sedittiness in the office of a *true* (a word he likes) economic account of class and its significance in the abjection of the black American majority.

Dyson has no intention of committing class treachery or justly pronounc-ing that Bill Cosby is an assimilationist menace to the black majority. In his attacks from a bully Christian pulpit, he "gangsters" the black poor in ways far more scandalous than any gangsta rapper has so far managed.

In the many years that Bill Cosby had some measure of creative control in the production of his famous and positive-image-bearing television show, how many times did *he* bring forth a single, intellectually cogent address to the plight of the desperate class? *Assimilados* are never reliable moral wit-nesses to the condition of the besieged majority. They invariably point to the sweetness of what they perceive as a verifiable and all-pervasive black freedom of opportunity and possibility in America. Simultaneously, they work fiercely hard to avoid discussing the ongoing dominant society's war against the poor. Dyson's focus on values, and not pointed analysis, in *Is Bill Cosby Right? Or Has the Black Middle Class Lost Its Mind?* represents just such avoidance.

Come Hell or High Water is Dyson's appropriation of one of the greatest natural disasters to strike the United States. I say "appropriation" because Dyson's text contains almost no hint of the agency of black Americans in saving their own and their families', friends', and fellow sufferers' lives during or after the storm. Though he places quotes from Katrina survivors on inter-leaved pages of his book, he seems to possess little knowledge of black groups and individuals—working 24/7 (in the present)—to rebuild and reclaim Af-rican American life and property in New Orleans. Most of *Come Hell or High Water* is simply a reprise of what even the most neophyte black activist knows: government in America is supremely indifferent to the miserable state of the black majority. Dyson once again signals in his Katrina book a class bias that cannot disentangle itself from what Michel Foucault calls "governmentality." Governmentality is a paradigm that attributes all agency to the ruling pow-ers that be, suggesting that the internalization of such regulatory power by the populace enhances its controlling and surveillance effects.

Dr. King was not a govermentalist; he commenced his liberatory labors by welcoming and endorsing as primary the aid, wisdom, and work of the black majority. That majority was always at the forefront of his labors. His guiding premise was that the federal government was, indeed, morally out of kilter, wrongly placed, malformed, and unaccountable. This for King was a truism. What needed to be formulated was a new, nongovernmental crusade of independent moral authority based on the needs of the many. Dyson's writing provides little sense of similarity to the determinations of Dr. King. Dyson suggests no processes of connection nor any plan of coalition between the middle-class audience that is his bread-and-butter and the post-Katrina black majority. He offers only a tiresome catalog of the *true* failings of the federal government. While his gangsta-rap-inspired eloquence of presentation, stand-up-comedy instincts, macho flair, and rapid-fire delivery have made Dyson a kind of black public intellectual icon, it is not really possible to consider him a CNN for the black world. Ultimately, his production is neither an elaboration of nor a new analytic on Dr. King's legacy. Short on intellectually interesting propositions and rigorously argued points of view in the service of ameliorating the plight of the black majority, Dyson's is a rap completely foreign to the most efficacious articulations of Dr. King. "Betrayal" may be too strong a word to use here, but it is probably close enough.

In the next chapter, I further explore the ideology and work of Cornel West. I read his labors and those of his former colleague at Harvard University Henry Louis Gates Jr. as yet another variation of the troubled category, black public intellectual. The combined and collaborative labors of Professors West and Gates, mark, for me, a deeply problematic centrist discourse that certainly bears little resemblance to the best of Dr. Martin Luther King Jr. Of course, for Dr. King and his cohort, there was no 24/7 media industry, no abundant funding during Black History Month, no ample budget from the Black Student Association, no Charlie Rose, no BET, Brian Lamb, or Larry King show hungry for instant and abundant race talk. The first wave of eighties black public intellectuals were far more inclined—as a function of the institutional desires and media's demands of their era—to go on stage, seize the mic, and greet the media cameras with hip-hopping, ministerial showmanship that put some lesser Hollywood actors to shame. They preferred this to assessing analytically the imperiled frontlines of black majority life and needs in America. At those still imperiled frontlines, well researched and thoughtful intellectual articulations can be of service, particularly if they issue from bona fide and well-regarded public sources. However, just as in idyllic lyrics of romance "love conquers all," so too the prospect of producing accessible celebrity sound bites on race for a 24/7 media not only conquered but also utterly ruled the attention of the first wave of post–Civil Rights era black public intellectuals.

In their capitulation to an eager audience of media admirers, these first-wavers were not essentially different from their white American, talking-head compeers. Their black public intellectual failure was in large measure a result of the very structure of public intellectualdom in the United States characterizing their era. In *Public Intellectuals: A Study in Decline*, Richard Posner writes:

> It is not at all certain that these or other sources of market failure [by which I mean, a complete absence of public accountability on the part of public intellectuals to anyone] are present to a significant degree in the public-intellectual market. [But] if I am right that the consumers in this market protect themselves by not relying on what the public intellectual says, this implies that they value public intellectual work for entertainment or solidarity rather than for guidance or direction, and it is not obvious that they aren't getting what they pay for.[12]

"Entertainment" resounds here with the echolalia of a sound pronouncement from the chief jurist of some classical temple of the laws. It is a fact not to be discounted that the first wave was resolved to outentertain even professional entertainers and to outpreach the most seasoned holy leaders of the flock. The showmen and -women of the first post–Civil Rights era public intellectual generation represented a giant step backward. Their intensely personal and decidedly economic agendas were far in arrears of the efficacious labors of the precursor Civil Rights and Black Power movements that made their lives in public possible.

But, how much was really lost or compromised by the first wave of hip-hop ministerial black public intellectuals? Certainly, despite the entertainment bent of their race writing, there was also available to the American public a more than ample stock of serious, comprehensive, scholarly work. Black studies in the academy saw to that. Moreover, under assault from a scurrilous neoconservatism, there was indisputably a clear need for *someone* to speak counteroffensively about the efficacies of race. The nation needed someone to counter the preposterous lies, shabby distortions of our history and national doctrines emanating from neoconservative think tanks and conservative media op-eds. If we ask in this light why there was sometimes a paucity of scholarly detail in the work of our first-waver intellectuals, there is a simple answer. They were battling a seriously ideologically overwrought, historically distorted, polemical, and ad hominem neoconservative barrage. The culture wars were everywhere!

One of my strongest memories of the "culture wars" is the negative emotional impact of a former white colleague at the University of Pennsylvania daring to send out copies of a strictly-for-entertainment, bombastic speech against academic inclusiveness and curricular expansion to the entire arts and sciences faculty. This man, Alan Charles Kors, had presented his cheaply insulting speech to the inaugural meeting of the National Association of Scholars (NAS), an institution whose board members currently include Irving Kristol and Shelby Steele. The agenda of NAS seems then and now to be to close down in the name of freedom every salubrious opening of the American academy to multiculturalism, expanded curricular offerings, affirmative action, and, access to the comprehensive truth. Let neoconservative freedom (meaning hegemony of predominantly white and libertarian males) reign. Simply stated, NAS holds that men and women of a peculiarly neoconservative stamp should politically and ideologically take over the academy in the name of liberty. A visit to the organization's Web site is like a walk back down America's neoconservative memory lane. What is most appalling to me—and persuades me to offer some apology for the theatrics of the boisterous race talkers of the first wave—is that the University of Pennsylvania administration at large seemed to endorse the anti-intellectual, vilifying, ideologically, and racialistically retrograde polemics of Professor Kors. We needed a black drum line to counter such aberrancy.

To their credit, the first-wavers did not let miasmic sources of historical distortion and ad hominem attacks such as those of the NAS off the hook. Nor, thank heavens, did they (save for the rare midwestern exception or southern misstep) actually become members of such an institution or endorse even its most seemingly innocuous calls for all Americans to abandon affirmative action in the academy and elsewhere. What ideological bent the first-wavers assumed, and the financing they received, came, I think, in combination with an implicit faith on their part in the cultural wealth and potential socially revolutionary expressive and creative wealth of the black majority. If asked, that is to say, Professors West and Dyson would almost certainly have averred that they were, in fact, speaking on the register of and in behalf of interests of the black majority.

And yet, by the nineties, Professor West and other prominent black intellectuals would make no such claims. They rolled with alacrity toward the center. At a time when debate over the interests of the black majority divided between the claims of the structuralists and those of the behaviorists, prominent black public intellectuals hovered with eager and smiling restlessness in the shining antechambers of neoconservatism's more stately mansions. They were often far more prone to endorse the logic of the behaviorists (those who posit that the abject condition of the black majority is a result of their own "bad behavior") than the structuralists. Dr. King was a structuralist; he believed global legal, political, social, and economic structures had to be revolutionarily readjusted if the Little Africas of the world were to become domains of the good life. In the next chapter, I turn to the discursive strategies of the national debate between behaviorists and structuralists and the role black centrist intellectuals assumed within it. In recent years, the debate has brought socially and rhetorically surprising occasions and actors to the foreground of U.S. life and culture. It has shaped a discursive universe where a comedian can be taken quite seriously as a race talker, and a Harvard professor can be read out in some of his influential writing as a comedian, or at least, a great American jokester.

IN 2004 THE COMEDIAN Dr. William Henry (Bill) Cosby Jr. sparked a public furor when he remarked to an assembly commemorating the *Brown v. Board of Education* decision: "I can't even talk the way these people talk. . . . '*Why you ain't, Where you is?*' . . . Everybody knows it's important to speak English except these knuckleheads." Cosby was referring, of course, to black youth in America. The comedian provoked further vitriol when he responded to the outrage his remarks occasioned (voiced principally by black Americans) in Chicago a few months later. In July 2004 at the Rainbow/PUSH Coalition & Citizenship Education Fund's annual conference, he continued his rhetorical jeremiad: "Stop beating up on your women because you can't find a job," he preached to the assembled audience. Cosby assured all who would listen that it was not he who should be blamed for "airing dirty laundry": "Let me tell you something, your dirty laundry gets out of school at 2:30 every day, it's cursing and calling each other n—— as they're walking up and down the street. They think they're hip. They can't read; they can't write. They're laughing and giggling, and they're going nowhere."[1]

Dr. Cosby was not without compeers in what seemed to be a year of black public assault on the young men and women of America's inner cities. At the 2004 Democratic National Convention, Illinois senator Barack Obama suggested that black inner-city parents needed to be reminded to supervise their children's schoolwork. He spoke as well to the baleful myth that succeeding in inner-city schools is tantamount to "acting white." Senator Obama's implicit chastisement of low educational expectations and standards in the ghetto drew glowing admiration from Dr. Henry Louis Gates Jr., who served as a guest writer for the *New York Times* during the convention summer of 2004: "Why has it been so difficult for black leaders to say such things in public, without being pilloried for 'blaming the victim'? Why the huge flap over Bill Cosby's insistence that black teenagers do their homework, stay in school, master Standard English and stop having babies? Any black person who frequents a barbershop or beauty parlor in the inner city knows that Mr. Cosby [and, by association, Senator Obama] was only echoing sentiments widely shared in the black community."[2] Under Gates's prose ministrations, Cosby's assault is transformed into vernacular wisdom of the barbershop variety. A scathing verbal assault on black people becomes black everyday common sense. As guest writer for the *Times*, Gates implores readers to forgive the sixty-seven-year-old comedian for referring to today's black youth as "knuckleheads."

Dr. Cosby and Dr. Gates emphatically remind us that ghetto youth are woefully undersupervised. Young black men and women do not possess even basic knowledge of their culture and heritage. And they seem shamefully comfortable with Ebonics (the "axe" for "ask" syndrome of the natural language known as African American Vernacular English). Gates and Cosby see the black community's woes preeminently as a *behavioral* problem. And a behavioral problem, with its locus in the individual, does not require government intervention. According to the two black doctors, the black community just needs a dose of straight talk and (seemingly) a corrective kick in the seat of the pants. Something on the order, I believe, of a ghetto trip to the principal's office to whip young black "strays" into standardized shape for good old all-American low-wage, entry-level employment.

In his book *Jim Crow's Children: The Broken Promise of the Brown Decision*, Peter Irons tells a story radically different from tales spun by Gates, Cosby, and Obama. Professor Irons argues that the educational deficit in today's inner city can be traced historically and unequivocally to willful and documented failures of American conscience and conscientiousness with respect to education for the black majority in the United States. The causes for low educational expectations and achievement are decidedly not behavioral, in Irons's account, but structural.

In other words, "shiftlessness" (a favorite word of Miss Ophelia from *Uncle Tom's Cabin*) on the part of the black community did not create the "axe" for "ask" syndrome or the fact that after school, black youth have no place to go other than the streets. Even the public libraries of America have been shut down by the absence of government funding. Where can young people go? Their schools are burnt-out, leaky, crumbling, musty structures suffering from years of neglect. Armed security guards with metal-detecting wands patrol the halls. The textbooks available are (as one student tells Irons) "older than your grandmama." The teachers are cynical and often undertrained. Material and structural realities of black inner-city educational life from Los Angeles to New York, Kansas City to Miami, are *abject*. More money is spent on security than on computers. The black educational enterprise often seems much more like imprisonment than enlightenment.

There have been some educational reforms in recent years—attempts to secure fitter buildings, better trained teachers and administrators, and state of the art informational technology. But these reforms have not addressed the serious problems associated with what Irons calls the "total environment" of the urban ghetto—which is home to nearly half of all black children in the United States.[3] Educational reforms simply do not touch issues like high crime rates, poor cultural resources, meager incomes, or the increasing prevalence of households in which the sole provider is a single woman, perhaps barely literate herself, with scant time or energy to devote to helping her children with their homework. And, before we are sidetracked by questions such as, "Well, why are these *children* having children?" or "Why is single motherhood so prevalent in the ghetto?" consider this statistic from the eminent urban sociologist William Julius Wilson: "Between 1980 and 1992, when the rate of births outside of marriage increased nationally by 54 percent, it rose 94 percent for whites and only 9 percent for blacks."[4]

Most recent efforts at educational reform have relied on standardized testing to measure and ensure "results." Professor Irons notes: "One consequence of 'teaching to the test' is that school officials pressure teachers to rely on old-fashioned methods of rote learning, the mainstay of Jim Crow schools before the *Brown* decision. Creativity, curiosity, and critical thinking are stifled."[5] Professor Irons's emphasis is not on blacks behaving badly (or badly performing), but on standardized testing—a structural issue—as a costly, misconceived, and retrogressive educational practice.

Unlike Cosby, Gates, and other public intellectuals we might call "centrists" (in that they unfailingly defer to moderate, commonsense, American moral notions of individual responsibility), Professor Irons resists a pious, moralizing caricature of a black underclass unwilling to pull its own weight.

He argues persuasively that the disaster of present-day black American education has assignable and easily discernable structural causes:

> The blame rests with the "dominant race" in America. Whites created the institution of slavery; whites fashioned the Jim Crow system that replaced slavery with segregation; whites spat on black children, threw rocks at buses, and shut down entire school districts to avoid integration; and white parents abandoned the cities when neighborhoods and schools passed the "tipping point" and became too black for comfort. This is not an indictment of a race, merely an acknowledgment of reality.[6]

A further acknowledgment of this reality appears in the work of William Julius Wilson. In his gripping book *When Work Disappears*, Wilson writes: "The residents of . . . jobless black poverty areas face certain social constraints on the choices they can make in their daily lives. These constraints, combined with restricted opportunities in the larger society, lead to ghetto-related behavior and attitudes—that is, behavior and attitudes that are found more frequently in ghetto neighborhoods than in neighborhoods that feature even modest levels of poverty and local employment."[7] It is social structure that produces "ghetto-related behavior" in Wilson's account and in Irons's analyses. In an America in which hundreds of billions of dollars can be expended "spreading freedom" in a country thousands of miles away while children at home are starving and millions are without health care or insurance, someone clearly needs to take a serious look at the nation's structure!

Wilson reminds us that in areas like Chicago's North Lawndale blacks once led a life that included at least a modicum of hope for achieving some measure of the American dream. Disaster struck more than four decades ago in the form of an American polity's decision to go global, restructuring the nature of work inside the country's traditional borders and outsourcing millions of American jobs abroad. This is the principal economic narrative of the past half century. It is now a twice-told tale: production and unskilled jobs disappeared either overseas or altogether. Service and high-tech skilled positions requiring competent educational achievement took their place. American rust belts proliferated as the country became decisively postindustrial. Here is Wilson on North Lawndale:

> Since 1960, nearly half of its housing stock has disappeared; the remaining units are mostly run-down or dilapidated. Two large factories anchored the economy of

this West Side neighborhood in its good days—the Hawthorne plant of Western Electric, which employed over 43,000 workers; and an International Harvester plant with 14,000 workers. The world headquarters for Sears, Roebuck and Company was located there, providing another 10,000 jobs. [These employers and most of the support economy that accompanied them disappeared by 1987.]

. . . In 1986, North Lawndale, with a population of over 66,000, had only one bank and one supermarket; but it was also home to forty-eight state lottery agents, fifty currency exchanges, and ninety-nine licensed liquor stores and bars.[8]

Work disappeared, and with its disappearance, *hope* became a lottery ticket. Survival became almost completely dependent upon underground (home hairdressing for hire) and illegal (drug trafficking) economies. What, then, motivates "bad black behavior"? The structural answer is inescapable: "It's the economy, stupid!"

Wilson writes: "Regular employment provides the anchor for the spatial and temporal aspects of daily life. It determines where you are going to be and when you are going to be there. In the absence of regular employment, life, including family life, becomes less coherent." Perhaps it is precisely because the parent of one of the students from Washington, D.C.'s Shaw Junior High School interviewed by Irons *knows*, deep in her soul, about the effects that economic constraints will have on her son's education and life chances that she tells him: "It's better to have a big heart than a big head."[9] This is sad consolation, to be sure. Yet, when structures of opportunity are bankrupt, such a maxim is a handy parental poultice for adults who desperately hold down seven dollar an hour jobs requiring three winter bus rides even to show up. And you can forget about benefits. Here is an excerpt from the full and varied ethnographic data collected by the *Urban Poverty and Family Life Study* that anchors Wilson's book:

> Clifford has been working for several years as a dishwasher for different employers. He now cooks, mops, and washes dishes for $4.85 an hour. He has held this job since February of 1985 without taking a single day of vacation. . . . On the day of the interview, he had had a molar pulled and was in great pain (partly due to the fact that, not having any money and having already borrowed cash to pay for the extraction, he could not buy the prescribed pain-killers); yet he was . . . reluctant to call his boss and ask for an evening off.[10]

It takes a big heart indeed to handle such indignity. But black centrist intellectuals like Henry Louis Gates Jr. and others seem entirely capable of ignoring the structural heart of the matter of present-day black immiseration, rolling off into the profitable, middle-of-the-road, nonoffensive, nonposition of the center.

This virtual center, eagerly occupied by public spokesmen, politicians, and errant representatives of the new black intelligentsia is an almost exclusively rhetorical ground. It enables them to pass easily between the Scylla of structure and the Charybdis of ghetto-related black behavior with deft avoidance of the facts and incumbencies of the former. Centrist territory is a rhetorical demilitarized zone where honest, committed, and historically informed proclamations on cause and effect regarding race, culture, morality, and gender in the United States can be studiously avoided, fudged, or simply made to suit the audience on hand. It is a domain where well-placed and articulate public men of America abide, as it were, all questions of racial commitment. Certainly, they abide the kinds of soul-wrenching inquiries about structural injustice and the Little Africas of the world that moved Dr. King to action.

I once adamantly announced to a colleague and friend that she was invoking improper standards to judge the political and theoretical position of a politician I was energetically defending. "You just don't *get* his position," I insisted. "He is a *centrist*." To which she responded: "You, Houston, are the one who doesn't get it. Don't you see? The *center* is no position at all!" In the current political bailiwicks of the United States we have reduced a mouthful of definitions of the center to two words: *flip* and *flop*.

Booker T. Washington tells a well-known story in his autobiography, *Up from Slavery*. It seems a black confidence man presented himself as an applicant for a teaching post in a southern community of newly freed blacks. Nattily dressed and wondrously well spoken, he entered the room for his interview. When asked by the chairman whether he endorsed the geocentric (sun around the earth) or heliocentric (earth around the sun) view of the universe, he responded that he had been comprehensively and fully educated. At the pleasure of the community, he was prepared to teach either view. It was all, for him, a matter of what would enable him to get paid in full. No story, perhaps, offers a fitter characterization of the black centrist sensibility.

Where does the responsibility for black educational deficits reside: in *structure* or *behavior?* Centrists can provide an answer favorable to either view. Centrists are fully and comprehensively educated in alternative responses. Does a candidate support abortion and a woman's right to choose, or does he believe in rights of the unborn that commence with conception? Some candidates for high office are prepared to sign onto either/or while diaphanously floating in the center. "Flip" and "flop" are marvelous tools for acceding to the profit motive, whether the gain is votes or cultural and economic capital from a paying constituency. What gets lost in all of this, of course, are the proper politics and policies for effectively improving the life chances and material conditions of the poor and the black majority of the United States of America.

The unbearable lightness of the center is the equivalent of a "Mr. Either One," a perhaps apocryphal character about whom I learned during childhood. My mother used to tell the story of a young black couple in Danville, Kentucky, who chose two different boys' names when the wife became pregnant. When their son was born, the doctor visited the maternity ward room of the still-groggy mother and asked: "Well, Susan, there are two boys' names here. Which do you prefer for the birth certificate?" Susan replied, "either one." My mother's tale is perfect for characterizing black centrist intellectuals. They are arch examples of the poet Paul Laurence Dunbar's wearers of the "mask that grins and lies," capable of endorsing any available position.

The Civil Rights Movement, affirmative action, executive orders, new legislation, Black Power, black studies in the academy, and the rise of a new black middle class have brought all sorts of grand opportunities to the black intellectual domain in recent years. The past has been prelude to well-financed, handsomely resourced, and altogether capable young black men and women. This cadre has secured every possible articulate opportunity within American institutions to set the record straight and commit themselves competently to defining the actualities of American history and ameliorating the misery of the American black majority. They have been positioned, by the type of work against white supremacy in which Dr. King so vigorously engaged, to move dramatically away from ascribing the black community's woes to behavioral problems.

Centrists are the "Mr. Either Ones"—the crafty maskers—of present-day American public media life. An either/or sensibility is their stock in trade. They glide around history's sharp edges and throw up faux-ethnic salutes to their best-paying customers. The only thing they do not seem to need for a good night's sleep is the respect of the black majority.

Before turning to a close, critical analysis and critique of two representative black centrist intellectuals, I briefly consider the life and work of Edward Curtis, one of America's most celebrated photographers. Curtis was an ambitious and fiercely talented worker, befriended by Theodore Roosevelt and financed by J.P. Morgan and Andrew Carnegie. When Curtis died in 1952, his ethnographic and photographic accomplishments were known and respected by a select coterie of photography aficionados and anthropological scholars. But since the 1970s, his artistic reputation has expanded as brightly as a firework on the Fourth of July. What was Curtis's project? He set out to provide photographic and ethnographic documentation of American Indian life in all its rapidly vanishing nobility and glory. His aim was to establish a historical and anthropological record of a race. He traveled a long way toward that achievement. He left a legacy of more than forty thousand photographs, twenty volumes of text, and a full-length documentary film. His masterwork comprises the volumes of the series titled *The North American Indian*.

To read and view pages of *The North American Indian* is to encounter an exquisite display of photographic nuance and texture, and an almost complete immersion in "American Indian reality." Indian reality, that is to say, as it has entered our consciousness from sites of American myth manufacture, spanning the centuries from William Bradford's *Of Plymouth Plantation* to the reissue of Forest Carter's *The Education of Little Tree*. We would not want to be without the splendid artistry of Edward Curtis.

Yet, facets of Curtis's work complicate our judgment and evaluations. The photographer, who grew up in abysmal poverty in Minnesota, was an inhabitant of the center. Curtis rhetorically, technically, and boldly understood how to mine the gold in the American marketplace. He was a contemporary of Booker T. Washington, and the two men shared the patronage of the same robber-baron millionaires to accomplish their labors.

Having honed his photographic artistry in his Seattle portrait studio, Curtis took to the open road of Indian country. He knew what Indians were supposed to look like, and he knew precisely what kind of portraits of Indians would sell. What is problematic about his artistic and pictorial practices is what might be called the fold they navigate between the bleak and brutal realities of day-to-day Indian life and the American marketplace's national, mythic expectations. He knew Americans wanted to hang on their walls a mythic Indian nobleness of mien and action, and he knew they were willing to pay handsomely to do so. One sympathetic critic of his work describes what Curtis's artistic practices failed historically to do:

Curtis's photographs capture only a part of American Indian life. They do not show the desperation of Indian people starving after the buffalo were gone, or when rations promised to them in treaties were not delivered. We do not see missionaries preaching in the plazas or on the Plains in his pictures, or medicine men being arrested for performing outlawed ceremonies, or Indian children being hauled off to boarding schools, or the abuse they suffered there. Curtis wrote about these things and he lobbied for Indian rights, but in his photographs he portrays only the traditional aspects of Indian life.[11]

Curtis portrays only the nobleness, first because it fits most challengingly the methods of his pictorial ambitions. But also because that is what *sells*. Curtis carried always with him a kit bag of Indian effects. He methodically doctored scenes of abjection, asking Indians to change out of tattered every-day calico and denim into costumes of an exultant history. But the history Curtis ultimately recorded was only *his* story. It was a representation of no-bility in its untrammeled state—a drama of derring-do, bravado, and ener-getic genre-play. Reality is unseen. Even if things in Curtis's photographic tent (where he had louvers to adjust for light and shadow) did not go so well, even if a modern wristwatch or clock was discovered in a developed print, it was not a major challenge. He merely had to crop or burn the negative to get rid of intrusive reality and make another print.[12] It was a simple, golden manipulation.

The example of Edward Curtis provides a significant analogue for the work of the black centrist intellectuals who have drifted away from their ear-lier progressive moorings in recent years. I say this not in condemnation of the photographic masterpieces of Curtis, but rather to emphasize the mythi-cal, manipulative, market forces that seem always to condition popular rep-resentations of race in America. Like Curtis, black centrist intellectuals wish to lay hands on nobility (in their case the nobility of blackness), all the while denying that essential blackness exists, and paradoxically condemning all bad American ghetto behavior as decisively black and a burden to racial progress. They invoke notions of racial progress while arguing that there is no essential reality called race. If today's black centrist intellectuals were capable of doing so, they would assuredly keep black denim and desperation out of sight—scrubbing the negative clean. For they seek to appropriate for their itinerant kit bags only the brilliance and nobility of the black arts. They are stunningly disingenuous in their heroic representations of themselves and of the arts and entertainment sectors of a race they claim to know. Two intellectual productions—Henry Louis Gates Jr.'s memoir *Colored People* and Cornel West and Henry Louis Gates's coauthored *The Future of the Race*—demonstrate clearly the nature of the black centrist intellectual project. They are second-wave black public intellectual productions par excellence.

Henry Louis Gates Jr.'s memoir recounts the story of his "colored" life in Piedmont, West Virginia, from the year of his birth to his departure for the Ivy League and his enrollment at Yale. The book's preface is a letter from Gates to his daughter in which the author states that he wrote *Colored People* in order to answer the question of "just exactly what the civil rights movement had been all about."[13] This is fine salesmanship. For who would not want to read an incisive and honest assessment of the Civil Rights Movement written by a well-known scholar like Gates?

However, *Colored People*'s opening letter is not emblematic of the book that follows. Gates's memoir unfolds in scenic episodes. It contains portraits of his ancestors, treatises on everyday black life in the '50s and '60s, personal accounts of strife and worry, and sometimes painful confessionals from the author concerning his own self-image. The plot of *Colored People* is not exactly original. The story is that of an unathletic young boy named Louis Smith Gates. The boy's father deplores his son's lack of sveltness and athleticism. The son, however, comes into his own through an unlikely combination of native smarts, Black Power, and interracial amour. In the spirited finale, the hero (single-handedly) performs feats of integration in his Piedmont, West Virginia, hometown. He bids the town adieu and heads out for Yale.

The hero's mother is represented as an earnest, heavy-hearted spirit. She dearly loves the narrator and his older brother "Rocky," the athletic captain of the basketball team. Yet her hatred of whites illuminates for the narrator precisely what he must never become. In a radical act of self-determination, the Gates of the memoir (college-educated and athletic-grace-challenged) marries a white woman. His preference for white women drives his misogynistic uncles absolutely nuts. They are driven to sheer buffoonery when he seats this white wife at their traditionally all-black dinner table at his grandmother's home on Thanksgiving Day. Sadly, black female relatives of the interracially married hero then cater to his wife as though she were a white angel. His dark uncles, embarrassed, grin and bear it, laughing, "hee, hee, hee."

At last—in a real-world Jacob-and-Esau legal tableau—the narrator (Louis Smith Gates) changes his name to his father's (Henry Louis Gates), effectively displacing his fearsome older brother "Rocky." (In the biblical story, we recall, the younger Jacob fools his older brother Esau into selling his birthright for a cup of stew.) Gates's mother dies. Integration apocalyptically wipes out the "colored" world.

But there is much more to Gates's memoir than can be gleaned from a synopsis of the plot. Since we are interested in the marketing and effects of centrist intellectualism in America, we must pay close attention to what *Colored People* makes of the Afro-American past. If we are careful readers, we quickly learn never to infer the character of colored people from descriptions by the narrator, Henry Louis Gates Jr. Instead, we read the nature of colored people from the acerbic judgments of "Pop."

Pop is the character Gates makes his father into. He is essentially a comedic version of Henry Louis Gates Sr.—sort of the Chris Rock of Piedmont, West Virginia. He makes quick work of the local black folk. "Niggers are crabs in a barrel: if [Pop] said that once, he said it to us a thousand times. My father was hard on colored people—and funny about it too" (83). He tells a young Gates: "There's enough niggers in your mother's family . . . to cast a Tarzan movie" (39). Concerning a citizen of colored Piedmont who had been cuckolded by his wife, Pop says: "He ain't chained to that blue-gummed woman. She sure must have some sweet *pussy* . . . cuz she's two-timing, funky, and ugly with it. Um, um, um" (159). On gay and lesbian life and manners: "queers."

Pop offers no inspiring views of fatherhood, black ancestral cultural wisdom, nor, of course, of colored people. As readers, however, we are given no idea about the actual views of Gates's real father. Pop is simply a caricature—the village commentator, a black man who, alas, has watched too many episodes of *Amos 'n' Andy*. With spirited vengeance (resulting presumably from Pop's scorn for his clumsy son "Louis Smith Gates") Henry Louis Gates Jr. portrays his father as a "dummy." "My all-time favorite Christmas present," Gates writes, "was a Jerry Mahoney ventriloquist dummy and a tap-dancing black minstrel known as Dancing Dan the Colored Man" (31). Pop is that Christmas present—an astonishing combo of minstrelsy and ventriloquism.

And Gates becomes, like Ralph Ellison's character Tod Clifton in *Invisible Man*, a huckster pushing Sambo dolls. Minstrelsy and ventriloquism translate into marketable black defamation. Whenever *Colored People*'s narrator wants to voice contempt or mockery toward the black majority, he craftily employs "Dancing Dan the Colored Man," namely a caricatured version of his own father. With autobiographical artfulness, Gates thus "formally" turns the world of his youth on its head. His seeming inadequacies are transformed into the put-downs of a race-bashing father who lampoons the black majority for what "Pop" sees as its relentless primitivism, wanton sexual attitudes, and rejection of the very values that move *Colored People*'s "unlikely hero" to concluding acts of derring-do: "There's just not a lot to do in a small town. And most people there never did mind too much about fornication as a sin, or getting pregnant out of wedlock. Which is not to say that everyone had a healthy, or satisfying, sex life. It is only to say that just about everyone seemed to be sleeping with somebody, or at least that just about everyone spent lots and lots of time talking about sleeping with somebody" (57). And next in the blame-dad frolic of Pop: "One day, I heard Daddy and Roebuck [Johnson] do a genealogy of my friends' and neighbors' proper and unlawful parentage, house to house, row by row, from Water and Paxton streets on Back Street, to Erin Street and Rat Tail Road up on the Hill. I was devastated. It seemed that virtually *nobody's* daddy was his daddy, and everybody in town (except me, apparently) knew" (176). Illegitimacy in blackness. Male boasting and pretense. The naive narrator (Louis Henry Gates) discovering a profligate sexuality in the barbershop. In the landscape of *Colored People*, the barbershop appears little more than a sex shop, where haircuts are a kind of secondary dispensation. A little shop of black-baiting horrors.

Are we surprised that *Colored People*'s intended subject—the Civil Rights Movement—inspires almost no positive action on the part of Piedmont's Negro citizenry? Colored people scarcely have time, one infers from Professor Gates's book, for nighttime organizational meetings; they are too busy sneaking and peeping, crawling into one illicit bed or another. They are lewd deacons of the dark: "Whatever tumult our small [television] screen revealed [of Civil Rights events in the United States] . . . the dawn of the civil rights era could be no more than a spectator sport in Piedmont. It was almost like a war being fought overseas" (*Colored*, 27). And who is the most contemptuous of all when it comes to the buoyant public-sphere activism of Civil Rights? Why, Pop, of course.

Pop cynically responds to the courage, organization, rebellion, and fortitude of the Little Rock, Arkansas, black community's decision to integrate its Central High School: "They handpicked those children. . . . No dummies,

no nappy hair, heads not too kinky, lips not too thick, no disses and no dats."
Gates assumes the role of the misled victim: "At seven, I was dismayed. . . . It
bothered me somehow that those children would have been chosen, rather
than just having shown up or volunteered or been nearby in the neighborhood" (26). Pop's attitude, indeed, is one step away from those hysterical cries
of well-placed whites who charged that black Civil Rights activism was initi-
ated by outside agitators. "Normal" black people, in the judgment of both Pop
and those white hysterics, were either too dumb or too complacent to bring
off colossal black liberation triumphs like the Little Rock integration miracle.

Black public-sphere organization and resistance skills seem alien to *Colored People*'s narrator. The theme here seems to be that colored people are
promiscuous dummies, too busy fornicating to engineer resistance. And just
when we think we have discovered the reason why colored people in Piedmont did *not* launch their own Civil Rights initiative, we unearth yet another
mortal Negro sin. Colored people are marathon eaters! They devour fried
chicken, greens, corn pudding, hot rolls, mashed potatoes, sausage, bacon,
eggs, biscuits—anything fat, fiberless, and cholesterol laden. Such dark glut-
tony is elaborately detailed by *Colored People*. How do these colored people
approach eating? One instance is sufficient to capture the tone: "They'd hit
those ears of corn like pigs on slop, pushing and shoving and elbowing their
way to the center of the table, tossing those too-hot-to-handle ears back and
forth between burning palms, until the palms got numb or the corn husks
cooled, and then the real work'd begin. They'd rip the husk right down the
corn, tossing the silk aside but leaving the husk to hang like an unbuttoned
shirt still secured by your trousers" (171). With this much energy expended
eating, no wonder there was only a small reserve of strength left for black
Civil Rights initiatives in Piedmont. ("Pigs on slop" is a denigration of the
black majority worthy, I think, of Bull Connor.) Hence, the paper mill's craft
unions remain segregated. Black people cannot own property. Black and
white are separate and unequal. The scope of *Colored People*'s big payback is
breathtaking—the black majority is reduced to rip-roaring minstrelsy, "niggers" and "coons" doing not much more than having sex and eating corn.

And yet, *Colored People* does offer affecting accounts of the black centrist intellectual as a young man. We learn how Louis Smith Gates acquired
knowledge about the Negro in lieu of playing sports. We watch the portly
young man make his way expertly into black literacy, rhythm and blues, jazz,
and popular song. And the memoir is insistently charming when it details

the boy's adolescent frustration, wonder, and hyperbolic desire for sexual favors. This desire, in fact, holds much of the book's tapestry in place. Desire joins forces with joyous recollections of countless public school successes: Gates's superb test scores, scads of As, a white grade-school sweetheart. Altogether, the quieter and more personal strands of *Colored People* engage us. It is only when the book moves to depicting colored people as a race that it slips over the edge into minstrelsy. There is almost no connection at all between the sophisticated ribaldry of the Yale graduate and *Colored People*'s depiction of the black, roughneck, primitive, dim-witted, wheezing, and rutting Piedmont majority.

The personal realm of Gates's memoir introduces us to a remarkably intelligent little boy who loves his mama. Her psychological suffering and thorough hatred of white people make her an intriguingly American character. She deserves a dedicated novelist's skill or at least the sober labor of an honest autobiographer. Gates, however, seems virtually incapable of elaborating the feminine side of his life. He seems unable to move into a gender-diversified cultural voice. This may be the case, of course, because all of Louis Smith Gates's "loves," as he proudly tells us, are white women: Linda Hoffman, Maura Gibson, and his betrothed, the woman he seats at the dinner table on Thanksgiving Day.

Nevertheless, the personal offers rich drama. At times, it even neatly connects with the anthropological—the sociology of everyday black life in Piedmont. For who has not experienced the sharp sweet smell of black hair "being done" as described by Gates? Who can quarrel with his description of chilly, early-morning awakenings to a day of fishing? What southern-reared black boy fails to relate to Randy's Record Shop—that black musical-cultural paradise in Gallatin, Tennessee? Unfortunately, these redeeming moments of the personal are too few, not nearly enough to redeem the race or make its representation in *Colored People* at all winsome.

In its most energetically noisy moments, *Colored People* offers up a black American past and history that contains almost no hint of organized public-sphere opposition to white supremacy in America. What *Colored People* contains—in rich abundance—is dark, minstrel fun at the expense of Piedmont's black majority. But who really can laugh at such a sad commentary on colored people as Gates's memoir? "And *everybody* [in Piedmont] loved *Amos and Andy*—I don't care what people say today. For the colored people, the day they took *Amos and Andy* off the air was one of the saddest days in Piedmont, about as sad as the day of the last [segregated] mill pic-a-nic" (22).

Amos and Andy were characters modeled from American minstrelsy. Two white male actors portrayed white America's phobia about an all-black world where "darkies" diurnally sneak and peep, scheme and gorge themselves, mispronounce the King's English, and seem to relish kicks in the butt. Gates insists that black people "loved" *Amos 'n' Andy*. And perhaps some did. But how bizarre does this report seem in a memoir supposedly dedicated to the legacy of the Civil Rights Movement?

The "pic-a-nic" to which Gates alludes when he speaks of *Amos 'n' Andy*'s final show is also a conclusion in its own right. It is the final segregated summer occasion financed for the colored people of Piedmont by the paper mill. The owners of Westvaco Paper Mill—acting under the impress of new Civil Rights legislation in the United States—announce to the colored people that Westvaco can no longer finance or endorse a segregated black picnic. The law has said there can be no more separate and unequal in Piedmont. Gates's colored people are undone by this announcement, this "forced integration" of their West Virginia lives. And who can doubt the truth of Gates's account? If the black folk in Piedmont really do love *Amos 'n' Andy* so much, perhaps they'd prefer to remain in their segregated colored zone of containment for all time. Why wouldn't they relish a segregated world of wanton sex and hot buttered corn?

Colored People's conciliatory portrayal of the black past is haunting, uncannily similar to the idylls of Negroes presented to white America by Booker T. Washington. But it is not Washington who is the model for Gates's book. Gates's reference to the mill picnic and *Amos 'n' Andy* reminds us of Paul Laurence Dunbar's "Chrismus on the Plantation." In Dunbar's poem, slaves have just been told they are free and cannot be provided a living wage by Ole Marster. The slaves' spokesman responds to this announcement with a view of the past and future that, even in this new millennium, remains terrifying for prospects of black public-sphere activism:

> Look hyeah, Mastah, I's been servin' you' fu' lo! dese many yeahs,
> An' now, sence we's got freedom an' you's kind o' po', hit 'pears
> Dat you want us all to leave you 'cause you don't t'ink you can pay.
> Ef my membry has n't fooled me, seem dat whut I hyead you say.
> Er in othah wo'ds, you wants us to fu'git dat you's been kin',
> An' ez soon ez you is he'pless, we's to leave you hyeah behin'.
> Well, ef dat's de way dis freedom ac's on people, white er black,
> You kin jes' tell Mistah Lincum fu' to tek his freedom back.[14]

Of course, Dunbar's poem goes far beyond mere conciliation. His slave narrator would like nothing more than to climb right back into bondage—just as Gates's colored people, who love the minstrel talk of *Amos 'n' Andy*, want to avoid the new freedom of the Civil Rights Movement.

How bizarre is this *Colored People*! Taken on its own word, it is a book that ultimately renders West Virginia's Civil Rights era as a minstrel comedy. A book for Gates's interracial daughters that ultimately reduces their cultural heritage to *Amos 'n' Andy*, fatty foods, and segregation nostalgia. One imagines *Colored People*'s white audience bursting with warm feelings for the darkies, just like Ole Marster in Dunbar's "Chrismus on the Plantation." For Gates's work is a gift to white people intent on the eradication of a dignified black past from the annals of American history. *Colored People* goes a long way toward that erasure. And what adds insult to this injurious sale of a Sambo-ized black past is that Gates strives to present himself as the *lone* exception to the black rutting rule of his West Virginia township. One of his community college instructors tells him: "Sin boldly." And certainly, as a memoirist, Gates does just that when at the end of *Colored People* he presents a seemingly dyspeptic and unathletic black as a Black Power hero.

In the concluding pages of the book, Gates tells us that his interracial love affair with Maura Gibson helped sway a mayoral election, resulting in the success of a "soulful" white candidate. Soon, a young, afro-crowned Gates takes charge of the personnel office at the Westvaco Paper Mill. Singlehandedly he integrates the craft unions. Black-Power Gates and the "fearsome foursome" of Piedmont invade a segregated dance club and ultimately force its closure. Action heroes all!

The rambunctious heroics of *Colored People*'s concluding pages may be entirely true and actual, real-world matters of single-person effort and fact. In the context of the book, and in my opinion, however, they seem an improvised heroics. Even the novice interpreter of texts should recognize such self-aggrandizing autobiographical heroics as uncharitable tales of *exceptionalism*. Given the wrath *Colored People* rains upon the heads of the black majority, how can the book really expect us to believe that a lone colored boy wins the day?

Another unfortunate point about Gates's memoir is that it does not choose to accentuate the efforts and voice of the mother as representative of a stable, activist energy of black resistance and liberation. Gates writes: "Some years before I was born, Mama and practically the whole colored town led a civil rights march demanding the right of the colored to be educated, if only in their own schools. The way it had been, you went only to the eighth grade in the one-room school, then had to ride the bus to Cumberland to attend George Washington Carver School, which is where Daddy met Mama" (*Colored*, 188). Indeed, this march was successful. Piedmont's blacks won the right to full public education, and the one-room former school became the Holiness Church.

How different is the legacy of Pop from the mother's public-sphere activism:

> No one colored was allowed to [sit down at the lunch counter in the Cut-Rate store], with one exception: my father. . . . You were supposed to stand at the counter, get your food to go, and leave. . . . I believe [the reason Daddy was allowed to sit] was in part because Daddy was so light-complected, and in part because, during his shift at the phone company, he picked up orders for food and coffee for the operators, and Dadisman [Cut-Rate's owner] relied on that business. At the time, I never wondered if it occurred to Daddy not to sit down at the Cut-Rate when neither his wife nor his two children were allowed to, although now that I am a parent myself, the strangeness of it crosses my mind on occasion.
>
> (*Colored*, 17–18)

Here, the parental past becomes a colored man's acceptance of the privileges of "light complectedness." Pop passes. He intentionally masks his blackness. He moves in the commercial sphere in ways unavailable to his family. Lo, an "ex-colored man," Pop proceeds mindless of segregation's public disgrace to colored people and, finally, the private disgrace represented by his own smug, thoughtless complicity with what the "cut-rate" market will bear.

I believe it is ultimately improbable that we can credit the Black Power heroics of Gates's concluding pages (my readerly opinion only). Rather, we are likely to see the product of his labors—the book *Colored People*—as a sad commodification, a package of robust minstrel entertainment that enables Gates to sit down at the American commercial lunch counter—a space still off limits to so much of the black majority today. The book's characterization of Civil Rights, black history, and everyday black life in the United States might well be labeled a "sin" against both history and the black autobiographer's traditional arts of liberation—arts that have their origin in heroic narratives such as Frederick Douglass's *My Bondage and My Freedom*. Gates's work is a betrayal of both black history and black art at its liberatory best.

Colored People demonstrates precisely what a black centrist sensibility makes of the black past, presumably for purposes of entertainment and market value. Black centrism elides a troubling and complex history, making it more palatable, thereby profitable. Black centrist intellectuals spin a tale of nostalgic Americana, replete with unkempt masses of jolly blackface darkies and a few rugged individualist heroes who beat the odds to earn themselves a seat at white America's table.

The black centrist sensibility, however, is not confined to revising the past. It dares to tread where even some of the better angels of our historical commonsense fear to fly: namely into prognostications and prescriptions for the black future. How do such futurist voices sing to each other? *The Future of the Race* coauthored by Cornel West and Henry Louis Gates Jr.—who once shared Afro-American studies territory at Harvard University—seems an ideal site to excavate for centrist intellectual notions and representations of a future black America.

Judging from the title, *The Future of the Race*, we might expect this to be a book that shows us what black America might, indeed *should*, become, in the eyes of its authors. We might expect the forecast from the dream team of black Harvard academics to be postmodern, mirroring, in fact, the form of the book itself. Structurally, *The Future of the Race* appears to be multivoiced, free-associative, fragmented, variable in tone, and disciplinarily scattered. There appear to be, in fact, at least six different authorial voices at work in *The Future of the Race*: two Harvard essayists of the 1990s, two voices of W. E. B. Du Bois (one of 1903, and one of 1948), and the creators of, respectively, the preface and an appended essay titled "W. E. B. Du Bois and the 'Talented Tenth,'" which bears the signature of Gates. Tonal, contextual, and authorial discrepancies on the theme of the black future make the book a strange hybrid collaboration.

The intention of *The Future of the Race*, as explained in the preface, is to provide, in a single volume, reflections on the views, talents, strategies, and leadership responsibilities of the educated black "elite" in the United States. These reflections, we are told, are like prose summations of conversations shared by Professors Gates and West during their strolls through Harvard's black studies corridors. The authors tell us they have no intention of submitting a policy treatise, containing programs and recommendations for addressing the present state of the Afro-American nation. No, the intention of *The Future of the Race* is to represent Gates and West *representing*—providing our era, that is to say, a take on the major black texts of the past and their relevance for the future. No text seems more worthy of such men's intentions than W. E. B. Du Bois's famous essay "The Talented Tenth," drawn from his classic collection *The Souls of Black Folk* (1903). Hence, *The Future of the Race* contains versions of Harvard conversations, reprints of Du Bois, and a stated avoidance of policy recommendations. Now that's postmodernism at its finest.

This future is starting to look suspiciously like a humanities honors seminar at Harvard. Certainly, it represents a strange fabrication of art and allusion, cultural appropriation and personal opinion, masquerade and allegorical rhetoric, likely geared toward being an eminently purchasable volume. Gates and West occupy and represent Du Bois's spirit, as it were, and effectively pretend to *be* him. They provide a simulation of Du Bois's black vision, leadership, social commitment, and prophetic ability. When the book discusses the desperately unhappy state of the Afro-American world, it takes very little analytical account of the deleterious effects of the Reagan-Bush era. In fact, according to Professor Gates, the unhappy state of black affairs is the fault of liberalism: "Through an excess of gallantry and zeal, liberalism itself created the alienated 'them' that deeded the Republicans the White House."[15] Moreover, Gates and West appropriate the work of Professor William Julius Wilson to bolster their claim that the problems that have beset black American life are only partially a structural result of U.S. polity and policy. They insist that half the blame lies with black America and is a direct result of bad black behavior: "We do know that the causes of poverty within the black community are both *structural* and *behavioral*, as the sociological studies of William J. Wilson have amply demonstrated, and we would be foolish to deny this" (*Future*, xiii).

Now, is it true that American social science has refined its methods sufficiently to make a demonstrated connection between certain designated behaviors and poverty? Can social science now codify such behaviors in verifiable racial ways? Is this what William Julius Wilson would claim "amply" to have demonstrated? Maybe so. But it seems a great misstep to attribute such behavioral science to Wilson, who is usually quite careful about the nature, extent, and proof of his claims. Gates and West just keep rolling along with exhortations to the black majority that even Dickens's Gradgrind would have found absurd and amusing. Mr. Gradgrind is a man, after all, of *fact*. ("With a rule and a pair of scales, and the multiplication table always in his pocket

...he seemed a kind of cannon loaded to the muzzle with facts, and prepared to blow them clean out of the regions of childhood at one discharge," Dickens wrote.) Showing little regard for the basis of their assertions, Gates and West stroll forth and gallantly proclaim:

> It is only by confronting the twin realities of white racism, on the one hand, and our own failures to *seize initiative and break the cycle of poverty*, on the other, that we, the remnants of the Talented Tenth, will be able to assume a renewed leadership role for, and within, the black community.... Not to demand that each member of the black community accept individual responsibility for her or his behavior [plight?]—whether that behavior assumes the form of black-on-black homicide, violations by gang members against the sanctity of the church, unprotected sexual activity, gangster rap lyrics, misogyny and homophobia—is to function as ethnic cheerleaders selling woof tickets from the campus or the suburbs.... Loving one's community means daring to risk estrangement and alienation from that very community, in the short run, in order *to break the cycle of poverty*, despair, and hopelessness that we are in, over the long run.
>
> (*Future*, xv–xvi; my emphasis)

Thus they define bad black behavior as a coequal cause for the current misfortune of Afro-America. Condemnation of such behavior from the campus or the suburbs is seen as a respectable, poverty-ending mantle to be taken up by the black talented tenth—if, that is, they are willing to agree that it is really blacks themselves who must break the cycle of poverty. What do Gates and West themselves plan to do to forward the work of the black defamation patrol for condemning bad black behavior?

They will urge leading Afro-American studies departments across the country to send "public service and community development interns" into inner-city black neighborhoods (something like, one imagines, those "peace patrols" that black urban radio stations dispatch into the inner city looking for cars with bumper stickers that read: "PEACE. I LOVE *power 88!*") (*Future*, xvi). It seems to me this strategy is not only an amazingly ineffectual one for the talented tenth; it is a clear throwback to what the Yale University black studies program attempted to do under its first leader, Dr. Roy Bryce-Laporte. Bryce-Laporte's internships were unsuccessful even then, when there was a romantic black rhetoric afloat about the natural bond between the black inner city and the Ivy League. Why would *The Future of the Race* assume Ivy League undergraduate interns are an answer to what they call the utter nihilism of today's inner cities? Alas, Gates and West have no sounder recommendations. They tell us that in the future black people will need jobs. However, if the future of black America is buttressed only by the type of past projected by *Colored People* and by the personal essays of Gates and West in *The Future of the Race*, we may all soon be well out of jobs. I believe it is fair to say *The Future of the Race*'s recommendations are overly simple and starkly self-incriminating—scarcely more than vague representations, if Du Bois is the model for comparison.

Gates's contribution to *The Future of the Race* is an autobiographical essay in which he recalls his undergraduate days at Yale. Perhaps he intends the essay to resemble Richard Wright's *American Hunger* or an excerpt from his own *Colored People*? Are we not a little concerned, even at this point in *The Future of the Race*, that the venue of blackness in America has somehow been shrunk to the walled cities of the Ivy League? We see the cloisters of Harvard, hear the carillon harmonies of Branford College at Yale, and wonder: What's Yale got to do with the future of the black majority? Gates is all too eager to reveal the redemptive value of his own insightful experiences in New Haven. The crux of his memoiristic project on the future reads as follows: "The fundamental challenge of my years at Yale would be whether or not to allow blackness to rob me of what I wistfully and portentously called 'my humanity'" (*Future*, 16).

Gates meets the challenge. The black freshman from Piedmont, West Virginia, removes himself from the influence of his two striking black classmates—Glen DeChabert and Armstead Robinson (who are black nationalist "pole stars" when Gates arrives on campus). Gates molds himself into something of a black undergraduate enigma (practically an Ivy League Tar-Baby) who knows just how to act when "sitting across the desk from some white man whose wallet you're trying to persuade him to share" (*Future*, 46). Gates also portrays himself as one of essentially three black undergraduates at Yale who gave point to the university's black nationalist founding of black studies and its politics of militant change. When Louis Smith Gates entered Yale in the late sixties, Afro-American studies had been planned, staffed, and was soon set in operation under the leadership of Professor Bryce-Laporte. There were links between Yale and two New Haven black urban communities surrounding the university—links that had been intelligently and sometimes passionately forged by Yale Law School and Yale Drama School students. Black professors and administrators on campus included Ken Mills, Austin Clarke, Arna Bontemps, John Clarke, Paul Jones, James Comer, Richard Goldsby, Elliott Paris, and others. (And, yes, I was there too.)

There were cooperative programs in effect between various Yale undergraduate colleges and several local public high schools and other community institutions. There was an intricate and dense collaborative of community politics, black studies standards and opinions, and expert intellectual guidance. There was a Yale Summer High School program meant to provide remedial academic work for students from inner-city high schools to aid their admission to college. All these things were in place upon Gates's arrival in New Haven. Undergraduates like DeChabert and Robinson had taken their lead from the collaborative. They worked to formulate policies, campaigns, and opinions. Which is only to say there was a thriving black public sphere already in place at Yale and in New Haven in 1969. And this, arguably, was a chief reason Louis Smith Gates was privileged to attend Yale.

That such courageous black public activism is pointedly not mentioned in *The Future of the Race* comes as no surprise to anyone who has read *Colored People*. Nor will it come as a surprise that Gates's autobiographical account in *The Future of the Race* portrays the ardent black politics of the late 1960s at Yale as a black pathology, a secondary effect of a black crossover generation's anxieties about their worth and identity: "Yet throughout all our strikes," writes Gates, "and protests and steering committees, I tried to shrug off a vague sense that had these things [Vietnam, Cambodia, black urban rebellions, the Black Panthers] not been there, in the world, we would have invented them; or at least a sense that these things were doing double-duty for us" (17). One might say this observation echoes Bishop Berkeley, the English cleric who claimed that nothing actually existed outside his own mind. It also manifests the kind of studied indifference to black social reality that is a favorite gambit of the "trashers."

Is Gates suggesting that a commitment to black empowerment by young black adults in the United States—a commitment that consumed activist lives and energy both at home and abroad in the late sixties and early seventies—was simply a sideline activity (a secondary preoccupation) for an Ivy League crossover generation's amusement at Yale? No, not exactly. Gates simply is making up history as he goes. He is offering a charming case for why he bailed out on blackness. He insists he couldn't just relinquish his humanity for the cause of addressing social evil. Then, with surprising gusto, Gates reports the deaths of those who hung in there with the struggle. As he chronicles the premature passing of DeChabert and Robinson, he implies, that both of the men abysmally failed to attain the full reaches of humanity: "The most brilliant scholar of our set, [Robinson] completed his dissertation with difficulty; and then gave up the ghost. His book? . . . He never published the book, though, or anything much at all. . . . Instead of writing, it seemed, he put on weight" (*Future*, 48). And DeChabert? Gates says he was lost in "mad, emancipatory dreams." He then notes that DeChabert succumbed to lung cancer (*Future*, 47). Bitter, indeed, would seem the fruits of an enduring racial membership in the black liberation club. Nonetheless, there is cause for hope, Gates tells us, because today a new and fiercely non-black-nationalistic renaissance is afoot in the black arts. But what happened to history and politics and sociology and the leadership needed for an activist, black political public sphere of opposition? Gates would say the excesses of liberalism foreclosed mention of all such matters. Only the arts offer life and light for the Negro future. What, then, is this future?

Gates grants us a vision of independent, racially transcendent black creators and performers who do not think of paying dues for membership in anything so ridiculous as, say, a black arts club. He also leaves us with the enigmatic suggestion that white people sometimes, shockingly, call Gates himself a "hustler." "Bravo," one wants to shout. The artistic manner in which the talented autobiographer Gates works his way through a blackness versus humanity dilemma at Yale is, presumably, the key to how Afro-Americans in general (and in the future) can secure the white man's purse. And not die of a heart attack (like Robinson) or lung cancer (like DeChabert). Hence, Gates's memoir is a black man's guide to fitness and the white man's money, steering its readers past mad dreams and the sordid weight gains of being true to the liberation club.

Cornel West's contribution to *The Future of the Race*, an essay titled "Black Striving in a Twilight Civilization," is far less autobiographical. The millennial tones of the essay's title suggest, in fact, that West—a Harvard Divinity School man—takes the job of charting the black future very earnestly. The missteps of W. E. B. Du Bois must *not* be allowed to hinder Cornel's efforts:

> My fundamental problem with Du Bois is his inadequate grasp of the tragicomic sense of life—a refusal candidly to confront the sheer absurdity of the human condition. . . . Du Bois's inability to immerse himself in black everyday life precluded his access to the distinctive black tragicomic sense and black encounter

with the absurd. He certainly saw, analyzed, and empathized with black sadness, sorrow, and suffering. But he didn't feel it in his bones deeply enough, nor was he intellectually open enough to position himself alongside the sorrowful, suffering, yet striving ordinary black folk.

(*Future*, 57–58)

Du Bois's failures of empathy, analysis, and understanding, according to West, resulted from the Great Barrington Sage's intellectual commitment to ideals of the European Enlightenment. Du Bois comes up scholastically short for West, as well, because he endorsed Victorian English ideals of respectability along with a tenacious American optimism.

West's arguments do not need full rehearsal. It will suffice to sum them up as follows. Because Du Bois championed the "rational" (Enlightenment ideals) as the human norm and endorsed Victorian notions of respectability and the possibility of dramatic betterment and reform for human life, he was unable (in West's view) to assess or analyze black American life and culture. This is quite an odd claim: that rationality, respectability, and reform agendas disqualify one from understanding everyday black life? But undoubtedly, there is some truth to West's argument. It bears some merit in relationship to Du Bois's personality and beliefs.

In autobiographical accounts such as *Dusk of Dawn* or the more formal *Autobiography of W. E. B. Du Bois*, we hear Du Bois lamenting that his New England Puritan boyhood bequeathed him a certain Victorian "reserve" before the hearty black camaraderie of our old southern home. Du Bois was never one of those dark-suited, grinning, indefatigably backslapping, hail fellows well met—no one knew this better than Du Bois himself. Nevertheless, it seems curious to suggest that Du Bois—the scholar who produced brilliant analyses of spirituals and magnificently profound scholarly accounts of the black church, black fatherhood, and black psychological responses to American racism—could be described as out of sympathy with the ways of black folk. Why does West charge Du Bois with such failure? I believe there are two telling examples of West's proofs.

The first is provided by West's interpretation of Du Bois's response to his own son's death. The second is offered by West's interpretation of Du Bois's response to a black evangelical church service. "Of the Death of the First Born" is the formal elegy Du Bois composed upon the death of his infant son, Burghardt. West thinks this formal elegy amounts to the confession of a man who was constitutionally incapable of looking life's absurdity in the face and getting on with his social mission: "Despite the deep sadness in this beautiful piece of writing, Du Bois sidesteps Dostoyevsky's challenge to wrestle in a sustained way with the irrevocable fact of an innocent child's death. Du Bois's [Enlightenment] rationalism prevents him from wading in such frightening existential waters. . . . The deep despair that lurks around the corner is held at arm's length by rational attempts to boost his flagging spirit" (*Future*, 63). This rather awkwardly written assessment of Du Bois's personal feeling and strength-for-survival is predicated on a frighteningly literal reading of a formal literary event. It was never meant to be a kind of new age pamphleteer's account of "how I, Du Bois, feel about the death of my black son." Learning to read the symbolic texts of our black culture is reported, or advertised, as one benefit to be sought from *The Future of the Race*. The preface tells us so. How, then, is it possible for West to err so miserably? It almost seems as though he believes Du Bois should have been writing for *Essence*.

The second proof West offers of Du Bois's analytical failings in black cultural theory derives from West's interpretation of Du Bois's response to a black church service. Du Bois says the "frenzy" of black worship service—its energetic witnessing of the "faith of the fathers"—is "awful" (qtd. in *Future*, 59). West writes: "The 'awfulness' of this black church service, similar to that of my own black Baptist tradition, signifies for [Du Bois] both dread and fear, anxiety and disgust. In short, a black ritualistic explosion of energy frightened this black rationalist [Du Bois]" (*Future*, 60).

In truth, Du Bois invokes "awful" in the German Romantic sense: "filled with awe," or "invoking and itself being, the sublime." How could anyone versed in Du Bois, familiar with his deep appreciation for black ritual expression, conclude that Du Bois was "frightened" by a little bit of Baptist shouting? We may be dealing here with a failure of contextualization on the part of Professor West. There may be justification for an intellectual time-out. Or we may be witnessing West's inexcusable refusal to engage in the type of thorough analysis that marked the whole of W. E. B. Du Bois's career.

The complexity of Enlightenment ideals may surely have marked Du Bois's faith in reason. However, such ideals were aptly enriched by Du Bois's adherence to spirit. He loved German and English Romanticism. His captivation with Victorian respectability was fully commensurate with notions of black decorum that he copied from the more elegant members of the race. Men like Frederick Douglass and Alexander Crummell (perhaps in surprising contrast to Gates's challenge on the score) had no problem being both black *and* human. Moreover, they were keen on remaining card-carrying members of the black liberation club. Optimistic faith in the leadership potential of exceptional men is scarcely, for Du Bois, a gesture toward the monarchical rogues of, say, Thomas Carlyle's *Heroes and Hero Worship*. It is not a tyrannical, imperializing American exceptionalism. Du Bois's American optimism is, rather, a pure New World product of his own late-century wrestling with the same type of emergent polity that characterizes Ralph Waldo Emerson's "representative man."

If the foregoing elaborations of terms used by West are plausible, then it is difficult to avoid the conclusion that what the Harvard schoolman calls Du Bois's "failure" is but the shallow effect of the model of evaluation and judgment to which *The Future of the Race* subjects Du Bois and his scholarship. And, in fact, West reveals—in spite of his curious notion that the writings of Tolstoy and Kafka are more fundamental for charting the future of black America than Du Bois's oeuvre—his own deep indebtedness to and admiration for Du Bois in the second part of his essay.

In part 2, Professor West just cannot be done with citing Du Bois's opinions on the "soul life" of black folk. It is as though, after intellectual disappointment, he has fallen back in love. Insisting that black musicians have provided sounds, life examples, moans, and tonalities best suited for facing the existential absurdity of black life, West calls time and again on the writings of Du Bois to reinforce his own proclamations. He summons Du Bois to help convince readers that the black arts—black expressive cultural, vernacular, religious, and secular traditions—offer a vibrant repertoire for seeing our way through to the future. In his crescendo, however, Professor West narrows black future sages to a mere duo: the tenor saxophonist John Coltrane and the Nobel laureate Toni Morrison.

But what of the black middle-class talented tenth?

Only very few blacks will have the courage to avoid "black rage," says West, and strive in Tolstoyan fashion to articulate a "visionary (disproportionately woman-led) radical democratic vision." We must, therefore, "look candidly at the tragicomic and absurd character of black life in America in the spirit of John Coltrane and Toni Morrison; let us continue to strive with genuine compassion, personal integrity, and human decency to fight for radical democracy in the face of the frightening abyss—or terrifying inferno—of the twenty-first century, clinging to 'a hope not hopeless but unhopeful'" (*Future*, 112). It is hard to know what kind of hope West has in mind. It does not seem to be the same as the Reverend Jesse Jackson's, which always publicly urges the black majority and black leaders to work in common toward the "beloved community." The larger point, however, is that the futurist West returns us, in the manner of Gates, to the arts and entertainment section of the American house of life. Though I suspect West would also want to add a black praying section to his trail mix for the future, we are finally left with only the questions: Where are the analyses of, precisely, the structural (as opposed to black behavioral) factors that have produced current misery among the majority of black America? How do "exceptional" black moaners and articulators like Coltrane and Morrison help everyday black people of America's inner cities to entertain hope, or—to revert to Langston Hughes—to buy and eat their lunch?

In the postmodern market simulations of West and Gates, the black future is, finally, just a sales job. It turns out to be not much more than hawking the black arts as though there were no tomorrow for the black majority. The Ivy League oracles write as though no black activist public sphere of analytical, oppositional scholarship and politics is possible. Gates and West are like sidewalk vendors found outside the Metropolitan Museum of Art: they promote auras of black artistic roots originality as the real black future thing. They rip off what they consider the consumer- and white-approved best of the black arts and act and write as though they had discovered enlightenment for the future of the race. Black history, the Civil Rights movement, grand Afro-American scholars and traditions of scholarship, black studies, and Black Power all can be cropped away. It is not unlike Edward Curtis, studiously tidying up whatever is complicated, difficult, in serious need of benevolent funds and attention in the life of the "other." Gates and West want to claim and insert themselves into what ultimately they imagine as an "authentic" world of black art. But the rub (at least if Gates is to be believed) is that neither really believes in blackness or authenticity. Edward Curtis, I think, would happily have shared ethnic studio space and a market stall with mask-wearing centrist second-wave black public intellectuals like Gates and West any day of the American commercial week.

IT IS DIFFICULT TO imagine a young Shelby
Steele (in 2007, a senior research fellow at the
conservative Hoover Institution in Palo Alto,
California) agreeing with the late black journalist George Schuyler that opportunities for
Afro-Americans in the United States are legion.
Schuyler, a staunch black conservative, insisted
(without irony) that blacks in America have access to the "best schooling, the best living conditions, the best economic advantages, [and] the
best security" in the world.[1] When Steele was
growing up, he found scant evidence to support
Schuyler's claims.

Steele grew up in a bleak working-class suburb of Chicago. His school was rotten in every
way. He refers to the institution's teachers and
staff as a "menagerie of misfits." As for treatment, it seems pretty much to have been what
one would expect from a menagerie of misfits.
One day when Steele was in the sixth grade,
the new physical education instructor (a white
ex-marine) ordered him "to pick up all of the
broken glass on the playground with my bare
hands.... [The ex-marine] commandeered a
bicycle, handed it to an eighth-grader—one
of his lieutenants—and told the boy to run
me around the school grounds 'until he passes
out.'"[2] Steele's school was so bad that eventually
it was shut down.

As Steele recounts his early days, there are
few experiences that would seem to connect
him with the black American conservatism of
Schuyler or of Schuyler's most famous predecessor, Booker T. Washington. Both Washington
and Schuyler abhorred black political agitation
and all those black race leaders who perpetuated
it, believing that only diplomatic, interracial ad-
justments of race relations could improve race

A CAPITAL FELLOW FROM HOOVER

SHELBY STEELE

It came from my own heart, so to
my head,
And thence into my fingers trickled;
Then to my pen from whence
immediately
On paper I did scribble it daintily.

JOHN BUNYAN
Pilgrim's Progress

President Bush told the congressional black caucus he didn't know
anything about renewal of the
seminal 1965 Voting Rights Act last
Wednesday [January 26, 2004]. . . .
"He said he didn't know nothing
about it, and he will deal with the
legislation that comes before him,"
Representative [Jesse] Jackson
[said].

JOHN BYRNE
"Black Congressmen Riled by Bush
Ignorance of Voting Rights Act"

matters in the United States. Schuyler was unflagging in his condemnation of Civil Rights and Black Power initiatives: "[Their] proclaimed aims are defeated in advance. The prestige given to public nuisance and civil disobedience hurts rather than helps the Negro future. Racial adjustment is delicate and difficult enough without the efforts of all the sorcerer's apprentices who for the past half decade have devoted themselves to performing miracles that became shambles."[3] Washington proclaimed, decades before Schuyler: "The wisest among my race understand that the agitation of questions of social equality is the extremest folly."[4] Then there is the young Shelby Steele, Civil Rights agitator par excellence.

Steele followed the footsteps of his white mother and black father, who were activists. He marched and demonstrated, and was an ardent Civil Rights activist when he left Illinois for Coe College in Cedar Rapids, Iowa. He met his own white wife at a meeting of SCOPE, a campus affiliate of the Southern Christian Leadership Conference. His inherited bent for black political agitation even carried him into the ranks of a strident black nationalism during the sixties.

A path from Chicago ghetto youth to black nationalist young adulthood scarcely foreshadows the emergence of a middle-aged, black American, conservative Hoover Institution senior fellow. Something seems evolutionarily wrong with such a picture. Yet, Shelby Steele undeniably inhabits the handsome Stanford, California, tower of the Hoover Institution, one of the most sublime peaks of antiliberalism (and, dare one say, antiblack majority interests) in the world. What is one to say of the senior fellow who rode the affirmative action train through college, graduate school, and into a tenured professorship at a state college and now is one of affirmative action's fiercest public opponents? Steele—in the tiresomely self-serving traditions of American neoconservatism at large—wrote a punchy little book titled *The Content of Our Character*, where he did a sharp volte-face in the most loathsome American neoconservative fashion on his people and began climbing not Jacob's, but Irving Kristol's, ladder.

Steele has subsequently publicly denounced all black strategies of social and political agitation that emerged during the post–Civil Rights era. He has crafted a viciously denigrating portrait of the black majority, its aspirations, claims upon the American polity, and daily life. He has angrily denounced the rhythms, speech, poverty, and everyday life of the black ghetto. Steele stands as the representative anti–race man of his generation. He is ever ready to make a pharisaic display of himself before the white neoconservative lords of the land. The rewards for his labors have been substantial: Emmys, a National Book Critics Circle first, the National Humanities Medal from the hands of President George W. Bush himself.

But Steele's so-called vision of race in America—even though it possesses a certain captivating charm in its eloquently simple and simplifying formulas—is but a knockoff, a febrile translation, and copybook imitation of white neoconservative dogma as it has unfolded for three score American years. Conservatism seems an unlikely vantage for black American intellectuals. It is a relatively recent European ideology whose origins are generally defined as the English reaction to the French Revolution. Opposing radical and violent changes represented by the French Constitution of 1793, moderate English conservatives called for piety and respect for the elders—the way things used to be. This call for respect for the elders—the old ways—is most eloquently set forth in the writings of Edmund Burke.

Burke insists that state and society must never be overcome by theory or abstraction, both of which can work to turn the natural order of political arrangements into artificial collectives. He also insists that state and society must always be seen as human equivalents of nature. Nature represents a God-ordained ordering of the world, where constancy and change exist in equal measure. In nature, there is harmony and balance of forces. The stability and constancy of state and society, by way of analogy, are guaranteed by balance and harmony among nobility, aristocracy, church. Burke calls these three institutions "estates" and argues that they should always exist in equilibrium.

The "balance of estates" should never be subjected to abrupt or violent change (think: the French and Bolshevik revolutions). The balanced state, in turn, must be handed down as tradition, prescription, and mores. These guide and condition man's life as a freely governed citizen of the commonwealth. But here's the rub: Estates endure because they are founded on property. "Property" is a spooky word in Afro-American historical life and collective memory. The founding of the polity of the American Republic designated us, precisely, as property—chattel. And here is the glorification of property by Burke cited from his *Reflections on the Recent Revolution in France*:

> You will observe, that from Magna Carta to the Declaration of Rights, it has been the uniform policy of our constitution to claim and assert our liberties, as an

entailed inheritance derived to us from our forefathers, and to be transmitted to our posterity; as an estate specially belonging to the people of this kingdom [England], without any reference whatever to any other more general or prior right.... By a constitutional policy working after the pattern of nature, we receive, we hold, we transmit our government and our privileges, in the same manner in which we enjoy and transmit our property and our lives.[5]

"Property," "entailment," and "inheritance" are the defining moments of conservatism's existence not simply in nature, but also in ownership. Ownership is the fathers' privilege. The patriarchal family, therefore, becomes for Burke and conservatism an appropriately natural symbol for state and society: "In this choice of inheritance we have given to our frame of polity the image of a relation in blood; binding up the constitution of our country with our dearest domestic ties; adopting our fundamental laws into the bosom of our family affections; keeping inseparable and cherishing with the warmth of all their combined and mutually reflected charities, our state, our hearths, our sepulchers, and our altars."[6] Basically, Burke makes a claim here for the balance of all social institutions, based upon the model of an ideal family where the father is decisively boss, owner, and principal progenitor.

If Burke's polity is considered in relation to the founding of the American republic, we know that blacks scarcely appear to have any stake whatsoever in the commonwealth—intellectual or otherwise. Why? Because millions of African bodies were brutally transported by the transatlantic slave trade to America. These bodies were considered not citizens, but property. Black bodies as commercial property were not inheritors of anything. They enjoyed no fancy patriarchal rights of entail. In fact, they were the entailed inheritance, belonging by law, mores, and custom to white "fathers." African bodies were written by the best minds of the founding generation as an inheritance meant exclusively for the service of white inheritors.

The bonding in blood that Burke asserts as essential to the commonwealth family, then, is exactly what was denied to African bodies by American founding fathers like Thomas Jefferson. In his *Notes on the State of Virginia*, Jefferson effectively separates "Africans" from the commonwealth family on the very basis of their inferior blood. He writes: "The improvement of the blacks in body and mind, in the first instance of their mixture with the whites, has been observed by every one, and proves that their inferiority is not the effect merely of their condition of life." In Jefferson's account, African "inferiority" originates in black blood. And the presence of such blood is re-flected, says Jefferson, in an "unfortunate difference of [African] colour, and perhaps [mental and imaginative] faculty."[7]

The visual difference of blackness is thus written along the arterial pulses of America. At the level of blood, a visible blackness presents what Jeffer-son calls a "powerful obstacle to the emancipation of these people."[8] In a very dramatic sense, race is instituted in America by a visual, sanguinary dis-inheritance. This blood-disinheritance would seem to make conservatism's pious talk about fathers and justice and balance perversely self-defeating and racial-group-destructive if taken at all to heart (much less adopted as the gospel way) by black American intellectuals.

Burke proclaims that the intelligent citizen who seeks judiciously to re-form society "should approach to the faults of the state as to the wounds of a father, with pious awe, and trembling solicitude." "Justice" consists of each individual's profiting from the "joint stock company" of the commonwealth in accord with his initial investment. Everyone thus has a right to profit—but not equally. "In this partnership," says Burke, "all men have equal rights; but not to equal things."[9] Surely this rings true for African Americans; what did we (always absent forty acres and even a single mule) have to invest? So, in the matter of justice, we couldn't even inhabit the fringes of the joint stock company's quarters. And, therefore, logically, blackness could never be an en-titled agent in or for the commonwealth.

Conservatism counts us out of investing and common life on the basis of blood, color, and an assumed deficiency of faculty. In light of conserva-tism's logic of exclusion with respect to black or African bodies and voices, it would seem that only the most bizarre logic or reverie on the part of a black American would promote the idea that she could assume effective conserva-tive agency. Only a fantasy would convince a black intellectual that he could in any way, under the sanctions of conservatism, transcend race and have equal things in the joint stock company that is WASP sovereignty, power, and domination in America.

In black conservative talk, the masses are the very black incarnation of sin, evil, lawlessness, and disorder. The black conservative labors hard to conform to moderate conservatism's rules by privileging his or her I/eye before the collective black majority. He believes he has an undeniably greater contribu-tion to make to the stock company than those whom he deems (with rankly condescending self-regard) as less beautiful, less educated, less hardworking, less prolific, less insightful, and less orderly than he. Black conservatives assume they are natural aristocrats in the manner described by F.A. Hayek, the economist beloved by American conservatives:

> In the last resort, the conservative position rests on the belief that in any society there are recognizably superior persons whose inherited standards and values and position ought to be protected and who should have a greater influence on public affairs than others. The liberal, of course, does not deny that there are some superior people—he is not an egalitarian—but he denies that anyone has authority to decide who those superior people are.[10]

Black conservatives have no such scruples; they think of themselves as natural aristocrats—lords of the black social order—entitled to far more esteem and money than the black majority.

The Content of Our Character might well have been titled *Reflections on the Recent Black Power Revolution in the United States.* The book is actually a conservative reverie recounting the decline and fall of the Civil Rights Movement under the baleful assault of a psychopathological Black Power revolution. For Shelby Steele, the Civil Rights era was, in his own words, a time of "character," a period invested with "morality." Black men and women valued individual effort and sacrifice over special "group privileges." The high moral character of Civil Rights' advocates was evidenced by their generous faith in white America and the inevitability of social change. A harmonious, interracial future seemed on the horizon. This is Steele's story.

The phrase "the content of our character" is drawn, not surprisingly, from Dr. Martin Luther King Jr.'s dream speech delivered at the 1963 March on Washington. As Steele deploys the phrase, it might be considered a perfect example of conservatism's longing for the good old days. By defining and emphasizing character in a soft moral frame, Steele attempts to reinforce the by now familiar image of Dr. King as a Christian martyr who concentrated his efforts on quietist moral uplift and American conscience reform. In this image, King is seen as a brave, but gentle and righteous, man of character. Not as a man of race and revolutionary resolve.

Steele's characterological image of King has nothing to do with the scope, dimension, tenor, and global revolutionary magnitude of Dr. King's struggles in the whirlwind storm of white racist violence. We must, therefore, read

Steele's interpretation as an interested misreading of the Civil Rights Movement. For the sake and support of his own conservative agenda, Steele imagines and sets before us a Christian icon rather than a flesh and blood, historical Martin Luther King Jr.

In contrast to Steele, Martin Luther King Jr. would have decisively placed emphasis on the adjective *our*, rather than the noun *character*. King's effectiveness as a leader resided in his allegiance to black collective action—the ends and desires of our and we, the collective, the black majority. What made him such a brilliant leader was precisely his rapport with the masses, his relinquishing of personal authority to collective wisdom. Character, then, for King—even in 1963—was defined by collective black majority endurance, intelligence, beauty, productivity, courage, and creativity. This extraordinariness of the black majority was manifested for King by the masses' stunning capacity to believe (in the face of all evidence to the contrary) that white America did, in fact, possess a conscience and an ability to change.

Steele's handling of King and the word "character" is exemplary of one of black conservatism's favorite rhetorical and polemical strategies. The strategy is best defined as a disingenuous rejection of cultural history and present-day fact. What *The Content of Our Character* attempts to accomplish is a redefinition, for conservative ends, of the most collectively oriented black leadership and social action in the twentieth century. The author blithely portrays King as a sort of Civil Rights Saint Sebastian: a dispassionate, sacrificial black martyr for freedom. According to Steele, King understood that "racial power subverts moral power, and [King] pushed the principles of fairness and equality rather than black power because he believed those principles would bring blacks their most complete liberation. He sacrificed race for morality, and his innocence was made genuine by that sacrifice. What made King the most powerful and extraordinary black leader of this century was not his race but his morality" (*Content*, 19).

In light of Dr. King's life and work, how can we characterize Steele's portrait as anything other than a deliberate distortion of almost every detail of King's moral life and social leadership? Steele presents a colorless (or is it colorblind?) saint, his body pierced by arrows of merely unenlightened white perfidy, dying nobly after serving a humble, moral apprenticeship for freedom. There is nothing of the whirlwind and frenzy, betrayal and complexity of Dr. King and the actual Civil Rights Movement in this picture. The canvas represents the beautification for hire at which black neoconservatives excel.

It is certainly akin to the kind of airbrushed history and photographic leger-demain that marks the work of Edward Curtis.

Black conservatives are always substituting clean, well-lighted places of a fantastical imagination for actual dark corridors of American racial history. Steele's paean to King's character reads like a high school offering titled "Dr. King, Christian Dreamer." At best, his reading of King is inadequate biography. At worst, it is chimerical reverie.

Steele's beautification of black American reality during the past four decades is deeply allegorical. *The Content of Our Character* borrows liberally from Christian archetypes, popular psychology, and American free-enterprise mythology. The book is a black neoconservative's *Pilgrim's Progress*. It unfolds as follows. Once upon a time in the mid-sixties, America was graced by an epiphany—a Great Awakening to sin. The white citizen suddenly and miraculously realized he was living in a morally deficient and ethically bankrupt republic. A conscience-stricken white American majority finally acknowledged its "lack of racial innocence, and confronted the incriminating self-knowledge that it had rationalized flagrant *injustice*. . . . There was really only one road back to *innocence*—through actions and policies that would bring *redemption*." (*Content*, 79; my emphasis) There is an aura here of the scriptural burning bush. Barriers of ignorance tumble like Walls of Jericho, and trumpets sound all around. Carillons accompany symphonic choirs of angelic redemption. And self-knowledge rains down on white America like storms of grace.

But something critical is missing from this tableau: reality. There is no reality, no history, no fact in Steele's picture. There is not even a hint of that omnipresent site with which this book began: jail. The real, racial, boldly oratorical, jail-term-serving black collective action and energy that set white America on its heels makes absolutely no appearance in Steele's happy song of "grace abounding to the chief of sinners" (Bunyan's title for another of his allegorical works). The Civil Rights Movement may have been graced in many ways (especially by King's leadership), but we did not come to new freedoms by grace alone. Rather it was by countless days of work by black majority hands and boycotting and marching feet. Which person who has seen *Eyes on the Prize* does not understand the mass, body-on-the-line, "jail, no bail" energies that were brought to bear in order to secure to blacks constitutionally guaranteed rights? *The Content of Our Character* substitutes a Christian and agentless grace for such energies. It gives the sense that a great white American majority pulpit and congregation came, in holy conversion, to a redemptive white bestowal of rights on blacks. Presumably because those blacks had character. And as a reward whites gave them the Civil Rights Act of 1964.

According to Steele, the Civil Rights Act was vastly more significant for black freedom than the Emancipation Proclamation of 1863 (*Content*, 68). In fact, Steele asserts that the mid-sixties legislation amounted to nothing less than the bestowal of unlimited freedom and boundless opportunity on all blacks in America. Dr. King, on the other hand, regarded the legislation and its attendant Voting Rights Act as paltry gains in the overall struggle of a world revolution for justice.

We behold in Steele's phantasmagoric, allegorical overstatements the wedding of George Schuyler and the present-day senior fellow of the Hoover Institution. From picking up glass with bare hands on a littered Chicago ghetto school yard, Senior Fellow Steele has progressed to the fanciful claim that unrestricted good fortune is the lot of people of color in America. Presumably, those who were formerly excluded now have a chance to claim their inheritance. As Ralph Ellison exclaimed in one of his more famous essays: "Well cut off my legs and call me Shorty!" Greater love hath no white world population than that it guarantees to its blacks equality under the law (*Content*, 131).

The Christ-like largesse of white America was responsible, according to Steele, for a "twenty-five year decline in racism and discrimination" in the United States (*Content*, 157). Would a decline in racism and discrimination include the assassination of Dr. Martin Luther King, the deaths of scores of Civil Rights activists, the rewriting of the vast majority of crime in America as "black," disfranchisement of thousands of black "felons," destruction of the social safety net that allowed some security to much of the black majority, and the patently racist law-and-order mutterings of the Nixon and Reagan administrations? But perhaps these are only remainders that marked the perimeters of the great decline. What, then, is missing from Steele's vision of the fall of racism in America? Evidence.

It would be generous to say that Steele's logic of racism's decline is strained. He cites as support for his claims of unlimited black liberation the fact that Asian Americans have prospered in business and lifestyle during the past twenty-five years (*Content*, 69). Despite non sequiturs such as this, *The Content of Our Character* won first nonfiction prize in the competition of the prestigious National Book Critics Circle awards. Inaccuracy and allegory—if it is black and neoconservative—can, it seems, bring a black man laurels. Though such work is a fall from even rudimentary competence, it is happily rewarded, in the manner of John Milton's Adam.

In *Paradise Lost*, Adam declares that his own rebellious fall from God's will was a *felix culpa*, a "happy sin." Adam—after the announcement of his expulsion from the Garden of Eden for the apple incident—ironically re-joices in his sin (given all he wields dominion over, and all the magnificent material benefits he and his lineage will derive from his status as first man) and calls his incompetence a "fortunate fall."

In *The Content of Our Character*, white America's acknowledgment (through grace) of its own fall from fairness and justice produces an abun-dance of good things for black people, such as the 1964 Civil Rights Act. Blacks thus enjoy a kind of secondary grace—"more opportunity for devel-opment than ever before" (*Content*, 151). Paradise is almost regained. Ah, but there are serpents in the garden.

In Steele's American paradise of the 1960s the role of serpent is played by Black Power:

> The [Civil Rights] movement, splintered by a burst of racial militancy in the late sixties, lost its hold on the American conscience and descended more and more to the level of secular interest-group politics.... As a people not formed in freedom, whatever vulnerabilities we [blacks] had were bound to be triggered by the chal-lenges of new freedom. On one level black power, I believe, was a defense against [denial of?] the shock of vulnerability that came automatically with freedom.
>
> (*Content*, 19, 65)

Steele the allegorist might as well be speaking as God: "And I brought you into a plentiful country, to eat the fruit thereof and the goodness thereof; but when ye entered, ye defiled my land, and made mine heritage an abomi-nation" (Jeremiah 2:7). Having declared the achievement of such freedom, Steele then proceeds to chastise Black Power as the very monster of free-dom's loss. Steele seems to suffer intense assimilationist anxiety about the liberational power of the black ghetto, that is, the Black Power energy of the urban majority to do things by itself and for and in its own interests. So rather than writing Black Power as a further struggle for genuine revolution-ary black freedom, Steele denounces it as a secular politics of disorder.

The same old disingenuous charges so often made by white men in their calls for colorblind morality can be found in Steele's assault on Black Power.

He too implicitly voices a familiar white injunction to the black majority: "These things take time, Jimmy." His allegory is, I think, nothing more than tepid leftovers—microwaved white neoconservative racism served as award-winning black insight.

By the mid-1960s, says Steele, blacks en masse had withdrawn into psychopathological retreat from freedom. In the final analysis, this alleged retreat is the essence of what Steele arrogantly calls the "black mind." What emanates from such a mind? For Steele, all that comes forth is a "sharp *racial consciousness*" (*Content*, 18; emphasis in original). But Steele himself freely acknowledges that the publicly choreographed drama of race in America originates in one source alone—whites' quest for power.

Steele recognizes that in order to capitalize on power as it derives from the bodily racial dynamics of African skin and hair, whites had to convince themselves that they alone were entitled to brute domination over the African other. We recoil from this quick and dirty talk of differences of skin and hair that perhaps "misled" whites into rapacious sin. We sense the slippery moral slope of eugenics in the immediate foreground of Steele's drama. We shake ourselves awake to critical remembrance, calling to mind the actual premeditated and for-profit violence and horror of American chattel slavery. White slaveholders, did, after all, write the abjection of African bodies carefully and constitutionally into the founding documents of the nation. But Steele is prepared to sprinkle such momentous soul murder and human disregard with the allegorical waters of a mid-sixties grace, implying that the original sin was expiated by the Civil Rights Act. A new order of black freedom, in his account, cancels all debts of slavery, peonage, and incarceration executed by whites on the basis of color alone. The capital fellow of Hoover forgives the essentialism of white racism, while he scandalously takes the new credos of skin color—the revolutionary hairstyles and rhetoric of Black Power—to task for a psychopathological appeal to race. He also allows Mr. Jefferson his pragmatic secular politics of race while condemning the secular black-majority-interest enhancing politics of Black Power. The Christian quietism of a putatively reformist Civil Rights Movement is the only thing that is all right with Steele.

Implicit in Steele's pop psychology and shifty logic is the familiar white charge of "reverse racism," the reality of which no white American commentator has ever persuasively explained to the black majority. Steele's mission in *The Content of Our Character* becomes clear. He hopes to transform the founding gospel of the United States—white supremacy—into a chimerical allegory of Black Power sin. Hence, *The Content of Our Character* converts documented, murderous white American national racism and bigotry into a biblical romance of misguided white, essentialist cravings for power. (Something on the order of an inherited supremacist addiction that Dr. Phil might usefully address.)

Steele reads the white nation's will to racial power as a morally innocent mistake. Ah, "happy, happy sin" that found redemption for millions of murdered African lives in a Civil Rights Act. Bloodstained history is neutralized by moral abstraction. Murder becomes a holy musical melodrama, fit for off-Broadway production during, let us say, White History Month, if there were such a thing.

The Content of Our Character is evangelically disarming pastiche—disturbingly pseudoreligious pop psychology and black neoconservative pandering to white elites. The pamphlet has virtually nothing to do with present-day racial realities. It insists that the weakest claims to innocence come not from whites, but from blacks (6). In its allegorical universe, guilt and innocence are manipulated by blacks, who desire one thing only: power. Blacks, Steele claims, psychopathologically transpose white brutality—which is merely unenlightened (and entirely redeemable by grace)—into claims of black innocence.

Marianne Moore talks of poets who present "imaginary gardens with real toads in them."[11] In Shelby Steele's written world, the innocent and real white garden of America gets populated with imaginary Black Power toads. *The Content of Our Character* is full of fantastical Negroes—mythical creatures sprung like griffins from Steele's ghetto-traumatized, Chicago-ghetto imagination—who have no idea what to do with freedom. *Friends like these!*

The collective black mind, according to Steele, is nothing but a mournful mental repository of ideology, rage, and hopping resentment. Haunted by self-doubt and evasion, this black mind's Black Power instincts are always primed to bellow out illicit declarations of innocence. Whereas the (white) human mind constitutes a personal sphere at the core of one's character, inside the black mind, Steele argues, there are no private, individualizing principles of morality and guidance. The black mind is surfeited by a single presence—a collective and disabling sense of victimization. Hence, whenever Steele witnesses black men and women referring to race, championing the collective interests of black people, appealing to the actual facts of black

American history, insisting that the nation as a whole owes an immense debt to black America, he beholds symptoms of a diseased black mind.

There seems to be no space in *The Content of Our Character* for a healthy, empowered, black private-life and public-sphere agenda oriented toward collective public gain. In Steele's world, the only thing blacks bring to public discourse is a pathological mask of victimization. They can never be prime movers of a public sphere of enhanced and enhancing American citizenship. And black America's consumptive mental illness compels mentally healthy, beleaguered white people to respond with ineffectual moral gestures of guilt and polite goodwill. Under the net of black psychopathology everyone in the nation is trapped, according to Steele, in petty rituals of public appeasement—a cycle leading finally to the "resurgence of white racism" (20).

Black Power *never* denied whites their "morality," as Steele suggests. Black Power advocates worked to call attention to the voluntary, enduring immorality of whites—the bad faith of those who insisted on being identified as superior. Moreover, Black Power—in its most effective practices and results—was far less interested in playing the race card than in reclaiming a black cultural and historical legacy.

While it is true that the paramilitary style of Black Power and black nationalism was remarkably influential, black cultural and historical nationalism was the biggest beneficiary during the 1960s and early 1970s with respect to setting the American racial record straight in the public square. What Black Power and black nationalism attempted conscientiously to do was to interrogate precisely the kind of allegorizing of race that Shelby Steele cobbles together in *The Content of Our Character*.

Rather than denying racial anxiety, black professional and cultural nationalism attempted to demonstrate that models of explanation such as Steele's were limited, biased, and racially overdetermined—basically in need of serious correction by committed work in both academia and the American professional worlds (*Content*, 139). By overemphasizing the pseudomilitarism of Black Power and its "grandiose" claims, Steele writes the entire Black Power project off as a kind of mob violence, complete with invading forces seeking to eradicate character from American life.

Actually, it was calmer and more intellectually and strategically deliberative than Steele makes out. Black Power produced remarkable advances in precisely the type of healthy social and intellectual inquiry into American matters of identity, culture, markets, and history that Steele professes to love. The difference is that Steele works (as neoconservatism always has since its Trotskyist days) "on the pulses," with harsh Stalinist polemic, HUAC grand inquisitions, and intimidation, with scant historical or psychoanalytical scholarship to support normatively grandiose and vitriolic claims.

When Steele describes his own behavior as an American academic professional, we hear him mock students who believe black history is a necessary discipline for understanding the work of Toni Morrison (*Content*, 3). He also derides black students who express personal appreciation for the black English vernacular that is their first language (70). Steele finds his students' conflation of language and identity grotesque. And again, there is his so-called professional insistence that black students, in the aggregate, are underprepared, hooked on soul, and pathologically incapable of successful college and university matriculation. Such students are only in universities and colleges because "guilt-motivated" white administrators have provided the ineffectual goodwill of affirmative action (118–119).

Charitably, we might label Steele's professional unkindness to blacks a raw result of his own Black Power shock. I believe academic-door-opening Black Power and black studies movements were motivating factors in Steele's academic employment. Certainly, he moved on to tenured status in an English department without producing a single scholarly monograph (the mandatory minimum for tenure in most American colleges and universities). Black Power gave Steele the vocabulary and stability of self-empowerment in America. But the profit for blacks is nothing but Steele's mocking curse and seemingly endless contempt.

Where Steele's allegory and condemnation of Black Power are concerned, there is a far more grandiose American role at stake than teaching in California's state academic system. His larger American role, in my reading of his neoconservatism, is that of a black terminator, ideologically commissioned to take out Black Power. The public payoff for what he terms a "new vision of race in America" is the eradication of every vestige of Black Power's presence, influence, claims, style, and enunciations for a black "good life" in America.

Steele revises all the racist terror of his youth and early black manhood under the rubric of "white misguidance." Racism, in a morally culpable sense, had nothing to do with the dread, denial, and horror of white actions Steele witnessed in his youth. His attempts to find refuge in Black Power's identity politics proved simply a passive, unhealthy, and unfruitful means of addressing his own anxieties. White America is, thus, conciliatorily absolved: "It's not your fault, boss!"

LET US CONSTRUCT OUR own allegorical account of Shelby Steele's award-winning book *The Content of Our Character*. In so doing, we may discover a take on what the lustrous author of contemporary black neoconservatism ultimately offers as vision for a new American racial era.

We approach Shelby Steele ritual ground by climbing a small hill. What first greets the eye is a stage marked "Race." If we have attentively followed the allegorical progression of his book, *The Content of Our Character*, to this elevation we are not shocked or surprised to find that the first stage is pristinely empty. For, we know by now the implicit expository goal of his book (perhaps his life's goal) is to erase—eradicate unequivocally, through exposition and utterly, to terminate—race.

This first stage is merely a token monument to a once life-threatening and invasive pathology of the black mind. Gone, gone with the wind is race. Banished utterly from the kingdom of the saved!

We feel our way to another stage. The flats and mechanisms are technologically grandiose. Its lighting is so dazzling that it startles, encouraging the audience to erase all memory of ancient racial pathologies. We cannot resist; we draw ever nearer. Across the second stage's proscenium arch, bold bright letters are emblazoned: THE GOOD LIFE. With this blazon, *The Content of Our Character* reveals the holy goal of its restless allegorical energies.

We have arrived at the black and exalted Vanity Fair of Negro conservative publicity, celebrity, and purpose in America. Shelby Steele is master of the revels. He soothingly reigns supreme in black finery as the black man who escaped both the tentacles of Chicago black ghetto misery and the Black Power addiction that, I suspect, resulted in his first scholarly employment. He has been washed in autobiographical and ideological scarlet and become—neoconservatively—whiter than snow. Steele's pardon of those who in his youth racially abused or offended him offers fit testimony to his redemption from the hazards of race. He finds fault only with himself for "haranguing" guests he thought racially insensitive at a cocktail party and implicitly apologizes to them. The masochistic former marine who made him pick up schoolyard glass with his bare hands is let off the hook. The white professor who Steele believes, even at the autobiographical moment of writing his book, was an avowed racist is excused on the grounds of wizened ignorance (*Content*, 31–32, 40–41, 130–136).

The drama of *The Content of Our Character*'s second stage of progress commences with something akin to an exorcism—that traditional (and very American) practice of burning witches in order publicly to separate purity and danger. On hard-packed ground directly in front of Shelby Steele's second stage, dressed in hip-hop's gaudiest, most flamboyant black ghetto attire, are none other than: the black lower classes. Actually—in a frugal effort to minimize extras—there is only one. His name is Sam. Is this Sambo? It seems so. Sam is closely akin to historian Stanley Elkins's psychopathological archetype of African blacks is his book *Slavery*. Steele's Sam is a ripe incarnation and disgusting epitome of a pathological black mind symbolized as lower-class black American life:

> No one in my family remembers how it happened, but as time went on, the negative images congealed into an imaginary character named Sam who, from the extensive service we put him to, quickly grew to mythic proportions. In our family lore he was sometimes a trickster, sometimes a boob, but always possessed of a catalogue of sly faults that gave up graphic images of everything we should not be. On sacrifice: "Sam never thinks about tomorrow. He wants it now or he doesn't care about it." On work: "Sam doesn't favor it too much." On children: "Sam likes to have them but not to raise them." On money: "Sam drinks it up and pisses it out." On fidelity: "Sam has to have two or three women." On clothes: "Sam features loud clothes. He likes to see and be seen." And so on. Sam's persona amounted to a negative instructional manual in class identity.
>
> (*Content*, 98)

Suddenly, with a roar, there is a burst of lurid flames! Smoke clogs the air. And poor Sam is no more. Ghetto anxiety has exorcized him utterly. He has been burned as a necessary sacrifice. (Somebody has to pay for America's racial discomfort; why not Sam?) The immolation is an archetypically American ceremony presciently outlined by James Baldwin as the "theology of terror." Everybody is afraid of the big bad wolf of race in America. He has been sacrificed for the delight of white readers: a theology of termination. For Steele, there is absolutely nothing in Sam's existence that constitutes a distinctive and valuable black cultural style or legacy. The suggestion that Sam might in fact be the very embodiment of an alternative conceptualization of the American good life never enters Steele's mind.

In a thoughtful discussion of *The Autobiography of Malcolm X* in relationship to the black public life, Manthia Diawara says that Malcolm's classic autobiography is divided into two parts: the "fallen" state of part one, and the conversion to Muslim orthodoxy of part two. We should pay less attention, says Diawara, to conversion, than to the autobiography's vision of the black good life.[12] What does the black good life imply? I turn to Professor Diawara to attempt an answer that will help one better grasp the full import of Shelby Steele's black neoconservatism. The black good life consists of black cultural style, efficacious public institutions such as mosques and churches, performances by black musicians breaking the hold of white global systems of expressive domination on the black mind, secure social safety nets, meaningful and gainful employment, real wealth accumulation. Two protocols of black behavior are at stake. The first can be called "conversionist." "Conversionist discourses, whether they are motivated by religion, science, or politics, always underestimate *culture* or regard it as *pathological*. Conversionists, whether they are politicians or religious leaders, appeal to their audiences by blaming the *culture of the people they are trying to convert.* They always expect people to come to a revolutionary consciousness or a spiritual awakening, and walk out of their culture, shedding it like a shell or a cracked skin, in order to change the world."[13]

Of course, the sacrifice of culture instanced by Professor Diawara is the result of a serious underestimation of what precisely "culture" at its most sophisticated brings about in the world. Black cultural style can produce very, very wealthy and influential "homeboys." This would mean success stories like those of the Russell Simmons variety—the emergence of black women and men sophisticates and masters of the geographies of race, business, entrepreneurship, and even rich multicultural intimacies. Mary J. Blige, Kanye West, Beyoncé, and Jay-Z all fit this mold. They are among the best and brightest of the world music industry. Cultural knowledge like theirs can, as BET has so amply documented, virtually rule the world. Culture perseveres, preserves, creates windows into the black good life.

Shelby Steele's character Sam plays only the role of a deceived ghetto dweller, desperately in need of conversion. The author of *The Content of Our Character* seems incapable of even hypothesizing the type of culturalist black majority energies and profits suggested by the life and work of the great black nationalist and Nation of Islam leader Malcolm X—or by the life and creativity of an extraordinary artist such as Mary J. Blige.

What, then, does the ritual murder of Sam accomplish for *The Content of Our Character* and black neoconservatism? For whom does Sam's smoldering absence provide new space? Steele's symbolic, ritual murder of Sam in *The Content of Our Character* ultimately provides space for, I believe, a new black Adam. A new colored presence for a paradise regained. And Steele assumes that role in *The Content of Our Character*. Black, Adamic Superfly strides confidently forth onstage, declaring that

> it was not, for us [the family whose sport of choice was "slam Sam"], a matter of hating lower-class blacks but of hating what we did not want to be. Still, hate or love aside, it is fundamentally true that my middle-class identity involved a dissociation from images of lower-class black life and a corresponding identification with values and patterns of responsibility that are common to the middle class everywhere. These values sent me a clear message: Be both an individual and a responsible citizen, understand that the quality of your life will approximately reflect the quality of effort you put into it, know that individual responsibility is the basis of freedom, and that the limitations imposed by fate (whether fair or unfair) are no excuse for passivity. . . .
>
> Hard work, education, individual initiative, stable family life, property ownership—these have always been the means by which ethnic groups have moved ahead in America. Regardless of past or present victimization, these "laws" of advancement apply absolutely to black Americans also. There is no getting around this. What we need is a form of racial identity that energizes the individual by putting him in touch with both his possibilities and his responsibilities.
>
> (*Content*, 99, 108)

This declamation from the new black Adam is warmed-over white neoconservatism par excellence. It is Babbittry (a secular political name for the scriptural philistinism). Hence, the black conservative paragon, or new black Adam, stands before us—an American original, middle-class suburbanite, and comically grandiose. "*He,*" we exclaim, "is the new vision?" Having been promised we were bound for the glory of heavenly revelation, we receive only a dull tableau of free-enterprise morality. Steele's new vision translates as a nostalgic regurgitation of the way things used to be in America. His book is nothing more than retrofitted white American neoconservatism in gaudy blackface. Considering the global corporatist economy of our era's late capitalism, Steele's vision has as much economic immediacy and usefulness for the black majority as a medieval ballad or as Booker T. Washington's

craft-industrial economics advocated from Tuskegee in an age of Birmingham Steel.

Finally, then, we come to understand that it is not really a moral or even a
psychopathological malaise that, for Steele, supposedly mires blacks in a defensive retreat from freedom. Rather, it is agoraphobia. According to Steele,
blacks—especially lower-class blacks—are afraid of the free market. The allegory that is *The Content of Our Character* thus concludes with a viciously
conversionist, didactic gospel of the marketplace. Blacks are expected to walk
out of their cultural shells like a serpent shedding its skin. In reality, however,
this dramatic conclusion is really a kind of new-market beginning. Publication of *The Content of Our Character* and the lavish manner in which it was
received by one of the most significant prize committees in U.S. publishing
marked the beginning of a new and profitable black conservative celebrity in
America. And *The Content of Our Character* is not just a commercially successful rebuff to the Black Power movement. It is, in fact, a manual for national
abandonment of all significant public regard for the black American majority. The book—clearly, and without embarrassment or second thoughts—in-
stalls in the public sphere of the American marketplace a vigorously washed,
black-English-vernacular-purged, free-enterprise conservative black Adam
to replace the black majority.

On reparations, for instance, Shelby feels that even though the nation
recompensed Japanese internment camp victims from World War II, black
American suffering "cannot be repaid." The impossibility or, in Steele's view,
illegitimacy of reparations for blacks, in tandem with this implicit acceptance
of the legitimacy of reparations for the Japanese, represents the same type of
indigenous moralizing that marks his thoughts on the differential legitimacy
of skin color and hair texture in the cultural work of white and black America (119). Further, Steele declares, affirmative action simply reinforces black
pathology. The nation should bear no responsibility for the plight of blacks
and the poor because a "new spirit of pragmatism should prevail [in which
blacks] are seen simply as American citizens who deserve complete fairness
[like the Civil Rights Act] and in some cases developmental assistance, but
in no case special entitlements based on color" (91).

Predicated on an allegorical misreading of the Civil Rights Movement,
marked by disingenuous condemnations of Black Power, sporting bizarrely
outmoded models of economics, Steele's vision is purchased at the cost of
the utter immolation of the interests of the black majority. That such vision

as Steele possesses has become the nationally preferred mode of blackness in the past decade is scarcely surprising. After all, his stale, banal outlook is wonderfully appealing to whites—rich and poor. It makes no demands whatsoever upon critical memory—or upon the American national treasury.

The godfather of black neoconservatism in his grand rhetorical debut has produced nothing but an allegorical wash. The presumed black content of our character at the hands of Shelby Steele is imitatively whiter than snow. And there is more in the effusion of Shelby Steele titled *White Guilt*

White Guilt, another of Steele's offerings on the altar of black neoconservatism, is subtitled *How Blacks and Whites Together Destroyed the Promise of the Civil Rights Era. White Guilt* is a commercially crafted hybrid travel narrative—part Michelin Guide, part Chautauqua. It is perfectly puerile, accessible reading for a weekday afternoon. The book's through-line is inspired by the author's inquiry into events that were current when he conceived and wrote *White Guilt*. The hue and cry surrounding President William Jefferson Clinton's adulterous liaison with White House aide Monica Lewinsky provides background music, as it were, and backstory for Steele's narrative. *White Guilt* does not, however, provide any carefully researched legal, philosophical, political, or economic analyses of the Clinton/Lewinsky matter. The book merely appropriates that signal event to suture its reflections on shifting American racial and sexual mores from the presidency of Dwight David Eisenhower to that of William Jefferson Clinton.

White Guilt commences with the rumor that President Eisenhower occasionally used the word "nigger" in earshot of the public during golfing expeditions. Though Eisenhower's use of the N-word did not bring down his presidency or brand him a racist, Steele suggests that, had Eisenhower engaged in the puritanical fifties in any Clintonesque sexual malfeasance, his administration would have crumbled. By the time of the Clinton/Lewinsky scandal in the nineties, Steele says, American racial and sexual mores had undergone a profound revaluation. If, for instance, the media had caught Bill Clinton uttering the word nigger, his executive house would have immediately imploded. What accounted for this change in American values? Steele makes this query a "thought project" for his coastal drive from Los Angeles (a cityscape marked and marred in *White Guilt* by South Central's anarchic racial rebellion and unending social irresponsibility) to the Northern California splendor of Monterey, the author's peaceful hometown on the Pacific.

Now, if I properly understand the geographical, topological, and mental drift of the journey recorded by *White Guilt*, the narrator ultimately concludes that the dramatic difference in racial and sexual codes of conduct between Eisenhower and Clinton is a function of white guilt. As with other key terms in Steele's writing, it is somewhat difficult to comprehend the precise boundaries of white guilt's field of meaning. This is so because Steele's writings do not place strenuous demands (on themselves or their readers) for rigor or factual accountability. His books always convey a sense of easy recognition and fellowship because they are replete with "just so" segues leading from memoir into religious allegory, melodramatic declarations, and facile comparisons. Only by going to the book itself and surveying firsthand its account of the key concept, white guilt, can we test the validity of these judgments.

In its primary definition, white guilt signals a reaction formation resulting from white America's confession of its insupportable white supremacy—the brutal, doctrinaire racism that guided the nation's polity for centuries. The Civil Rights Movement of the fifties and sixties was responsible for exacting from white America a confession of its evil, racist sin. The movement could legitimately exact such a confession because, in its early phases, it adhered valiantly to professed American national principles: religious freedom, individual responsibility, and the inalienable right to life, liberty, and the pursuit of happiness.

However, the unintended consequence of white America's confession was, in Steele's view, a vacuum of "moral authority." Having been mired in the sin and evil of white supremacy for centuries, a postconfessional white American world found itself moribund and morally paralyzed by its resultant sense of historical guilt. Predicated on a doctrine of racial supremacy that promoted global terrorism against women and people of color everywhere, the white nation's erstwhile power revealed itself as deeply immoral. Despite the national conviction that only white men were ordained by God to rule the world, the power of white supremacy became a confessed sin.

Suddenly, things began to fall apart; the white national center of moral authority could not hold. Who, then, was left to provide moral vision, to step forward and radically articulate a new national polity? In attempting to provide philosophical background to answer this question, Steele offers an account of what Hegel calls "lordship and bondage" that varies in stunning ways from some commonly held notions of oppression and the oppressed. "Oppression, in itself," writes Steele, "pushes people neither to anger nor to revolution. If it did, black slaves would have been so relentlessly rebellious that slavery would have been unsustainable as an institution. . . . Slavery might never have ended had not larger America—at the price of a civil war—decided to end it. The slave's rage meant nothing and brought only the lash. Anger is acted out by the oppressed only when real weakness is perceived in the oppressor."[14] This remarkable declaration concerning American history implies that slavery and its abolition in the United States found blacks entirely devoid of agency. They took no active part in their own liberation, in securing their first freedom. Had it not been for "larger America" (read, white America) black Americans might find themselves chattel slaves in the twenty-first century. Similarly, had it not been for the agential confession of white America extracted by the Civil Rights Movement, black Americans would never have come to exist in a state of freedom. Steele admits that both American slavery and white supremacy were morally bankrupt; they were clear instances of evil. What is most significant for his psychology and philosophy of lordship and bondage, however, is that their immorality was a point of perceptible weakness, a point of structural vulnerability. And it is not so much the sin and evil as the *weakness* that motivated rebellion by the oppressed. Steele writes: "Anger is never automatic or even inevitable for the oppressed; it is *chosen* when weakness in the oppressor means it [anger] will be effective in winning freedom or justice or spoils of some kind" (*White Guilt*, 20; emphasis in original). It is not the agency of the oppressed (who cannot even be angry or morally indignant, it would seem, unless their masters are weak) but the weakness of the oppressor that creates conditions of possibility for black freedom.

Steele's account of the dynamics of bondage and freedom renders black liberation a deeply problematic social and moral occurrence. By his logic, black freedom is coexistent and coterminous with the field of white power because such freedom is purely derivative. It always travels in the shadow of the valley of white supremacy. This translates as follows: black freedom is—because it is engendered by the moral weakness of formerly empowered whites—infected by a dark Nietzschean impulse to evil, that is, a treacherous will to power and its corollary: lascivious demands for spoils.

Striking though it may seem because it strips all agency for their own liberation from the hands of the oppressed, the foregoing is in a nutshell Steele's putatively informed historical account of American racial dynamics. Now if black liberation and freedom are cast in the same mold as white supremacy, it is not surprising that the author declares that the void of moral authority created by white confessionals brings unhealthy national results.

Having pounced, as it were, upon the weakness of whites, blacks are hungry not for a responsible freedom, but only for spoils. Rather than absolve whites in the office of a newly enfranchising and more humane national polity, Black Power (and one might add, by inference, New Left, feminist, gay-and-lesbian, countercultural, academic activist, and black studies) seeks only unfair advantage and unseemly profit. In Steele's account, the power of the newly freed is avaricious, irresponsible, vengeful, greedy, mean-spirited, and self-regarding. In short, Black Power is insatiable; it hungers not to avail itself of boundless opportunities and clear responsibilities offered by freedom, but only to amass spoils of power from whites paralyzed by guilt.

Blacks and their progressive allies have not busied themselves—since they were freed by larger America—with paeans of gratitude to their former enslavers or programs of absolution for whites who have acknowledged their global sins. Blacks have not even engineered independent bootstrap programs for their own uplift. Instead, they have continuously insisted—despite what Steele sees as indisputable evidence to the contrary—that they are not yet free. They dare to claim that white supremacist sinners are not genuinely penitent and have yet to relinquish even a modicum of their powerful global supremacy. Blacks and their allies recklessly persist in assertions that systemic barriers constructed by white supremacy continue to demand—and fail to receive—structural-economic attention from an enduringly oppressive white power. Such structural and systemic claims from those who are free, says Steele, amount to no more than a vicious opportunism fueled by white guilt. They metaphorically kick truly penitent whites while they are morally down and ineluctably blue. In Steele's worldview, for the formerly oppressed to charge that white oppression is still as real as rain in their everyday lives—and furthermore demand economic and structural attention—is devastating to founding principles of the nation. *White Guilt* feels at times like prose nostalgia for white supremacy. At one point in the text, Steele even states that the evil of white supremacy notwithstanding, it provided gears, levers, and stunning achievement for a great world civilization.

Rites of confession, morality, sin, and guilt are at the affective heart of both *The Content of Our Character* and *White Guilt*. In *White Guilt*, Steele poses as the lonely prophetic journeyman by the sea, decrying Bill Clinton's sexual excess. He hails the nation from the gleaming Pacific, seeming to say: "Take heart, my people, for President George W. Bush is among us. His legerdemain has cannily brought national reprieve from the white guilt that had rendered us authority-less!" What Steele actually claims in *White Guilt* is that the "right has made itself *accountable* [today] to the democratic and *moral* vision of the early Martin Luther King . . . [and George W.] Bush is the first conservative president to openly compete with the left in the arena of ideas around poverty, education, and race. He has attempted to establish conservatism as a philosophy of *social* reform" (178–179; emphasis in original). I can think of two words that seem to contradict Steele's claim: Hurricane Katrina.

One certainly hopes in that the wake of the devastation of Katrina and the Bush administration's deep social and economic indifference to the disaster that Steele has revised his evaluation. He makes his assessment of President Bush an essential element of what he suggests is a new theory of present-day Republican conservatism. For Steele, this theory commences with and finds its glory in conservatism's "dissociation from the racist past through principle and individual responsibility" (*White Guilt*, 179). If Bill Clinton is synecdoche for a greedy, self-indulgent moral relativism that consumes the void once white supremacy's moral authority has been cast aside, then President George W. Bush is the epitome of a new psychology and program of reform. His path is that of a healthy and responsible dissociation leading to reform. President Bush is the epic avatar in Steele's account of Dr. Martin Luther King Jr. This is the same George W. Bush and administration that were and seem to remain deliberately indifferent to their callous failure to respond to the immediate needs of thousands of Hurricane Katrina victims. This is the president who opted for a flyby over flood-wracked territories of the Gulf and praised a wretchedly incompetent Michael Brown, whom he had appointed director of the Federal Emergency Management Agency, as hundreds of impoverished inhabitants of New Orleans suffered and perished all around them. The only way for one to arrive at a comparison of such a failed leader as Bush with such a genius of leadership as King is by following the twisted paths of right-wing, Republican disingenuousness, with its studied obtuseness to the social suffering of the American majority. Steele's bromides about individual freedom, upward mobility, and moral responsibility stand tendentiously in space that should be occupied by intellectual analysis—and plain common sense. In the wake of the Bush administration's dismal response to Hurricane Katrina, perhaps only such a substitution of cliché for common sense could maintain faith in what Steele reads as a new conservatism, a new theory of social reform. So then, what message does *White Guilt* ultimately convey, as its narrator comes home to roost in Monterey? Actually, the question better posed is: What is it that *White Guilt* fails to tell us as it journeys decisively away from South Central?

White Guilt is characterized by profound silence concerning the root cause and structural realities that produce and exacerbate the abjectness of black majority life in the United States today. During Bill Clinton's run for the presidency, campaign manager James Carville was queried about the focus of that contest. His response is legendary: "It's the economy, stupid!" One wants to elaborate on Carville's quip and say to Shelby Steele: "You have completely, and perhaps deliberately, ignored in your book the shifting national economics of the space between Eisenhower and Clinton that so intrigues you." The administrations of President Ronald Reagan and President George Herbert Walker Bush set in motion a by now nearly complete devastation of America's economies of national production, and substantial and compassionate networks of social safety for the underprivileged. Wealth was transferred upward in greater sums at greater speed than ever before in our national history. American industries were deregulated; American jobs were exported; and American organized labor was reduced to unseemly compromise by actions such as the termination of hundreds of jobs of striking American air controllers. A private prison-industrial complex was given sanction by zero tolerance, three strikes, and mandatory sentencing policies in American criminal justice and national jurisprudence. Black and brown men and women by the hundreds of thousands were fed into this private prison-industrial complex by the type of summary justice represented by the Rockefeller drug laws. These new "felons" of color have come to constitute a great migration from zones of bleak urban confinement like South Central into the privately financed and administered sites of the private prison-industrial complex. Public schooling in our era has reached an almost zero sum return on development and instruction because indifferent local and state governments have vacated expenditures for genuinely efficacious education. Health insurance is an unaffordable luxury for scores of millions of American citizens. The same George W. Bush presidency hailed by Shelby Steele as reformist successor to the legacy of Martin Luther King Jr. spends more in a week on its unjustified war in Iraq (which truly does represent a void of moral authority) than it has on all of public education and general public assistance and health care during its term of office. Hundreds of billions of dollars is not an account category that matches any American enterprise except war. Then, there is a multimillion dollar U.S. embassy being built in Baghdad that will take a billion dollars a year to operate.

How—given the ignominy of the aforementioned economies—can the nation expect to secure a purchase on morality and social justice? And how can the presumed analytical and responsible prose of *White Guilt* endorse the white legislative, business, and executive ravages of our national values that have marked the presidencies of both George Herbert Walker Bush and George W. Bush?

A signal promise of the Civil Rights Movement was that future black intellectuals and activist thinkers would commit themselves to rigorous analyses of, especially, the immemorial economic sins and failings of white supremacy, American slavery, and American governmental plutocracy. Martin Luther King Jr. was, after all, Dr. King.—a studious, activist Ph.D. always intent on speaking truth to power. To read King's writing is to discover his avid commitment to American economic redress to victims of chattel slavery; he called for a global redistribution of wealth in the name and service of social justice and the people farthest down. Dr. King unequivocally championed reparations, global restitution for white supremacy's brutal exploitation of the wretched of the earth. As one can glean from his writings, King did not advocate the transfer of wealth upward, nor did he expend energy recommending the exportation of American jobs, or signing trade agreements that denuded the American working class. He certainly did not lobby for the repeal of the estate tax. Therefore, when Steele compares George W. Bush to Martin Luther King Jr. he seems to be a black writer on the very edge of a half mad sycophancy before white power. He certainly does not display the logic or intellectual rigor of the Civil Rights Movement's promised activist intellectual bent on achieving truth, justice, and soundly researched conclusions. Martin Luther King and Shelby Steele would seem to have almost nothing in common.

It would be a serious error, however, to assume Steele is economically naive about his own distinctive genre of moralizing authorship/authority. By the time he reaches San Luis Obispo, he realizes that a fat wallet will carry him comfortably anywhere he wishes among whites (*White Guilt*, 9). On a variety of race-based public matters of the past decade and a half, he renders harshly negative judgments on everything from the verdict in the O. J. Simpson murder trial to the Supreme Court's ruling on affirmative action in *Grutter vs. Bollinger*. The race card played by Johnnie Cochran in the Simpson trial, according to Steele, was as much a plugging for advantage and spoils as was Justice Sandra Day O'Connor's pivotal argument for the continuance of legitimate forms of race-based admissions in the Supreme Court decision.

What lies behind Steele's race-denying target practice is, I think, a gainful authorial commitment to defending capitalistic privacy. He condemns affirmative action in the academy because he endorses the notion that seats in academe are private spaces, virtually labeled "whites only." They are not unlike—in Steele's argument—the private coach seat taken by Homer Plessy that triggered one of the most nefarious judicial proceedings in U.S. history. In fact, Steele avers that the "white blindness" manifested by Justice O'Connor in *Grutter* was more egregious than that marking *Plessy vs. Ferguson*, which gave birth to the "separate but equal" horrors of Jim Crow (*White Guilt*, 143–145). The comparison is not simply bombastic misrepresentation; it is pernicious melodrama for white consumption and approval.

The public and highly media-conditioned proceedings of the O. J. Simpson case exposed the racism of America's systems of criminal justice and jurisprudence to a global audience. Steele, however, implies that he for one knows that Simpson was guilty of murder. Had the proceedings been private, and limited to the control of an authority impervious to white guilt, matters would have turned out quite differently. Steele charges black Americans with willfully "generalizing" the "individual" and "occasional" police and judicial racism of the Simpson case, exacting a not guilty verdict through a kind of Black Power exploitation of historical white guilt. Given the incompetence, racism, and ineptness of the Los Angeles Police Department and the Los Angeles District Attorney's Office revealed in the case, it is perfectly amazing that Steele believes it was white guilt and not a racist white ineptness that wrought the exonerating verdict for O. J. Of course Steele doesn't actually revisit the case, he merely pontificates on it. He seems scarcely to have read (or to have believed) anything concerning the monumental incompetence of the LAPD and the misfiring strategies of the prosecution. But, then, this is the same Steele who accuses blacks of generalizing police brutality based on their viewing and understanding of the vicious beating of the black Rodney King, who was stopped by police for speeding. White officers then beat him severely with batons, Tasered him, and stomped on his shoulder. Steele suggests that the treatment accorded Rodney King was probably "necessary." Blacks generalized his treatment out of context. Says Steele: "Ingeniously, they [blacks] globalized what was very likely a necessary police beating into an agonized national debate on the state of black America" (*White Guilt*, 37). What is a "necessary" police beating?

Steele's harsh judgments on the welfare of blacks and the responsibility of the public sphere vis-à-vis social justice for them seem resolutely intended to defend white private property, white capital gain, and police state brutality meant to deter any menace to white authority and comfort. Steele is, in the vernacular, a hater of any law or order meant to prevent or ameliorate the traditional exclusion of blacks from higher education based principally upon scores from high-stakes standardized tests. The beating of black traffic-stop victim Rodney King by possibly racist officers of the metropolitan police force is "necessary" to keep Simi Valley safe for private, white domesticity. Advocacy for private property and capital gain is, I think, no sin. But what morally and dramatically subverts Steele's claimed disinterestedness and ethical fair play are his self-regarding economics as a black public spokesman.

Steele's capitalist alchemy turns the leaden void of white moral guilt into the profitable gold of his own authorship. He absolves a newly confessed white world by crafting an itinerant drama of Black Power, countercultural, New Left, and feminist disorder and social irresponsibility. Essentially, he simply, in the guise of a corrective, offers a right-wing pep talk for wealthy white Americans. "Why did you confess in the first place?" he seems bent on asking. "You should have known the majority of these power-hungry, searching-for-weakness 'minorities' out here have no merit, excellence, or cultural treasure to add to the world's store. It probably would have been better for American morality and its capital reserves had white supremacy never ended." (Again, my words.) But why would someone who feels as Steele does that the oppressed are marked by almost insensate numbness to insult, immunity to anger, and incapacity for agency—how could someone who believes this way have any reservations about the wisdom of white supremacy's continuing sway? "I am certain," writes Steele, "that racist rejections . . . do not cause low self-esteem in their victims" (*White Guilt*, 15). Clearly, this is black, neoconservative mainlining of absolution as an antidepressant for white American blues. Call it a cash cow gambit for Steele. Call it a betrayal of blacks, and history, and American progressivism for the rest of us.

There is much more that might be contested in *White Guilt*—the text's devaluation of black and ethnic literatures, its endorsement of Bill Cosby's denunciation of the life and culture of the black majority, its vicious mischaracterization of Dick Gregory—but it is best to conclude here with a glance at the book's unkindest cut of all. It comes when Steele staunchly defends his posture and life-world as that of a black conservative. He acknowledges that through his graduate school experience and early teaching days, he postured as a man of radical, leftist, black politics. But he claims he did so only to project a political identity, having no real knowledge of what such politics meant. His public displays of radicalism were a mask.

He calls the state of dissonance between the way he actually lived and the manner in which he carried himself in public "schizophrenia." Of course, this implicit attribution of mental illness to those who do not agree with conservative power is not out of keeping with Steele's Christian moralizing. In days of old, whole power structures of king and divinity were wont to see plagues visited upon their enemies as God inspired, the wages of their dissent from supremacy. But for a resident of Monterey and inhabitant of the prestigious Hoover Institution in Palo Alto to mistake—or mischaracterize—the venerable process of blacks wearing the mask as schizophrenia is, at best, ignorance. "By the mid-eighties," writes Steele, "the schizophrenia imposed on me as a black who was identified with the left had become unbearable. I had no interest in becoming a conservative. I just instinctively disliked the left's disregard of principles that had *always* been important to me. Worse, I had become terrified of the Faustian bargain waiting for me at the doorway to the left: we'll throw you a bone like affirmative action if you'll just let us reduce you to your race so we can take moral authority for 'helping' you" (*White Guilt*, 174; emphasis in original).

The politics of black liberation, the fortitude and mental discomfort they occasion in a racist land, not only prove too much for Steele, but also compel him to label those who engage such politics as victims of schizophrenia. Those of us who have lived in the presence of mental illness—its devastations compounding the everyday fraught reality of simply being black in America—must be appalled by Steele's ignorant insensitivity. He surely means to suggest of his felt "two-ness" of life and politics something on the order of "cognitive dissonance." But, as with so much of his writing, he pulls "schizophrenia" out of the hat and dangles it flashily before his white audience. Steele labels himself free of a disorder he does not properly define, announcing that as a conservative (i.e., healthy) black man he is empowered to damn all black radical leftists (i.e., the mentally ill) and the black majority with whom they labor. He seems to conclude that devils of schizophrenia will always plague and impoverish the black left. From the idyllic scenic description that concludes *White Guilt*, we may well infer that such a devilish fate will never befall at least *one* black citizen of Monterey.

IN AFRO-AMERICAN LORE, ONE of the best stories of the trickster concerns a slave who claimed he could foretell the future.[1] It turns out he had devised secret peepholes and monitoring devices while he worked as a house slave among white folks. Overhearing and overseeing their comings and goings, he was always on top of their agendas and could thus "predict" what they were going to do. Well, it seems the slave's master was so convinced by the slave's prophecies that he was willing to wager a substantial sum with a neighboring plantation owner. They agreed to hide something under a large pot and let the slave try and "see" what it was. The big day arrives. The event is public. The slave is truly in a tight spot. After stalling, delaying, scratching his head and muttering a lot of mumbo jumbo, he concedes, saying: "Well, he run a long time, but they cotched the ole coon at last." The slave's master is delighted. They raise the pot and out scampers a raccoon.

Of course, the comic end to the story turns upon words being spoken one way and taken another. The slave's "trick" is not just his surreptitious spying and scouting at the Big House, but also his way of speaking words that seem to mean something they don't. A confession is taken for a revelation. Who is this trickster? Jeanne Rosier Smith writes that "tricksters are not only characters, they are also rhetorical agents. They infuse narrative ... with energy ... [and] humor ... [and they can produce] ... a politically radical subtext in the narrative form itself."[2]

This seems a fine definition, with one caveat. Tricksters can also produce texts that are less radical and more preservative, even conservative.

REFLECTIONS

OF A FIRST

AMENDMENT

TRICKSTER

STEPHEN

CARTER

The presence of tricksters in the lore of every culture seems to be due to their rhetorical ability to manipulate sacred texts, founding documents, homespun wisdom, and hearthside truths. It is just such cultural lore that holds together the unified populations and institutions we come to call a "community." The way we know we belong to a particular community is through our ability to handle its defining texts. For example, it may be difficult for ardent patriots in the United States to acknowledge one's American-ness if one cannot handily recite the Pledge of Allegiance or belt out with gusto at least one chorus of "God Bless America."

Tricksters are characters of twice-told cultural stories; they manipulate and handle a community's sacred texts in ways that are supposed to preserve that community. Neoconservatism in America is a community replete with tricksters. And like the prophetic slave in the tale, neoconservatism's joint stock company of tricksters sometimes includes performers in blackface.

"Blackface" calls up that enduring, enormously popular, and archetypically American performance known as the minstrel show. Any Web site hosting images of college and university fraternity high jinks will show just how alive and well it is today. "Blackface" refers to the costume: burnt cork, rouged lips, wooly wigs, and the rags and tatters of Negro abjection. Even when African American performers (who were actually black!) took to the minstrel stage, they "blacked up."

The minstrel show offered a moment when the blackface performer would deliver a windy version of the "Gettysburg Address" or the "Declaration of Independence" in jumbled black dialect, infested with malapropism. Such performances were, of course, double-edged and tricky. Whites guffawed raucously, and the black performer—as with the prophetic slave of the trickster story—got paid in full.

The black minstrel's trick was to perform sacred cultural texts in a fashion that made the black majority (which the blackface performer was always held to represent) look ridiculous while the minstrel himself soberly got paid. His performance comforted white audiences, assuring them that blacks in the aggregate were definitely outsiders to the dominant community. Minstrel shows were simply one more "proof" that the black majority was unfit for citizenship (as if they could not get the tune or the words of the "Star Spangled Banner"). Minstrelsy confirmed that the black majority was not ready for prime-time American-ness and that the dominant white population's sense of its superior cultural and community belonging was entirely justified.

Which is only to say that the black minstrel trickster knows exactly how to handle his lampooning, conservative performance of white ideas, notions, and texts in a manner that preserves white community.

But none of this becomes usefully clear without example. We need to take a critical look at one of the most famous performers ever to grace the American neoconservative stage. That would be Professor Stephen Carter, author of a punchy guidebook to black neoconservatism in America: *Reflections of an Affirmative Action Baby*.

Professor Carter is the William Nelson Cromwell Professor of Law at Yale University. He has published seven nonfiction books, including *Reflections of an Affirmative Action Baby*. He also published a novel, *The Emperor of Ocean Park*, in a two-book contract that yielded a $4.2 million advance, making him by almost any standard a rich black man.[3] His second book seems decisively not to have emulated the success of his first. He is a member of the American Law Institute and a fellow of the American Academy of Arts and Sciences. He is a black media celebrity, having appeared on *Face the Nation* and other heralded television talk shows. He holds an array of awards and honorary degrees stunning for a scholar so young. In the face of such overwhelming accomplishment, Professor Carter is a man who could scarcely be accused of *not* knowing precisely what he is doing, writing, saying, or endorsing. Stephen Carter is a black man who can say of his tirade against affirmative action, *Reflections*: "I wrote that book a long time ago. I was a lot younger then and, like a lot of younger people, I was more prickly and more passionate about certain things. Some things that upset me then probably upset me a little less now, but a lot of people are still upset by them."[4] Is this in fact a wealthy black author saying: "I repudiate my guidebook to black neoconservatism in America"? It is, rather, a smart and celebrated black neoconservative intellectual who has made a ton of money and jump-started his career trashing the very greased skids by which he gained fame and fortune, trying, as it were, to disavow earlier damage to the black majority in the name of a youthful prickliness.

If Carter has conformed to and is as comfortable at Yale Law School as *Reflections* seems to imply, then it is difficult to fathom how he could have written, published, and reaped cultural capital from a book like *Reflections* without realizing (or at least considering) what an injurious monograph it would be to black majority interests. The realization that Carter is an enormously talented, superbly educated, and prolific black academic makes it almost impossible to imagine that he did not know he was traveling in volatile and consequential territories of race and law in America when he published his book—"prickly" though he might have been. Unintended consequences are always a possibility of academic writings and public positions. But given Carter's credentials, it is hard to imagine that he did not *mean* to deal a smart blow to affirmative action and its beneficial effects for the black majority. His success in doing so is, in my opinion, permanent, inexcusable, reprehensible, and irremediable.

"Tricky," perhaps, is the adjective that most aptly describes Professor Carter. (One of my gifted academic friends once advised me when I threw my name into the ring for a deanship that my politics would surely cancel my chances of success. "But," said he, "if it does come down to the wire and you might get power, money, and fame, just say: 'I no longer endorse my earlier views. They were missteps of a guileless youth.'") Unlike Shelby Steele, Stephen Carter does not rehash biblical rhetoric in his neoconservative campaign against affirmative action. As one might expect from a lawyer, he brings the Constitution of the United States of America to his defense as a "dissenter" from what he labels the "black party line." However, before analyzing Professor Carter's performance in *Reflections of an Affirmative Action Baby*, it might be useful to state, again, that Black Power, comprehensively read, does not seem in any way guilty of the narrow, provincial, authoritarian, xenophobic line of which Steele and Carter accuse it.

In its manifestation as black cultural nationalism, one of the principal ends of Black Power was global outreach. It worked in scholarly, creative, political, historical, and, yes, mythical ways to construct blackness as a marker of diversity. It was an open-ended, freely associative, inclusive liberation theology in at least one of its manifestations. It sought to reclaim and make known the voices of Africa, the Caribbean, Mexico, Latin America, and, indeed, all historical and geographical regions of the Americas where blacks have migrated. Never before, in so brief a span of American academic time, had there occurred the type of recovery, revised pedagogy, accelerated cultural distribution, and scholarly research that was motivated by black cultural nationalism, black studies, and Black Power during the 1970s and 1980s.

Presumably, it was the global extension of range under the sign blackness that enabled black world populations beyond the borders of the United States to apply blackness as an analytical category to an array of social configurations. Black British cultural studies, for example, and the now defunct use of black as a British sign for coalition politics, offer examples of the utility of Black Power's influence abroad. The scholar Paul Gilroy's energetic studies *There Ain't No Black in the Union Jack* and *The Black Atlantic* are recent illustrations of how capacious Black Power's writings of blackness have been. Rather than racial totalitarianism, Black Power and black cultural nationalism represented provisional efforts by activists and scholars alike to provide new evidence and methods in order to include new geographies for scholarship in the field of cultural studies.

For moderate and conservative America, the freeze-frame ideal of the Civil Rights movement is Dr. Martin Luther King Jr., poised at the Lincoln Memorial, dreaming a racially harmonious dream. For Stephen Carter that dream moment is farther removed. His ideal—pristinely frozen in time and space—is the inscription and adoption of the Constitution's First Amendment: "Congress shall make no law respecting an establishment of religion, or prohibiting the free exercise thereof; or abridging the freedom of speech, or of the press; or the right of the people peaceably to assemble, and to petition the government for a redress of grievances."

These words resonate with symphonic overtones of New World freedom for Stephen Carter in *Reflections of an Affirmative Action Baby*. Like all such words, however, they are abstract—statements of principle, declarations designed for specific circumstances, utterances shaped by varying interests. Anyone who freezes them into a pristine legal tableau of supposedly disinterested revolutionary white male intellectualism is a broker of fantasy and nostalgia.

James Madison's original aim for the First Amendment was to prevent the federal government from establishing a national religion and thus interfering with citizens' civil rights or their "full and equal rights of conscience." Madison and others sought to guarantee that government did not use religion as a justification for thought suppression. Despite Judeo-Christian predispositions, Madison and others knew that a "general" statement would be more likely to secure consensus and ratification of the Constitution than a more elaborated code of prohibitions and sectarian considerations concerning religion. Implicit for Madison and the other founders, nonetheless, was a "general" notion that Christianity would be well encouraged by the states.

New World overtones of freedom translate, therefore, at least in the instance of the First Amendment, as a dramatic multiplication of meanings and intentions. The same may be said with respect to the First Amendment's provision of "freedom of speech." Conservative nostalgia strives to interpret the

First Amendment's free speech provision as implicitly filled with Madisonian and libertarian original grandeur. Such a clean and aesthetically satisfying vision of the First Amendment is what some critics call a misprision—a kind of deliberate mistake or tricky intentional misunderstanding for rhetorical advantage in an argument. Indeed, the First Amendment was not unequivocally meant to guarantee anybody's right to say whatever he or she pleased, so long as it did not present clear and present danger to civil society. It was not meant as a libertarian manifesto. Had it been, "hate speech" and "love speech" alike could be launched into the world with impunity; politicians and governments could be vilified at will; summons to violent overthrow of existing authority could be dispatched without punishment. We know all such unchecked willfulness is, of course, prohibited under the rule of law. The First Amendment does not protect licentiousness, libel, or anarchy.

No, what free speech seems to have meant to the founders was freedom from "prior restraint"—defined as that pre-Revolutionary necessity for newspapers and journals to pass inspection by licensers and censors. A check, therefore, on censorship of thought, not a warrant for anybody and everybody to do and say precisely what they pleased, with equal tolerance for sense and nonsense alike. This historical view of free speech as pragmatic openness is more sobering by far than the conservative's boast of free-range libertarianism as the amendment's original intent. Indeed, provisions on "sedition" and "espionage," McCarthyism, and an image of the Black Panther Bobby Seale bound, handcuffed, and gagged in an American courtroom reveal that, implicit in the assumptions of the founding fathers, was at least the thought that not all, or indeed any, speech was inherently free—existing in rarified ether, liberated from dictates and demands of power and the effects of cultural and financial capital. Uneven development (the rich get richer, while the poor abide their lot) in various sectors of the U.S. population, and uneven degrees of freedom (a Voting Rights Act required in 1965!) has made some speech free and other forms of talk rigidly subject to both prior and consequent restraint. The uneven and differential effects of "free" might be suggested by summoning that old chestnut that no citizen is free to shout "Fire!" in a crowded theater. On the other hand, the black writer Amiri Baraka boldly, and perhaps quite accurately, asserts in one of his most powerful essays of the 1960s that were he to stand on a corner in downtown Manhattan—regaled in all his blackness—and loudly and repeatedly proclaim "I'm a *free* man!" he would be dead or in prison by nightfall.[5]

The nobility of the ideal of free speech—completely open public discursive assemblies—in a fully participatory marketplace of American ideas is, at best, an allegorical reverie where blacks, women, Native Americans, Asian Americans, Mexican Americans, and non–property owners in the United States are concerned.

Time, litigation, judicial tests, trials, and tribunals have, of course, left a mixed record with respect to the First Amendment in American jurisprudence. There is much in this history that is edifying and honorable. But the fact remains that there have always been those who are more free to speak than others. And any visualization of a frozen moment in time when Chief Justice Oliver Wendell Holmes's ideal was the actual existing reality for all is rhetorically manipulative nostalgia. In his dissenting opinion in *Abrams v. United States*, Justice Holmes asserted:

> But when men have realized that time has upset many fighting faiths, they may come to believe even more than they believe the very foundations of their own conduct that the ultimate good desired is better reached by free trade in ideas—that the best test of truth is the power of the thought to get itself accepted in the competition of the market, and that truth is the only ground upon which their wishes safely can be carried out. That at any rate is the theory of our Constitution.[6]

Even Justice Holmes, in his shrewd dissent, acknowledges that no matter how exactly free his own personal standards may be, freedom of speech—conceived as fair, truthful, marketplace competition available to all—is theory.

Stephen Carter's elaboration of what I call the doctrine of the "natural aristocrat" takes the form of a First Amendment self-defense and rhetorical counter to the authoritarian party line supposedly held in place in the United States by Black Power. Carter rails against affirmative action (as an outgrowth of Black Power), because affirmative action is an affront to a natural black aristocracy of which, naturally, Carter is one of the chosen members. *Reflections of an Affirmative Action Baby* begins autobiographically and traces, with finger-thumping conviction and often stirring eloquence, how affirmative action *hurts* the black aristocratic few.

Born in the valley of the shadow of Cornell University, Stephen Carter was the smartest kid in his class. And through his "prickly" days, he was unfailingly annoyed by traditional Civil Rights and Black Power agendas that confused his individual, undeniable, unmistakable "smartness" with the color of his skin. This confusion is a direct outgrowth of a party line. As the product of a party line, it has brought disastrous consequences to middle-class, smart men of color like Stephen Carter.

In Carter's account, black Americans, oppressed by discrimination, were being driven to an intolerant, racially defensive majoritarianism. By this he meant, in 1992, that the black majority has always displayed a keen sense of collective unity in defense of its interests and has not easily tolerated those who urge it toward gradualist suicide or assimilationist self-extinction. Carter feels it is unhelpful to *his* interests that the black majority has always demanded special preferences as recompense for years of unpaid suffering and exploited labor in America. Of course the black majority refers to this not as special preference but as entirely justified reparations.

Carter believes that American recompense to blacks, offered in the form of affirmative action, only results in quite unnerving behaviors on the part of the white majority. For, in his early days, he felt that whites assume—and sometimes state in public—that blacks who have benefited from the recompense or reparative mandates of affirmative action are not as qualified as whites who are (in their view) hired, admitted, and professionally promoted on the basis of merit alone.

Reflections details the author's personal embarrassment, his individual discomfort in the face of affirmative action. At times, it appears Carter's personal discomfort alone prompts his recommendation that America eradicate affirmative action. Carter repeatedly tells us that he suffers near-paranoid distraction at the thought that white people might give him an A not because he has merited it, but because of the dark color of his skin. And this paranoia, he seems to believe, plagues him perhaps more than such merit anxieties trouble others.

Reflections sketches for us the calm material fullness of its author's life: suburban residency, academic scholarships and professional degrees, Christmas parties for black Yale law students (to show his solidarity), special status as one of the meager population of black authors in the United States. Surely, these trappings of the good life qualify their bearer to track the monstrous offspring of a black party line to its lair and slay it. Affirmative action must die. It confuses folks about who Stephen Carter is—a man of achievement, a man of class difference, a natural aristocrat. Carter wants America to know he is a well-heeled and independent thinker. He will never be a majoritarian follower of colored gospels. His beautiful life—complete with the self-bestowed privilege of dissociating from the interests of black Yale law students whenever principle demands—reinforces his notions that he is not like other Negroes, who are racially defensive and, perhaps, emotionally oversensitive: "The black conservatives, so-called, are quite comfortable in their tenured academic positions and other posts, which is, after all, what academic sinecures are for. Despite the name calling of their critics, they will not be silenced. Nor should they be. A central message of *freedom for even hated and hateful speech*—a message missed equally by those on the right who would ban flag burning and by those on the left who would ban racial epithets—also holds true in this case: silencing debate solves no problems; it simply limits the range of possible solutions."[7] The constitutional allegory thus commences, discovering Carter drawing a definite "allies line" between his personal politics and an idealistically nostalgic evocation of the First Amendment.

Carter wants his readers to endorse his conviction that the class and occupational status he holds is a result of merit alone. And if this is true, then his blackface status as a dissenting performer of the First Amendment is middle-class minstrel work par excellence. Under the umbrella of the Constitution, the author of *Reflections of an Affirmative Action Baby* is safe from the party line storms of black majoritarianism.

He is black, smart, and dissenting. He feels he and his black conservative brethren should be admired for their rugged neoconservative individualism—their suburban market savvy. Carter's rhetorical performance of the spirit of '76 makes him the peerless anti-affirmative-action baby for American consumption and profit. America will ravenously devour Carter's critique of black communism (for, what else does "party line" suggest in the annals of U.S. neoconservatism) and define him as a First Amendment Messiah. In fact, he could probably do without an audience, since he does write himself with bold egotism as the country's best First Amendment metaphor. Individualistic, tenured, and dissentingly outside the hurly-burly of reparations, reform, and black majority causes in general, Stephen Carter is a stark, black symbol of how to hate and hurt "your own," while ever being mistaken for "one of them." The hubris toward white privilege that streams into Carter's New England household compels the author of *Reflections* to portray himself as Saint Stephen, apotheosis of black dissent. Yet at least Carter's writing is refreshingly provocative, sometimes original, and usually energetic.

On a plane far less exalted than a self-anointed sainthood, Carter implies that black Yale Law School students should humbly commend his free ideological leanings when he writes:

My sympathies generally run toward freedom, and I would oppose efforts to regulate racism that is reflected in simple speech, even when the racist views are insulting, offensive, or painful. For example, I would fight, forcefully if unhappily, for
the right of students to express the view (in the classroom or in the dinning hall or
on wall posters, signed or unsigned) that black people display a tendency toward
criminality or are intellectually inferior. Cruel and insupportable such views might
be, but they are plainly speech.[8]

Again, Carter plays the First Amendment Saint. But I believe we can read
his defense of white supremacist speech as a rhetorical maneuver (under the
cover of the First Amendment): a clear, personal, elitist abdication of local
responsibility. I say "abdication" because it seems to me black professors with
a sense of the realpolitik of the American academy of the 1990s were able
to fall back on libertarian notions of free speech only by refusing to see the
battle actually at hand for black people everywhere. Speech, in the racial climate of the past half century, is not as free to some as it is to others.

First Amendment fairness is scarcely the rule—of ethics, policy, or intellectualism—when, for example, an act of hateful speech issues from a black
Nation of Islam advocate precisely in the halls of the academy. During the
first quarter of 1994, a loathsome, bombastic speech by Khalid Abdul Mo-
hammed was delivered in an academic venue. The speech was anti-Semitic,
flamboyant, and rancorously racist. Rather than being, in accord with Carter's
notions of the First Amendment, intellectually tolerated as "clearly speech,"
Khalid Mohammad's effusions became a target of a media frenzy. Whites
worked to compel every living black soul in the United States to condemn
Mohammad's "hate speech." Our national legislature even took time out to
pass a resolution condemning Mohammad's college campus speech. Does
Carter not realize that such anti–First Amendment venom exists in white
America? And if he does realize this, how could he be so obnoxiously smug
about racist posters in the halls of Yale?

Battles rage even into the twenty-first century to shut down black-uttered
hate speech of that black religion represented by the Nation of Islam. Post
9/11, the fury of our white national consciousness—secular and religiously
right—has ballooned. We do not like that which white racism designates as
"camel jockey," "raghead," "cowardly," "fanatical," "terrorist." The Middle East
and Southside Chicago (headquarters of the black Nation of Islam) have
become evil twins on the American "Axis of Evil" radar.

The unprincipled shiftiness of white American standards of merit, excellence, rights, and debate seems not to trouble Carter. He appears to feel that by championing what he personally considers fair and legitimate modes of behavior he is in touch with reality. For example, he surely believes he is buttressing a nonrelativistic American norm of First Amendment free speech when he asserts that he would "fight, forcefully if unhappily, for the right of students" to display white racist posters in the Yale Law School. His implicit anxiety and confessional angst amount, I think, to an abandonment of Yale black law students.

Black students at Yale Law School petitioned the administration for an out-of-classroom means of registering their problems with instances of white hate speech (or, better perhaps, racial harassment) in the classroom. Professor Carter immediately made it known that he thought the black students' request was ludicrous. After all, other (read: normatively white) students feel free to take issue with professors in the classroom. Why shouldn't black students feel and act the same way?[9]

Black students responded by saying they felt constrained in classroom situations because white law school professors represent a power base that forecloses all possibility of a fair hearing for black student dissent. "Nonsense!" suggests Carter. Black students need to grow up. Yet, Carter himself—after a moving and passionate rehearsal of the sufferings of black intellectual dissenters who refuse a party line—cries: "But … the dissenters [black neoconservatives] lack a black power base from which to intimidate their opponents."[10] Carter's chagrin at his personal situation is both hypocritical and manifestly jejune.

What in heaven or on earth could persuade the black American majority to serve as a power base for the dismantling of affirmative action? Affirmative action was not instituted principally to guarantee admission to elite law schools for the smartest black kids on the block. It was instituted as a proposed remedy for years of discrimination against the black American majority. During the past three decades, affirmative action has been vigorously effective, providing jobs and job training for thousands of black people in the United States. So why would black people—who indisputably suffer the highest unemployment rates in the nation—want to empower Stephen Carter to shut down whatever vestiges are left of affirmative action?

Does it seem at all rational for Carter to solicit a black power base when the whole philosophical bent of his rhetorical performance is precisely to disempower the black student population of the institution where he wields his greatest local influence? If Carter's rhetoric—in its local instances—is contrary to black emotional, intellectual, and group interests, why would he dream of securing a black majority power base for his views? My answer is that Carter once dared to promote such an outcome because he, like Shelby Steele, is no more than a man of misprision in *Reflections of an Affirmative Action Baby*. He quixotically and trickily dreamed the indisputably impossible (and eternally harmful to the black majority) dream for the entertainment and solace of a white audience.

Specifically, he claims that Martin Luther King Jr. was opposed to Black Power and black nationalist movements. He even implies, quite strongly, that if Dr. King were alive and well, he would—in the name of black Christian morality—reject the economic benefits of affirmative action. Such claims seem uninformed by an awareness of Dr. King's real and adamant calls for economic justice in his post–March on Washington years.

Professor Ronald Turner notes that in a 1965 interview Dr. King was asked whether a "proposal for a multibillion dollar program providing preferential treatment for Blacks or any other minority group was fair." The great black Civil Rights leader responded as follows: "I do indeed [feel it is fair]. Can any fair-minded citizen deny that the Negro has been deprived? Few people reflect that for two centuries the Negro was enslaved, and robbed of any wages—potential accrued wealth which would have been the legacy of his descendants. *All* of America's wealth today could not adequately compensate its Negroes for his centuries of exploitation and humiliation."[11] Turner concludes as follows: "One cannot fairly derive a colorblind principle from King's total message and philosophy. Such a derivation could only be achieved by omissions, distortions, simplification . . . and an overall lack of familiarity with King's views."[12] The scholarly incompetence that Turner identifies is everywhere present in Steele's and Carter's notions of King's intent.

The institutionalization, flourishing, and global work of Black Power also seem to be a zone of ignorance for Carter. However, the author of *Reflections of an Affirmative Action Baby* seems no less optimistic about the American racial future than Shelby Steele. If only integration shock and Black Power's party line can be eradicated, we're in for a colorblind, racially harmonious good time. Carter claims that "systematic subjugation of black people as a group" is an "oppression that is passing into history."[13] His optimism is premature, at best. Nevertheless, oppression has left a "frightful legacy."[14] This legacy is not what one might expect. Given the horrors of chattel slavery, its Reconstruction aftermath, and the holocaust of spectacle lynching in the United States, one would expect Carter to reference the resulting poverty, disadvantage, and mass imprisonment of blacks in the United States. But no, that is not what he means. For Stephen Carter, the most egregious legacy of white American racism is a monolithic black Civil Rights agenda—a party line blatantly out of touch with merit-based, dissenting, free-speech black intellectuals. What is there to say in response to such a willful disregard of the long-term social, economic, and political consequences of white racism?

But let us, for a moment, grant Carter his premises. For him, the allegorical ideal is the intellectual:

> Part of the responsibility of the intellectual is to try not to worry about whether one's views are, in someone else's judgment, the proper ones. The defining characteristic of the intellectual is not (as some seem to think) a particular level of educational or cultural attainment, and certainly not a particular political stance. What makes one an intellectual is the drive to learn, to question, to understand, to criticize, not as a means to an end but as an end in itself. An intellectual believes in criticism in the purest sense of the word, and understands that to be a critic is not necessarily to be an opponent; an intellectual, rather, is an observer willing and able to use rational faculties to distinguish wisdom from folly.[15]

Modern thinkers (such as Marx, Nietzsche, Carlyle, Du Bois, Sartre, and Hannah Arendt) who have turned attention to the character of the intellectual have understood that any claim to pure and disinterested reason on the part of any human being is the signal for rational men and women to break out the steel helmets to protect themselves from minstrelsy and tricksters' ribald craziness. In one of his more self-revelatory moments, Ralph Ellison argued that when someone begins to proclaim that a self-violating erasure of one's own emotions, affect, and everyday common sense is "disinterested intellectualism," history is about to boomerang. Watch your heads, black folks!

Carter's definition of the "intellectual," in other words, is an alibi, a sellout for his neutron-bomb clearance of Black Power's everyday work from the American landscape. What replaces it? Nothing, nothing at all save that supposedly dreaded term of conservative intellectuals: *ideology*. Here is his rhetorical apparatus with respect to black intellectual history. He insists that Booker T. Washington is to a traditional Civil Rights agenda what W. E. B. Du Bois is to Stephen Carter. We read: "The argument that dissenters from orthodoxy do not speak for the black community is an old and vicious form of silencing. It was used to shattering effect in the age when Booker T. Washington was the only black *intellectual* whose views mattered."[16]

Booker T. Washington is portrayed by Carter not only as an intellectual (though he in no way conforms to the author's own definition of the term), but also as a thinker who symbolized a Civil Rights agenda concerned with the collective welfare of the black majority. Carter's lively portrayal of Washington and Du Bois contains more than one false note. My freshman Afro-American studies majors would instantly notice his sleight of hand. Undaunted, however, by the historical facts, Carter continues his disingenuous comparison by misreading the black intellectual legacy of W. E. B. Du Bois. Implicitly comparing himself to Du Bois, Carter points out that Du Bois was a dissenter, a black intellectual who believed that pure black rationality could be employed "not as a means to an end, but as an end in itself."[17] Carter's characterization of W. E. B. Du Bois simply is contrary to fact.

W. E. B. Du Bois's lifetime dedication was to black sociointellectual activism. His activist mode—from student days at Harvard to final labors in Ghana—was unceasing, put-you-in-jail, Civil Rights agitation, and always radical political anti-white-supremacy asceticism. Du Bois did not sell out his talents in the name of black merit or sell his soul for a mess of pottage. He was nothing like the Carter who serves as character witness for the hero of *Reflections of an Affirmative Action Baby*. Carter bullishly sutures Du Bois, the sage of Great Barrington, to his own narrow, anxious, black conservative personalism.

Other than problematic, grandiose, and bogus comparisons of himself to "the greatest black generations," what does Carter offer? His recommendations are twofold. First, he calls for the complete dismantling of the affirmative action apparatus of the United States. Second, he calls upon our nation to educate and promote a cadre of black professionals who are so excellent, so proficient, and so productive that white America will concede they are "too good to ignore."[18]

We might charitably say that these recommendations are based not only on a misty First Amendment nostalgia, but also on Carter's own peculiar personal yearnings for an absolutist set of standards that define merit. In the final analysis, Carter seems to abandon the Constitution altogether and to join Shelby Steele in the Hoover fellow's biblical pulpit. However, his self-righteous First Amendment posturing never suggests how this excellence can be (apolitically, ahistorically, unemotionally, and disinterestedly) conceived. The only way, I think, for the world to accord with Stephen Carter's fantasy is not through the forest of intellectualism or rational dissent, but by way of the shouting-and-frenzied neoconservative church of divine white ordination.

Excellence becomes, in the allegory of Stephen Carter, transubstantial with an Irving Kristol God. This God's servants on earth are none other than black natural aristocrats of conservatism in New Haven, like Stephen Carter. If such a mundane, Christian, anti-intellectual reading of his project is *not* what Carter intended, I am at a loss to understand what he means at all.

Certainly the smartest black kid on the block knows that corporate America—in recent years and under direct scrutiny of affirmative action—has paid huge sums in reparations to black employees. This same corporate white racism—for example, Denny's and Texaco—has freely admitted that it has denied black employees promotions and raises on the basis of skin color alone. Excellence, in American corporate culture, seems quite easily ignored.[19]

If we accept that Stephen Carter understands American corporate and expressive economies (he has claimed in countless post–*Emperor of Ocean Park* interviews that he is an inveterate reader) then it appears that what our trickster Yale professor really wants to alleviate are his own personal symptoms of black conservative lamentation syndrome. "Woe is me! I am smart, smart, smart, but white people only see me as black, black, black. Woe is me!" I believe that Carter can only comfortably occupy the stage of the good life as the smartest kid in the class when he encourages a national campaign to eradicate affirmative action. The disappearance of affirmative action will obliterate all his (and other black neoconservatives') formless little fears that race is the only purchase they have on America's attention.

Carter's rhetorical comparisons and his "just so" racist stories in *Reflections of an Affirmative Action Baby* are, ultimately, only personal tales of his own neoconservative racial anxieties. *Problems des riches*, as one of my friends in the academy has phrased it. That Carter invokes the U.S. Constitution to dramatize for profit his personal role in sending poor black folks up in smoke probably would not have surprised James Madison or Chief Justice Holmes. Those savvy whites knew all too well the vagaries of men's free deployment of speech.

In the typical about-face mode of his white neoconservative allies, this is what Stephen Carter had to say of free speech in 1998: "The proposition that all speech must be protected should not be confused with the very different proposition that all speech must be celebrated."[20] It would seem that his turn toward civility and his trade book on the topic have made Carter realize that not all speech is equally free in America. You have to fight hard to be heard—especially if you are black. Alternately, you can simply surveil the white establishment like the trickster slave of lore and figure out—within the economies of American minstrelsy and national sacred texts—what exactly you need to be dirty rotten filthy stinking rich—and then write it.

IN *LOSING THE RACE: Self-Sabotage in Black America* (2001) John McWhorter set out in no-nonsense fashion to discredit the notion that systemic white American racism is alive and well. While not going so far as to claim racism has been completely eradicated, McWhorter asserts that what remains of it is merely "residual." Since the sustaining legal conditions of racism's existence were exterminated by acts of Congress in the mid-sixties, he argues, notions of white racism as a barrier to black advancement in America really hold no intellectual or historical weight. Black America's urban ghetto malaise, for McWhorter, is a product not of racism but of a black psychological pathology and behavioral dependency he calls "victimology." When blacks claim the abject conditions of their lives are the result of centuries of chattel slavery, legal segregation, horrific spectacle lynching, and dehumanizing Jim Crow in America, McWhorter retorts that during the past forty years, black Americans have been freer than in any other epoch in our nation's history. Moreover, he claims, blacks have been graciously blessed during these years with more opportunities, rewards, and life-enhancing benefits than ever before. They have profited immeasurably, for example, from the largesse of both private philanthropy and federal and state government handouts. As recipients of such lavish generosity, blacks—in McWhorter's opinion—cannot rationally or justifiably claim to be victims. Any such assertion is, for him, an insidious manifestation of the plague of victimology.

How did the author of *Losing the Race* find this denunciatory voice and rise to rail against the black ghetto in America? McWhorter re-

MAN WITHOUT

CONNECTION

J O H N

M C W H O R T E R

counts his epiphanic moment: "Shelby Steele's *The Content of Our Character* was a formative experience for me on the level that *The Autobiography of Malcolm X* has been for so many other blacks, articulately and bravely expressing feelings of mine that had been pent up since childhood."[1] So the scales drop away from his eyes, and McWhorter becomes a partisan of the antiblack jeremiad, issuing screeds like *Authentically Black* and *Losing the Race*.

This kind of liberational moment is a familiar trope in the slave narratives. A restless, aggrieved narrator discovers a document, book, or mentor and learns to read the world in self-liberatory ways. His dungeon shakes; his shackles fall off. One of the most famous examples of this trope appears in Frederick Douglass's *Narrative of the Life of Frederick Douglass: An American Slave*. Douglass's moment of truth occurs when he discovers *The Columbian Orator*. This late eighteenth-century collection of speeches, essays, dialogues, and poems was used widely during the nineteenth century to teach schoolchildren. When young Frederick discovers the collection, he immediately hones in on a dialogue between a master and slave in which the argument and oration of the slave win him his freedom. Another favorite of Douglass's is Parnell's declamation on Catholic emancipation. The veil is lifted from the young boy's eyes; his feelings of bafflement about the reasons for his enslavement disappear, and he becomes reasonably certain that Providence did not create him or any man to be a bondsman in perpetuity.

Douglass went on to become his era's preeminent advocate for the liberation and freedom of the black majority. "Free your mind, and your body will follow." This was the implicit mantra of Douglass and his nineteenth-century cohort. The same mantra guided activists in America during the days of black nationalist organization and Black Power resistance, especially in ghettos across the nation. By contrast, John McWhorter's serendipitous discovery of the neoconservative revelations of Steele seems a noisy parody of Douglass's eloquent encounter with *The Columbian Orator*. McWhorter, by his own account, does not draw himself up from the quicksand of white impressments. Rather, he shakes from his sandals the dust and residual grime of black American victimology. With an oratorical straight face, McWhorter posits a compulsion to this so-called victimology as a natural black cultural trait—an innate drive that compels blacks to blame white racism for all their failings. From McWhorter's burning bush moment of *The Content of Our Character* forward, he seems to resolve to take personal responsibility for defending the national polity, the economy, and corporate America against the specter of victimology. He also provides cover for the drug-industrial complex, the U.S. Congress, the president, and the national educational enterprise. Essentially, McWhorter mounts a constructive defense of all white people against black blame.

Where the ghetto is concerned, McWhorter's feelings are explicit: He has no sympathy for those who remain there. Why? McWhorter recounts his own experience: his mom moved him and his sibling out of North Philadelphia, by way of West Mount Airy, to the suburban respectability of Lawnside, New Jersey. If work disappears, why not follow the jobs? McWhorter reveals in his plenitude of anecdotes that he has a penchant for the dramatic. He is generally inclined to illustrate his points with loquacious theatricals that bear little resemblance to American reality. I believe the question of McWhorter's commitment to analytical, academic, empirical evidence is at the heart of his dark parody of classic African American literary, critical, and creative traditions represented by the slave narratives.

In the preface to *Authentically Black*, McWhorter explains that in his race writings he does not hold himself to an academic/scholarly standard. Perhaps this helps explain how someone like McWhorter, felicitously gifted with degrees and access to the public square, can resolutely assert the existence of an empirically verifiable thing called victimology. McWhorter does talk about victimology's actual, natural existence and infectious quality. And he explicitly claims victimology is a black cultural trait. But with respect to an academic standard of analytical and empirical proof, McWhorter seems rhetorically caught in a whirlpool of intellectual retrogression, devolutionary spiraling downward in wit and reasoning. To make claims for both the natural and cultural inferiority of blacks with respect to civilized, grateful, and responsible behavior on the basis of a phantom victimology seems remarkably irresponsible. Such clearly stated claims bring the very premises of *Losing the Race* dangerously into accord with the discursive universe of mid-nineteenth-century experimental efforts to ferret out criminals on the basis of cranial measurements and to indict ethnic minorities with the click of calipers. Creepy stuff, this. What is McWhorter thinking?

Transparency and good faith are not what his work reveals. Instead, we see a young man delineating a worldview and philosophy based on nothing more than anecdotal evidence and the ideological interpellations of Shelby Steele and other think tank oracles of neoconservatism in America.[2] The Hoover

Institution is McWhorter's lighthouse, and he rows mightily to carry us to its rocky shoal before victimology takes hold. *Losing the Race* might as well be McWhorter's completed take-home exam in a course called Black Neo-conservatism 101. McWhorter is so eager to excel in class that he gleefully adopts the neocon buzzword "victimology" as the shifty foundation for his polemical house of black majority condemnation.

Why would McWhorter cast black victimology to play the evil alter ego, the flip side of the coin in a world of level playing fields and meritocratic accomplishments? Victimology is a useful, gothic, ghostly blast of air, meant to distract us, I think, from the truly bad national news of the past forty years. It is a ruse. It is summoned to divert our attention from, for instance, national economic disasters such as the beat-down of the American middle class, the export of tens of thousands of American jobs, and the outrageous expenditure of hundreds of billions of dollars on unjust wars.

"Victimology" is a buzzword that seems full of scientific import. But it is a chimera that shares target space on neoconservative firing ranges with other straw man constructions like "welfare queen," "reverse racism," "political correctness," and "tenured radicals." Such spectral abstractions (some of which, one knows, were cannily appropriated from the radical left) are not useful concepts for reporting what's really going on. They are merely anti-intellectual prompts urging ideologically overloaded neoconservatives to commence fire. After his epiphany with *The Content of Our Character*, McWhorter simply follows Steele. Like Steele, McWhorter posits a direct cause-and-effect relationship between legislative passage of the Civil Rights Act (1964), the Voting Rights Act (1965), and the extermination of bigoted white racism in America. He faithfully echoes Steele in his proclamation that the Civil Rights Act undeniably and indubitably resulted in unbridled black freedom.

Both McWhorter and Steele cast law and jurisprudence as concrete universals. They rely on the premise that the effect of a law once enacted is direct and uncomplicated. In their world, the Civil Rights Act—meant to free African Americans—can have no unintended consequences and will at once be comprehensively applied and enforced. All laws are, in effect, social stories of the way things should or ought to be if prudent men exist (and are to continue to exist) in an ordered society. In this sense, laws are idealized and encouraging fictions that have the power to condition our behavior. But as social fictions, they are always contingent, unstable, and ever varying. Laws are conditioned by time, events, and the hearts and minds of the judges who interpret and enforce them. Laws are never perfect or guaranteed in their operation. Even a cursory review of the jurisprudential histories of the Fourteenth and Fifteenth Amendments should make the matter clear to thinking men of good faith and analytical integrity everywhere.

Dr. Martin Luther King Jr.—a prime mover of the black mass movement that motivated (or, more precisely, forced) passage of the Civil Rights and Voting Rights acts—characterized these legislative acts as the spare, tenuous beginnings of a journey toward black freedom. His views have proven prophetic. Effective job training, decent housing, and safety nets for the poor have become but shadowy national presences since the mid-1990s. The true history and chronicle of enforcement of the two congressional acts praised so highly by Steele and McWhorter have only thrown into dramatic relief the seemingly infinite economic, political, and psychological rows that must be hoed before a genuine black freedom becomes a reality, even in twenty-first-century America.

Black cultural life is marked by complicated perceptual fields, the residue of historical trauma, and intersubjective chronologies of connection that have little to do with simple legislative acts. For example, the Emancipation Proclamation—which declared all (approximately 4.5 million) enslaved blacks in Confederate states free—had a profound psychological and affective impact on black culture but did not yield anything approaching a tangible freedom or a safe mobility in America. Similarly, congressional acts of the mid-sixties have only minimally affected the life possibilities of the black American majority. That majority remains immobilized, demoralized, miserable, and poor, not by creation, but by design of the white plutocracy that has ruled our nation for the past forty years.

In McWhorter's disclaimer about his race writing, he asserts: "When wearing that [race-writer] hat, I intend my writings as what we might call informed editorials. I certainly consider myself responsible for the factual accuracy of anything I present to the public. I furthermore attempt to found my opinions upon open eyes, wide reading, and careful reflection."[3] You will not find any disinterestedness in McWhorter. He is always beating his own drum and patting himself—his life, his friends, his sense of humor—squarely on the back. In his race writing we learn so much more than we want to know about McWhorter, who tiresomely rehearses for readers his University of California at Berkeley days, his disciplinary adventures as a linguist, and his

Stanford University student theatricals. He details with utter sanctimoniousness his own personal freedom from racism as he shops freely in American commercial establishments. He touts his mastery of classical British novels. He gives himself a shout-out for the regular recognition he receives from clerks and toll-takers who have seen him on television. He excruciatingly details his elementary school science fair projects and the correspondence he receives from hundreds who adore his writing. He also provides an itinerary of his multiple childhood family relocations, from North Philly to West Mount Airy, then to Lawnside (complete with a roll call of his New Jersey black neighbors).

Rather than autobiographical critique what McWhorter proffers is anecdotal self-storying as somehow, we must infer, useful common sense. Anecdote is supposed to offer, in his account, clear-eyed editorial proof of the writer's unquestionable authority on race in America. But his anecdotes are all meant to demonstrate that blacks in our present era are consummately free as a result of a single legislative act that occurred in 1965, the year of McWhorter's birth. McWhorter's natal freedom, one might say, is an earnest signal to white America that if given more than half a chance, *all* black Americans have a least a shot at living large and liberated like the author.

McWhorter's race writing—in the literary critical domain elaborated by a robust black studies discipline in the past forty years—can be compared in style, theme, and autobiographical content more appropriately to the self-caressing output of Booker T. Washington than to the elegant analyses of W. E. B. Du Bois. This is not meant to invoke the clichéd charge of Uncle Tom-ism so often leveled against Washington. But the proximity and affinity between the black classical writings of Washington and the books of a prolific neophyte such as McWhorter are ideological and rhetorical. *Losing the Race* pontificates (too casually, I think) on the natural and the cultural with respect to black American life. In almost carnivalesque fashion it announces the rampant pathologies of the black majority. And its author champions the ethical virtue of ignoring racist insults. But the seas of these personalisms and moralisms coming from McWhorter lack academic finesse, kinship, compassion, and straightforward economic truth telling. Here is a classic enunciation from Booker T. Washington, the master of Tuskegee Institute: "Ever since I have been old enough to think for myself, I have entertained the idea that, notwithstanding the cruel wrongs inflicted upon us, the black man got nearly as much out of slavery as the white man did" What, exactly, did "we" get? We learned the habits of brutally hard, yet careful, work: "The slaves, in many cases, had mastered some handicraft, and none were ashamed, and few unwilling, to labour."[4] Washington was writing for a turn-of-the-nineteenth-century philanthropic white audience. His work brought him thousands of "personal" dollars from such whites, who designated the money specifically to be deposited in Washington's bank account. Wealthy white men and women repeatedly praised and rewarded Washington for taking on what they described as "our work." And Washington gave them, in turn, a representation of the black majority as a horde of culturally misinformed Negroes who did not grasp the principal revelation that (in his words) "merit no matter under what skin it is found, will be recognized and rewarded."[5] Washington was certain this was a universal law.

The style, modes of proof, orders of logic, multitudinous and boring personal anecdotes, and the semiauthoritarian tone of Washington's *Up from Slavery* are uncannily mirrored in McWhorter's *Losing the Race* and *Winning the Race*. An ominous tingle should run up the spine of any black majority partisan after even a cursory reading of McWhorter. In part this is because McWhorter, like Washington, seems to have cast off repressed feelings in some revelatory moment, but neither writer is able to curb his propinquity for deliberately suppressing the darkest racial truths of our national past. (For example, was chattel slavery in the United States really a beneficial, vocational, good time for 4.5 million blacks?) While reading McWhorter, we of a new millennium are aware that what does *not* appear in his books is precisely what white American wealth has made of our country during the past four decades. The author buries such truth under a flood of trite personal anecdotes about freedom. This is what I find is most disconcerting about McWhorter's preachments. It is also what gives authentic and informed autobiographical critique—as well as critical historical logic and analytically superb sociological race writing—a bad name. To illustrate, take the following hypothetical scenario. A nattily attired, influential, handsomely paid, suburban white man stands before two tenured black professors and asks: "How's the black race doing, guys?" McWhorter answers: "Never better, Bob. Black men who are working and black women who are not single moms on welfare are finally getting on with that freedom you gave them. We have CEOs and outrageously wealthy athletes, films that depict us in a positive light, lots of nice homes and cars, and children attending Harvard and Yale." Professor number two pipes up: "Never been worse, Bob. Never been worse. Because an underprivileged and discriminated-against black majority is profiled daily and incarcerated by night. That majority is tragically undereducated, desperately housed, imminently unsafe, and miserably paid. More importantly, that majority is a metaphor for our national future." Which of these professors do we think Bob is going to finance, publish, and promote onto bestseller lists? Bookerite rhetoric is as ideologically welcome and handsomely profitable at the present moment as it was at the turn of the nineteenth century.

Here is McWhorter on achievement: "At the end of the day, it is a *human universal* that achievement only comes from within. It would be nice if there were another way, but there simply is not. If anyone says otherwise, their ideology is bankrupt unless they identify a single person in America or even world history who have [*sic*] risen from anything but their own efforts" (*Authentically Black*, 30; my emphasis). But the American multibillionaire Warren Buffet freely admits that his economic advantage in life was a result of winning the "genetic lottery."

Here again is McWhorter (who devotes at least 20 percent of *Winning the Race* to himself): "Although I try to argue on the basis of evidence from as many corners as I can find, I cannot even begin to claim that my writing on race is not founded, at heart, upon my personal experience."[6] McWhorter's elevation of personal experience at the expense of a catalog of causes of our national failure would be laughable if it were not so appalling. He never comes close to addressing, much less critiquing, the dismantling of our civil rights in America post 9/11, nor does he have anything to say about the gross bad faith of our national corporate sector with respect to the middle and working classes. There is no time or room enough here to detail even a fraction of the brutal excess and greed of Enron, WorldCom, and Halliburton. Their names do not appear in McWhorter's prose. Moreover, he says not a word about the general increase in violent crime in the United States that has resulted, some argue, from the diversion of municipal and even state police forces to national security and homeland security rather than *hometown* security assignments. McWhorter does not, in short, address the clear and present dangers posed to majority interests by the governmental and corporate alliance that has ruled our world for the past forty years. Instead he dances about, attempting, in his own imagined ring of shadows, to defeat racism with anecdotal jabs.

Here is McWhorter on his hometown life: "I can't speak for the eighties and nineties, but at this writing I have lived in New York for three years and take cabs often. And I can honestly say that not a single time have I been bypassed by a cab, even though I have been highly attuned to the possibility, given how much one hears about it. When I put my hand in the air, a cab stops in front of me on a dime, just like for everyone else, day or night, wherever I am going" (*Winning the Race*, 209). Perhaps New York taxis halt for John McWhorter because their drivers—like the clerks and toll-takers he encounters—have seen McWhorter on TV and can't wait to tell him how much they appreciate his writing. McWhorter is so busy with himself that he simply refuses to provide readers with an academically sound account of our national history or a truthfully articulated account of our present-day economic malaise.

American jurisprudence and congressional fiat have always played African Americans false in the New World. For example, the Civil Rights and Voting Rights acts were journeys back to the future: postbellum constitutional amendments that proclaimed instant freedom had to undergo a murderously costly do-over in the 1950s and '60s. The intervening years were rife with illegal violence against the black body, mind, and spirit—from lynching and Jim Crow to redlining and inner-city police brutality. Now, mind you, all this time black freedom was on the constitutional books, but pushed by society to the quotidian backburner. If we acknowledge even this brief account of racist white bad faith, how can we muster huzzahs for the guaranteed freedom and opportunity McWhorter gushingly extols in *Winning the Race*? Or are those in the majority who distrust mere legislation the ones who have the rational edge? Where history is concerned, the answer is clear. Laws and regulations only appear guaranteed. And in one reading of black reality, laws and constitutional enactments have been as problematic in their American guise of archways to freedom as the trademarked arches of McDonald's are in their promises of decent employment and healthy comestibles.

The distance between black and white in America—and the gulf in economic and institutional equality occasioned by it—has been boldly and honestly chronicled during the past forty years. Courageous, analytical, and historical critique has emerged from what I think of as a robust new consciousness (in the academy, in media, in publishing, the arts, and other public spheres). This new consciousness is a direct outgrowth of the energies that marked the countercultural moment of the sixties. But both Steele and McWhorter unleash their fire on what they consider the moral laxity and pathologically infectious misdirection bequeathed to black folks by the white sixties counterculture. And in this, they are in alignment with the developmental history of U.S. neoconservatism and its targets of attack. But Steele and McWhorter's genuflection to their own set of ideological precursors misses the real historical point. For, can there be even the remotest doubt that it was, in fact, blacks who in their activism and critique were the very engine of the countercultural sixties?

Rather than leading and misleading blacks in the sixties, what young whites (and some not so young) did was run riot and talk as fast as they could to catch up with the juggernaut of a black mass movement like no other witnessed in our national history. These are the facts. We set the style, terms, and in many cases, the agenda for what young whites came to believe they wanted. We issued the critiques, lit the flames, and gave black voice to the *j'accuse* that made the nation take stock of its infamous past and extant social injustices. They loved our songs, dance, aesthetics, hairstyles, and efficacious activism. We were not passively duped evolutionary biological clones of a white countercultural movement. We were militant and moral in our leadership for America, and it scared the hell out of all those who exercised corrupt and oligarchic power. Witness J. Edger Hoover foaming at the mouth and tearing his vestments, declaring the Black Panther Party to be the greatest threat to American law and order on record. Think of the New York City Police official who declared Malcolm X the "most dangerous man in America." Why? Because, at least in the instance of Malcolm X, we saw a scintillating, articulate black consciousness that autobiographically called the hand of all the plutocratic, conspiratorial, philistine, parochial, and complacent white players at the table—those who believed blacks would be pacified en masse and forever by mere passage of a congressional act. An act that was a (re)granting of a black freedom that was supposed, already, to be guaranteed. One might say that the countercultural sixties were really the black leadership sixties. That decade produced a fiercely astute, prophetic, and self-consciously academic critique of all that was wrong with America. If that critique was sometimes too heady, it was never without unshakable grounding in history or studied empathy with the black majority. At Dachau, there is a statement of memorial purpose that reads: "That the dead shall be remembered, that the living shall never forget." Nor shall we, who (admittedly) write from a point of view of black, radical, autobiographical critique, forget.

In the sixties, black people did not abdicate their willpower to white radicals. Nor did they, even under threat of death, relinquish their newly public right to bear arms, memorialize their past, assume leadership, and set forth the black academic studies tools for a new writing of American history and culture. A new black consciousness led the activist, intellectual, and critical way of the counterculture. As this consciousness has radically morphed, worked and developed, published, documented, and transformed during the past forty years, what has emerged is an American voice never heard before on land or sea. It is fearless and it has flow. It carries smooth and critical cultural resonance. These are the facts—facts that terrify a formerly exclusively white academy and are targeted for disappearance by black neoconservative snipers like Shelby Steele and John McWhorter.

What did the consciousness bequeathed to white America by Black Power and black activism in the sixties produce? I think it yielded an antiestablishment courage that today buttresses articulate critiques of an unscrupulous, greedy, and violent set of American practices variously referred to as neoliberalism, globalization, welfare reform, omnibus crime control bills, wars on terror and drugs, and "no child left behind" educational testing. In our nation, middle-class economic well-being has become an oxymoron. The same is true for dignified black underclass employment, sound educational systems, and guaranteed freedom and opportunity under the law.

Yet John McWhorter insists that young black Americans are not effectively educated because they are resistant to education, because they believe that comporting themselves in scholarly ways will subject them to their peers' charge that they are "acting white." Hence, according to McWhorter, black children, by their own irresponsible bending to peer pressure, are miserably educated. Statistics telling us that almost 60 percent of black American fourth graders are functionally illiterate seem to support McWhorter's denunciation of the "acting white" hypothesis. But a mere forty years ago, the American education system was flexible, generally efficient, and emulated worldwide. Now it has deteriorated to the point where we are producing more dropouts than graduates. We are far less successful in confronting poverty and overcoming it in our educational practices than India and China. (One may explore the controversy surrounding our standing in relation to developing superpowers such as India and China at the National Education Association Web site, or in works by Gerald Bracey, Charles Krauthammer, and Joel H. Spring.) The state of our educational enterprise vis-à-vis international competitiveness—despite regular infusions of federal cash—is dire. American teachers make less than half as much as it is speculated might be required to induce the best and the brightest to join the pedagogical workforce. Our public school buildings (in all but elite and still highly segregated domains) rot on their foundations. Incentives to stay in school are, at best, minimal, even for the most talented black underclass students who are loath to meet injury or sudden death in the halls and locker rooms of creaky old buildings.

Given the indelibly national character of our educational disaster, why do McWhorter's big books make absolutely no mention of this collapse? Why does McWhorter focus only on the personal failings of black inner-city youth? Busily promoting himself and seemingly oblivious to historical realities, McWhorter follows the party line of his great revelator, Shelby Steele. He believes that black majority youth are free, but that they do not take advantage of the vast American educational opportunities freedom has bestowed. W. E. B. Du Bois would be aghast at such flagrant parochialism and ideologically prompted intellectual dishonesty. And even Booker T. might look askance at the monumentally glaring silence of McWhorter on the dreadful national state of our educational system.

A new, plutocratic, conspiratorial, and violent national polity inaugurated by corporate America and its bellwether, Ronald Reagan, gave birth to the heyday of wealthy interests in the United States. George Herbert Walker Bush followed President Reagan to office. And the Reagan/Bush compromise of inverted national values and priorities was in place. Jobs disappeared. Taxes were disproportionately raised for the middle class. Public education was in shambles. Safety nets for the neediest were in shreds. A fit and aerobic American dream became a nightmare in the industrialized nations' race to achieve decent standards of living for the majority. One can justly say, I think, that the documented educational plight of the black majority in America is wholly commensurate with the devastating Reagan/Bush compromise of majority interests. And John McWhorter wants to charge the educational failure of black children to a fear of "acting white"?

Further, the mass exportation of American jobs as a function of trade treaties during the past forty years has made the grand old U.S. song "Look for the Union Label" a standing joke. The Clinton presidency's decimation of welfare "as we know it" has made a well-housed, financially resourced, and relatively safe life virtually impossible for, say, a single mother in any of the bleak zones of confinement that mark the lives of the black majority. That mother's nights—whether navigating Waffle House incorrigibles as a waitress or burying her kids under their bed to avoid bullets of the neighborhood drug trade flying through her walls—are a living nightmare. A high school diploma from our nation's rotting educational system and an admirably plucky Booker T. belief that merit is always rewarded will not keep that mother and her children safe, nor help her move to a fine place in Lawnside, New Jersey. With the dramatic increase in the incarceration of women in the United States, our hypothetical mother is more likely to land in jail than in the safety net. She can expect no dramatic boost from an *equitable* and long overdue rise in our national minimum wage or a reasoned educational grant to an urban university that would allow her to train as, say, a social worker. While our hypothetical mother and her fellow residents of the black ghetto have desperately flailed about for subsistence during the past four decades, American economic wealth has soared exponentially upward.

The keys to our new plutocratic minority's billions in assets are not difficult to discover. The first is, à la Warren Buffet, legacy wealth. The second is the eradication and disabling of all restraints on corporate expansion and merger, export of jobs, compliance with fiscal and environmental regulations, and of course, war profiteering. In short, the Enron-ization of America. Business, in America today, is government, and vice versa. Black neoconservatives scapegoat inner-city residents as slothful, pathological terrorists, endangering national peace and security. Meanwhile, American corporations (a buoyant support base for conservative think tanks and presidential politics) steal and conceal billions globally.

Meanwhile, black neoconservatives hunker down in front of their think tank computers and denounce the "violence" of the black ghetto and the "obscenity" of rap music as though such matters are chief causes of both our internal strife and the hatred so much of the world has for us. No one who is even reasonably media savvy credits such pedestrian attribution of black causality to our national anxiety and bitter discontent. Corporate America and its bought-and-paid-for government, its countless billions of dollars circulating every nanosecond, have everything to do with it. Those megadollars are a direct outcome of the Reagan/Bush compromise that made business the true government of the United States.

McWhorter and his black neoconservative cohort are deaf, mute, blind, and clueless vis-à-vis the national disaster of our American polity. Their disingenuously insensate behavior seems especially troublesome in McWhorter's case. He declares in *Winning the Race* that precisely what is absent from the intellectual and scholarly repertoire of black America is a dutiful, articulate attention to history. McWhorter demonstrates no such attention in his books.

The inconsistency of McWhorter's silent consent to the causes of our national disaster in the past four decades (while blasting, in deep-voiced pious-
ness, the black majority) speaks most clearly, I think, to his betrayal of everything Dr. Martin Luther King Jr. held sacred. The razor-sharp integrity of
King's critique of American governmental and corporate failures is a matter
of record. King sought global freedom from poverty and war. He knew his
black activist goals required far more than a simple act of Congress for their
accomplishment. McWhorter's silence regarding the American betrayal of
all that Dr. King gave his life for seems to be insidiously and transparently
dishonest. How can any black man with a university education in America
write as follows:

> What killed black neighborhoods was neither The Man nor economic forces, both
> of which black people had known all too well long before the late sixties. The key
> was what was new to the late sixties: a new way of thinking that infected blacks
> and whites alike. It effected a massive transformation in cultural attitudes that
> discouraged millions of blacks from doing their best, while at the exact same time
> teaching concerned whites that supporting blacks in this was a sign of moral so-
> phistication.
>
> (*Winning the Race*, 75)

McWhorter's conclusions about the death of black neighborhoods are
premised upon his rudimentary deployment of evolutionary biology as ex-
pounded by the British zoologist Richard Dawkins. In crude shorthand (and
meaning no disrespect to a discipline that boasts so many smart and fashion-
ably nonreligious adherents) I will say that in McWhorter's presentation of
evolutionary biology in *Winning the Race*, cultural memes replicate Mende-
lian genes. He ascribes memes with Darwinian heritability as moving forces
of black history. McWhorter constructs a gross conflation of memes and
cultural traits. He posits that memes (abstract notions of cultural behavior,
such as, "welfare dependency") in themselves dramatically overdetermine the
lifeworlds of whole populations. For McWhorter, such determinations pass
unstoppably through time to successive ghetto generations.

One brief response to McWhorter's invocation of biology is to note that
he is treading intellectually on what the old hymn calls "sinking sand." The
casual deployment of natural evolution as the basis for establishing cultural
biology is sometimes described by philosophy as the "naturalistic fallacy."
Given the moral, ethical, and rational agency of human beings, it is a mistake

to attempt to found a science of human behavior on evidence and methods designed to address nature. We might think of McWhorter's biologism—especially since it is applied with vigor to tarring an entire black American culture—as having as much intellectual legitimacy as nineteenth-century race science and its craniological chronicles of ethnic criminality. McWhorter's race writings commit themselves, with anecdotal abandon, to the naturalistic fallacy.

Winning the Race takes the lead in this by holding in the first and last instance to a faith in pseudoscientific biologism to attempt to rebut not only putative black claims of victimology, but also the findings of American academic sociology's careful ethnographic work on black urban life that has emerged in the past forty years. McWhorter attempts to appropriate biology to confer a natural validity on his cultural musings. But it does no such thing. McWhorter has no comprehensive, materialist notion of black culture as a whole way of life. *Winning the Race*'s construction of an evolutionary biological causality makes it useful for the ideology of the neoconservative firing range. It seems to kill two birds that annoy the think tank intellectuals with one supposedly scientific shot: the despised white counterculture and the genetic, "memic" agency that enabled that counterculture to infect black inner-city culture with the welfare blues. Such postulations offer a melodramatic racial exposé, but little more. *Winning the Race* is, I think, an expository prose imitation of tabloid television.

When open-ended welfare became available—and that welfare was monumentally in excess of what could be earned from available menial labor—why would blacks not choose welfare? If that choice was in disharmony with pie-in-the-sky idealism that insists (à la the film *Cinderella Man*) "better to break your back and fists, and subject yourself and your family to chill starvation than accept charity," so what? There is not much that is noble about self-chosen starvation and misery. And welfare was not only a rational choice, but also legally sanctioned and in accord with the prevailing safety net expectations of the time. McWhorter's response to this historical choice, however, is to compose a book of black mourning, all decked out in grim shades of biologistic regret at the black majority's nourishing rationality.

Many things in *Winning the Race* distract us. First is the book's king's ransom of effusive and overweening personal anecdotes. McWhorter is convinced that the life he lives is both inherently interesting and always and indubitably proof in point of the ritualistic, black neoconservative historical

fables he devises. Second is the author's melancholic ahistoricism, his disin-
clination to regard the past as prelude. *Winning the Race* presents a chronicle
of disconnections masquerading as a cohesive exposition of black cultural
history. I call it "neo-Reconstructionism." An identifiable school of letters
in the South called the Plantation School—often associated with Thomas
Nelson Page and Joel Chandler Harris—implied that until black slaves were
freed from bondage, they were a noble and amiable lot. They were Booker
T. Washington's loyal, efficient, self-sacrificing laborers who would rather
die than turn from their masters. McWhorter seems to link arms with the
Plantation School, reading black Indianapolis before the sixties as a kind of
genteel urban plantation, blacks strumming and humming all evening before
going to dead-end jobs early in the early morn. The Plantation School felt
that freedom spoiled our black ancestors; carpetbaggers and damn Yankees
ruined them with teachings of liberation. Our ancestors, entranced by a freedom they were biologically incapable of handling, acted out and made it
necessary for whites to lynch them to restore order. McWhorter reprises this
mendacious narrative in *Winning the Race*—blacks newly freed by the Civil
Rights and Voting Rights acts act out under sway of white carpetbagging
radicals who use them as pawns against the establishment, resulting in their
(justified?) reincarceration. Dare one say, reenslavement?

Bringing to our attention black ancestors who faced far worse odds and
indignities than we, *Winning the Race* seems to set up a coherent line of black
descent. It sketches, for example, an engaging portrait of black Indianapolis
as a historically representative black ghetto where, during the first third of
the last century, blacks strove for self-sufficiency, worked menial jobs, and
sent women forth to break their knees shining white women's floors to a
brilliant gloss. There was structure and dignity in this Indiana black enclave.
There were colored newspapers, refusals of charity, and robust chastisements
of young women who got pregnant out of wedlock. Churches and respectability flourished. Children got reasonable educations. This was all accomplished with fortitude, courage, and interminably long trips to and from
low-paying jobs. Black Indianapolis survived, declares McWhorter, despite
segregation and redlining; it was never duped into passivity by special handouts from anyone. Perhaps most commendably, it held its own in the very
face of "unfreedom."

Where, McWhorter wants to know, did the black pluck and impervious-
ness to insult and injury that historically sustained black Indianapolis dis-

appear? Who, or what, banished those old noble black impulses to tolerate quietly all manner of suffering and indignity? We can agree that the picture McWhorter paints of a segregated black Indianapolis in its glory is in plain accord with the brute fact that blacks certainly did sustain cohesive and productive communities. We were, one could even suggest, better provisioned and better educated. Certainly, this is Derrick Bell's considered and persuasively analytical point of view with respect to black education before *Brown v. Board*.[7] But doesn't McWhorter's elegy for the segregated ghetto contradict his lusty anthem for post–Civil Rights Act black freedom?

McWhorter wants to set before us a moral exemplum. Past racist obstacles were overcome in organized dignity by Indianapolis blacks with incredibly high tolerances for pain and deprivation. These blacks form the supporting cast of *Winning the Race*; its leading man is McWhorter himself. The book offers a nostalgic chronicle, a panorama that finds hearty black southern peasants pulling up stakes and relocating to the rotting, industrial, urban inner-city circles of American metropolises of the North and West.

But one has only to read Richard Wright's *12 Million Black Voices* to learn that southern blacks were never peasants, and they did not pull up stakes but instead were pushed out by southern white terrorism. McWhorter's retelling of the progress-through-immigration myth is his attempt to resurrect the American dream. He sees the American past as full of vicious brutality, denial, exclusion, and incarceration directed equally at *all* outsiders. But here is the shifty turn of rebuke that makes the moral point for McWhorter. Racism, ghettos, denial, lynching, police beatings, exclusion, and menial employment can cause the dignified, ambitious, and longsuffering soul to grow productively stronger.

McWhorter makes it clear in his patriotic fervor that he believes we have the greatest nation on earth. He holds that people of all persuasions want to come here and suffer their way to opportunity. According to McWhorter, it has always been the case (and it continues to be true) that only the black majority has refused to be as successful, responsible, moral, and literate as all the other longsuffering outsiders. Black culture on its lower frequencies is a national embarrassment. The memes and cultural lines of all other immigrants have carried ancestral accomplishments and heartiness to descendents into the sixth and seventh generations. But the nobility of black ancestral suffering (e.g., black Indianapolis) proved not to be inheritable for descendents beyond those dark ages of the ghetto sixties. Black history is, for McWhorter, an American anomaly. It is the aberration in the gallery of ghettos—the blot on the U.S. urban escutcheon.

For McWhorter, the post-sixties black ghetto has not only refused to learn anything from the noble suffering of its ancestors in Indianapolis but also betrayed almost everything noble in the rags-to-riches psychology of the American poor. McWhorter's chronicle has no place whatsoever for the American Indian. And his idyllic account elides any true account of black cultural history.

What we do *not* receive from *Winning the Race* are statistics on black infant mortality; life expectancy differentials between black and white Indianapolis populations; accounts of evictions and the out-of-door misery of the black Indianapolis world; the effects of desperately unequal municipal funding and salaries for black education; and the general light-dimming wear of day-to-day life under the impressments of a white supremacy fed on a legacy of historical American abuse of the black spirit. One is not at all disinclined to concede McWhorter's point that black American history has always seen extraordinary men, women, and children making a way out of no way. But what is also clear to the historically informed among us is that such men, women, and children were exceptions with respect to a majority that continuously took it on the chin, perpetually endured disease, poverty, infant death, and lives that were brutish, short, and nasty. McWhorter's view of black Indianapolis is more closely akin to shrewd nostalgia than it is to ethically well-grounded scholarship and adept intellectual analysis. His chronicle is not history. It is historicism. It is a project not in continuity, but in disconnection.

As for the plague of unemployment, sexual misconduct, crime, rotting schools, and drugs that have killed our bodies and brain cells over the past forty years, what we are experiencing are simply the local aftershocks of national deterioration. If it is true that as the black majority goes, so goes the nation, the reverse is equally the case: as the nation has gone, so have we. McWhorter is culturally misinformed, ideologically overzealous, and just plain wrong when he asserts the following: "The economy did not cause [the transformation of what was considered normal in the black community during the sixties], any more than it had created anything similar in black America before then during the endless ups and downs from the mid-1800s onward. What changed senses of shame and responsibility in black America was the countercultural shift among whites" (*Winning the Race*, 389). This is a kernel paragraph in McWhorter's project. It generates the grammar of his thought. It can easily be parsed into the selective argumentation of *Winning the Race* in its entirety. From this, the selective argumentation of *Winning the Race* literally sags under the tiresome burden of its Bookerite ideological misprision. It is all anecdotal loquaciousness in search of white approval.

The past, in *Winning the Race*, chastises and illustrates the antithesis of the shameful black present. The book's tone, method, and conclusions mirror such sentimental films as *Once Upon a Time . . . When We Were Colored* (1995) and *Miss Evers' Boys* (1997). These films nostalgically and with a guarded selectivity project brilliantly resilient and dignified black life under segregation. There is, of course, always at least one raucous scene of a black church or of street dancing and revelry by de boyz in the segregated 'hood. In *Miss Evers' Boys*, the boys danced tragically to their own deaths from syphilis sanctioned, implicitly, by Tuskegee Institute and explicitly by the National Public Health Service. Of course, Miss Evers, the black nurse knew penicillin would cure her "boys," but she kept them from it by any means necessary. Still, the NAACP presented Alfre Woodard (who played the nurse in the film) with an image award for her sanitized performance.

Chronicles such as McWhorter's black Indianapolis review and *Miss Evers' Boys* omit entirely from their representation of history the cost to the spirit of what I call "Little Africa reality." They minimize, that is to say (or even disappear from their stories) what the eminent black historian Nell Irving Painter so aptly terms the "soul murder" of the black majority that has been a daily and immemorial fact of African New World existence since the first Euro-slave-trading vessels sailed forth with their human cargoes.[8]

In one sense McWhorter creates—with abundant heartwarming morality and honest statistics—a black urban past that connects nothing with nothing. In the manner of his neoconservative fellow dissenters, McWhorter is resolute in dismissing all notions that American slavery has any place whatsoever in an adequate account of the forces and conditions that are engines of contemporary black ghetto culture. So we inquire: is slavery really important to an account of black culture? Is it vital for an account grounded in the whole way of life and structures of feeling of the black American ghetto? Absolutely!

"Slavery" is a term practically equivalent to "fire" in some camps of white Americans. Let a black person utter the word slavery, and the room instantly empties. One suspects that if the founders were revising the Constitution today, they would list mentioning "slavery" in a dark theater populated by whites as a First Amendment violation. Many white Americans move emotional and logical mountains to dissociate themselves from slavery. When they are absolutely cornered by it, they ask the president to apologize.

By contrast, most black Americans regard slavery as essential to any authentic account of the black ghetto, black majority everyday life in America, or black culture. It is all about structures of collective and connective cultural feeling. For, in its historical immensity—its enduring loss, mourning, and desire—slavery is the only foundational structure of feeling that has the effect and affect of eternality in African America's practices of a whole way of life. The violence directed specifically at the African in the Americas has entailed a forced dependency. Chattel slavery's brutality, surveillance, sexual assault against the black body; its caricaturing of the black intellect; its murder of the black soul are all-American originals. They were born in the USA. The profit of American slavery (as Dr. King so eloquently declared) is based on and has its being in black dependency, white profit, and racist white advantage. As the poet Amiri Baraka has it in one of his more dedicatedly political poems: "nobody's threatening anybody / that's just the way things are / boss."[9] In short, these are the cultural facts.

Slavery as the ur-generative condition for black culture's structures of feeling is not, however, a chronicle of unhealthiness. In the wholeness of black cultural psychology, slavery also occasions an inevitability for blacks to look back in the face of soul murder and declare a dialectical and resistant "No!" Acting out was the way for Frederick Douglass to secure his freedom (as it was for many a thousand who took fugitive leave).

McWhorter defines the so called paradigm-shifting 1960s as aberrant, beyond the black cultural pale, as in fact a whole new behavioral set that yielded a culture of poverty. His proclamation is coextensive with his book's perpetual eliding of the historical realities of ghetto life since its inception in the United States. It misses, most importantly, the actual black structures of feeling that black American culture conceived as a whole way of life. Specifically, McWhorter reads dependency on open-ended welfare as a paradigm shift that killed black neighborhoods. But, of course, the offices of such white open-ended giving are immeasurably more complicated if one brings to the table the reality of the structures of feeling that mark, specifically, American chattel slavery. What McWhorter wishes to substitute for what I am calling structures of feeling and culture conceived as a whole way of life is his own exposition putatively based on empirical truth and grounded in science.

What *Winning the Race* offers when it speaks of cultural traits, memes, and a deducible resultant called the culture of poverty is nothing more than scientism. Scientism is the rhetorical and philosophical posture that claims that the only knowledge that is really knowable and valid is knowledge that methodologically cozies up to the natural sciences and insists upon evidence without ever really defining what counts as such. McWhorter's proofs in *Winning the Race* and his other publications are often no more than self-congratulatory triumphal tautologies. This reads out as something like the following: "What I claim to be true is true because the evidence supports it. My evidence comes from science which is always true, because only scientific knowledge is *truth*." But whose truth?

McWhorter, interestingly enough, is not a positivist. We know this because the preeminent mode of proof he invokes is personal anecdote, his own life—and common sense, of course. So, we have a closet idealist and possible narcissist declaring that he has scientific proof to demonstrate that structures of feeling, cultural studies, and slavery have no knowledge-based authority and causality with respect to black culture as a whole way of life.

When blacks introduced major noise and upheaval into complacent white cultural structures of feeling during the Civil Rights and Black Power movements, they occasioned a radical need for adjustment. They forced the master to give materialistically more with the dialectical, in-your-face presence of a resoundingly resistant black "No!" The question of whether the black majority should have readily taken the "more" is moot in an account of black culture grounded in history and actual structures of feeling. The black ghetto's noise and acting out motivated freeing legislation. Prevailing relations of white/black interdependency had to be radically realigned. No giving, no peace! Yes, the ghetto accepted what was given. And in the revolutionary bargain that was the sixties, black ghettos fueled a white counterculture, creating global popular cultural codes of listening, movement, fashion, slang, and critique.

McWhorter is not a new Shelby Steele. He is a far more analytical and earnest researcher than Steele. But it is difficult to believe many people of color in the present-day United States would champion an author who believes black Americans of any class whatsoever have had so little positive agency in their fate for almost a half century. McWhorter's position is contrary to Dr. King's body-on-the-line faith in the black majority. It is contrary as well to what we witness of the extraordinary day-to-day creativity and courage of that majority—a demographic that has scarcely been silent—as they strive in the best everyday forms available to them to overcome American abjection. McWhorter's assertions of the black majority's passivity and irresponsibility are rendered completely suspect by even a cursory glance at world-shaking expressive black cultural innovation, canny underground economic institution building and management, and the brilliantly creative distribution strategies of self-help and cultural production. In *Off the Books*, Sudhir Venkatesh writes of his fieldwork in a black South Side Chicago neighborhood:

> I soon discovered that the seemingly random collection of men and women in the community—young and old, professional and destitute—were nearly all linked together in a vast, often invisible web that girded their neighborhood. This web was the underground economy. Through it the local doctors received homecooked meals from a stay-at-home down the block; a prostitute got free groceries by offering her services to the local grocer; a willing police office overlooked minor transgressions in exchange for information from a gang member; and a store owner might hire a local homeless person to sleep in his store at night, in part because a security guard was too costly. In one way or another, everyone here was living underground.[10]

Venkatesh goes on to describe informal community councils that mediate disputes, alley automobile mechanics who work expertly at deeply discounted rates, omnipresent vendors of goods that have "fallen off trucks," and preachers who are brokers of domestic labor for congregation members willing to return the favor by cleaning the church sanctuary without compensation. Viewed in train with the irrepressible global cultural capital enjoyed by hip-hop, the underground creativity of the ghetto is a canvas of energetic survival hues and innovative lines of connection and currency. All these innovative and expressive modes of cultural resistance are outcomes of black structures of feeling and, as such, decisively characterize black ghetto provinces during the past forty years.

McWhorter's condemnatory version of black American life brings rather more anecdotal heat than analytical light. But what of McWhorter on matters such as the departure of factories, crashing of major highways through main ghetto thoroughfares, and the entry of drugs into black ghettos? The author of *Winning the Race* attempts thoroughly to discredit any of these familiar academic explanations (or, in his view, I think, "excuses") for the deterioration of black ghetto life and culture in America. He is as persuasive as he can be. Yet I believe we are compelled to return to his disconnective predilections. For McWhorter can only be persuasive when he disaggregates the intricate complex of structures, policies, behaviors, and events that careful sociologists, urban studies scholars, policymakers, and black community activists never consider in isolation.

The failure of intellect and imagination that McWhorter reveals in his discourse on black culture as a culture of poverty disturbingly manifests itself, time and again, in his thumping rebuff of events, influences, relocations, and in-migrations (e.g., of drugs) that have been considered direct causes of urban ghetto deterioration in recent years. He quixotically flails at windmills of his own disaggregating. He does not make connections.

No single trait would ever be adduced by a left wing sociologist to be the lone, independent cause of ghetto misery, abjection, and deterioration. No rebuttal of a single, disaggregated causal factor could convince any attentive and informed reader or scholar that severely damaging structural and material reorientations of the American economy and polity at large during the past four decades have not had disastrous effects on black ghettos, and on American majority life in general. Even a race writer such as McWhorter who opts out of scholarly responsibility for his conclusions should not be satisfied with problematic, evolutionary explanations for black ghetto abjection and American national failures of responsibility. A savvy attentiveness to black cultural structures of feeling can bring us closer to a comprehensive understanding of black majority life.

Dr. Martin Luther King Jr. courageously modeled the project of the black activist intellectual in America. It was he who taught those of us who engage in race writing that the goal is not to win notoriety or monetary rewards. The goal is to stay the course, keep faith in the process of truthfully analyzing and reporting on the whole of black life, and never be afraid of negative public opinion of what we do. We are eternally obligated to realize precisely what structures of black cultural feelings—ones grounded in a historical slave trade and its holocaustic and traumatic aftereffects—can reap on the black body, mind, and spirit.

The project of *Losing the Race* and *Winning the Race* is not connected to the ideals of Dr. King's exemplary public intellectualism in tenor, spirit, or analysis. I believe, Dr. King would choose and endorse *The Columbian Orator* or *Dusk of Dawn* in advance of the labors of John McWhorter. The indictments of putative black self-sabotage in *Authentically Black* would perturb the good doctor no end. King would rather have us fully realize, I think, that any such exposition anecdotally seeking to demonstrate that Congress freed us, white radicals misled us, and hip-hop artists have single-handedly made us violent and sexually unsavory is but a self-indulgent, neoconservative fantasy. It connects nowhere with anything, and it can mean the black majority no good whatsoever.

MYTHS ARE GRAND STORIES cherished by groups of people. They are sacred cultural texts that explain the origins of nations, contain accounts of heroism, and draw vivid portraits of people of thought and courage. Myths renew nations in times of crisis. They also serve as information blackouts during bad times, keeping disastrous revelations at bay with songs of national glory. Myths are at their keenest when they proclaim, and imaginatively project, valued national cultural ideals, such as filial piety or colorblind justice, as existing realities. The Greeks had their dauntless, eloquent, and shrewdly inventive Odysseus. The Romans countered with Aeneas—reverent, pious, big-shouldered, founder of Lavinium. U.S. mythic notables include a cast of straight-backed, classically featured, white founding fathers. At center stage among them is the grand patriarch himself, the president of the United States. It is "Hail to the Chief" in white-majority chorus lines, from George Washington and Thomas Jefferson through Ronald Reagan, William Jefferson Clinton, and the Bushes.

The essence of the American myth (sometimes referred to as the American dream) is that our founding and subsequent fathers have always strived publicly, self-sacrificially, and honestly to give structure and reality to national ideals such as liberty and justice for all, equality before the law, inalienable rights, and charity toward all, enmity toward none. In our new millennium the recitation of the grand national American story is that we have presently come as close to the full realization of a colorblind, liberty and justice for all society as we have ever been. For example, in matters of our huge national dilemma of race, we are persuasively and statistically

AMERICAN

MYTH

ILLUSIONS OF

LIBERTY AND

JUSTICE FOR

ALL

"I was dispossessed, myself, back in thirty-seven, when we were all out of work. And they threatened me once since Wilbur's been in the Army. But I stood up for my rights and when the government sent the check we pulled through. Anybody's liable to get dispossessed though." She said it defensively.

RALPH ELLISON
"The Way It Is," *Shadow and Act*

told that we could hardly be more progressive. After all, there now exists a dutifully and profitably functional new black middle class. This population is substantial in its numbers, well-scrubbed, literate, articulate, tasteful, and not afraid to be just Americans. They are a miracle that could only have existed in the feverish, dismal swamp imaginings of, say, the great black Underground Railroad heroine Harriet Tubman or in the restless nightmares of the arch Arkansas racist Orville Faubus, who made such a grotesque gubernatorial spectacle of Little Rock Central High School integration. Many sons and daughters of the new black middle class do not believe they, personally, have any reason whatsoever to give any more thought to race than to imaginary unicorns. Surely this is astonishing national progress!

In addition to our fantastically portrayed state of national racial health, we are assured by myriad media myth purveyors that we are inhabitants of a strong economy, one that grows more evenhanded and just with each new session of Congress. On an international field of ideological play, our president declares that we are spreading democracy to a world eager to embrace it. In mythic accounts, Thanksgiving may soon be celebrated in Baghdad with the same solemnity that marks our national holiday in Boston.

Where American myth in the new millennium is concerned, those who sit on top of that obscene upward transfer of wealth and power that occurred during the past two and a half decades in the United States are decidedly *in*. Those who were permanently injured, dislocated, fired, sentenced to harsh prison terms, deported, deprived forever of health insurance and pensions, rendered irreparably homeless, and exterminated by uncontrolled state violence are indisputably *out*. They are simply gone, disappeared by the upward moving currents and currency of global greed. As an aggregate, those who are out constitute uncultured reality. Liberty and justice have bypassed their zones of abject isolation, their unresourced territories of confinement without so much as a train whistle hoot of good-bye. They are simply and decisively out for the new-millennial count. The U.S. census does not even trouble itself with the dispossessed, disappeared, locked down population created by the Reagan-Bush compromise. As Christian Parenti notes:

> When "discouraged workers" who have given up the quest for employment and the incarcerated are added to the equation, the real unemployment rate for African American men emerges as a brutal 25.2 percent. Among Black youth during the mid nineties unemployment was twice as high as among white youth. . . .

> Two major American ethnic groups [black and Latino] together make up 22.8
> percent of the U.S. population but account for 47.8 percent of Americans living in
> poverty. Overall 35.6 million Americans—40 percent of whom are children—are
> impoverished.[1]

It is definitely bad times for those who were not assimilated by the domestic
Pax Americana of recent decades.

The American grand myth is now a fabulous, allegorical tale told by white
neoconservative griots and their black public intellectual quislings. Such exalted storytellers sit in ruling seats of the academy, government, and commerce, spinning yarns and smoking cigars. They make up and legislate new
insider rules over taxpayer-financed, after-dinner brandy. Black and white
neocon mythographers jerrybuild their rule-book-for-profit-taking with
cynical abandon—in the absence of evidence, through distortions of history,
and relying always on information blackouts that an embedded media gladly
supplies.

Who, then, is out? Decisively out? A look at the National Urban League's
State of Black America for 2004 indicates beyond a shadow of a doubt that
if the gold standard of our national in-ness is comprised of whites, nobody
is more seriously out than the black majority. There are, of course, far too
many statistical and social problem books around to rehash all the telltale
numbers here. (In one of his essays, James Baldwin is told by a friend that
shelves in our bookstores veritably groan under the weight of social problem
novels. And that, says Baldwin's informant, is precisely why things will never
change. Because our reading and feeling bad about the dreadful situations
condemned in the novels suffices to satisfy our consciences and convince us
that weeping over the plight of the dispossessed persuades us that we have
actually done something! This is a bit of a paraphrase, but it preserves the
point.)[2] Still, the drawbacks of social scientific and problem novels number
crunching notwithstanding, it is worthwhile, I think, to turn to the Urban
League's *State of Black America*.

While the 2004 report unequivocally records the ascendance of a new
and very real black middle class in America, it also statistically and adroitly
rehearses for our new millennium the age-old American story of the black
majority. Members of this racial class make less money, die sooner, and possess far less access to quality education and public spheres of commerce than
the majority of white Americans. They hold zero wealth. Black men are

stopped, brutalized, intimidated, murdered by the "nation's finest" more often than whites are. Blacks are almost comically insignificant with respect to our nation's power elite. (There is one black cabinet member, Condoleeza Rice. There is one black senator, Barack Obama.) And as the brilliant black comedian Chris Rock observes: "We don't have any *wealthy* black people." Rock is not unaware of superrich black sports and entertainment celebrities; after all, he is one of them. However, he is also keenly aware that although Shaquille O'Neal owns jewels, cars, a yacht, a sumptuous Florida mansion, and high-end fashion enough to clothe a whole flock of black ministers and deacons, he purchases all of these luxuries on salary. Rock points out that Shaq is *rich*, but the man who "owns" him and pays his salary is *wealthy*. Despite my reluctance to rain down numbers, statistics may be helpful at this juncture. The following is from *The State of Black America*:

> There are troubling differences in the types of assets held. Of the $44.373 trillion in assets held by whites in 2001, 43 percent or $19.222 trillion were financial assets. Financial assets include stocks, bonds, and other liquid investments. Only 25.9 percent of white assets were held in their homes. Of the $1.493.3 trillion in assets held by blacks, 42 percent were held in their homes while only 33 percent were held in financial assets. On the liability side, blacks held nearly five times more installment debt than whites and nearly three times more debt than whites overall.[3]

We have no wealthy black people. Ditto for powerful black people if the standard chosen is the plutocracy of white America that was aided and abetted by the Regan/Bush/Clinton/Bush decades. The black majority is definitely out. Some might say the fate of the black majority was actually sealed when the founders released the Constitution from that Philadelphia assembly for national ratification: "The Constitution as ratified in 1787 was not colorblind. For eighteenth-century black Americans it neither ended slavery, nor enfranchised black freedmen. In fact, it literally prohibited Congress from interfering with the slave trade until 1808, in those states where it [slavery] flourished."[4]

When Martin Luther King Jr. was placed in a leadership role as both strategist and orator for Civil Rights, he knew in his conscience and consciousness that the grand story called the American dream was, at least temporarily, on hold for the black majority. He knew, as well, that it was in fact the black majority that indexed what the Urban League refers to as the state of black America. Dr. King knew the black majority's consensus in his leadership bestowed upon him a responsibility to move the index of black possibilities considerably ahead for that black majority. King was acutely aware that he had to remain ever watchful and a principal advocate for a deeply structural reorientation of American mind, policy, practice, and myth. He was not only a relentless and informed realist in regard to who in our society was historically and chronically out, but also a fearlessly cosmopolitan champion and advocate for the freedom and welfare of a global society brutally split between North and South, rich haves and wretched have-nots. While he certainly was not as worldly sophisticated as, say, Bayard Rustin, he was more fiercely wedded to the cause of people farthest down than almost any other modern black spokesperson for justice. Compassion, empathy, fearlessness, self-sacrifice, and a genius at living within modest means, King stood witness for the freedom of the black American majority and was a compatriot to all the wretched of the earth. When he referenced the great American myth in his scintillating homiletics for freedom, it was usually to reveal how exclusionary that myth is from its founding instance till the time of his assassination ... and beyond. He was a big-issues public intellectual who refused to avert his eyes from the harsh and enduring ill treatment meted out to the black majority by our national polity.

Black post–Civil Rights era public intellectuals have, in form, substance, style, ideology, and spirit, betrayed virtually every contour of the legacy of public intellectual leadership bequeathed by Dr. King. Their lively performances and earnest recommendations have, time and again, amounted to little more than a black-majority-vilifying, neoconservative, ideological pottage sold and fed to paying white audiences. They have, each in his or her own way, stewed up a gumbo of pseudocolored, high-sounding, black-majority-betraying, semimythic soul food designed to provide white people with what we might call post–Black Power relief. The books and performances I have chosen to analyze are only a select set of examples; others might have been put on the table. But surely the people whose works I have critiqued are among the most famous, representative, and, in the instance of the black neoconservatives, most injurious to prospects for the good life of the black majority at the present time. All of them blink the big issues, cast blame on the black majority, and happily do old-school buck-and-wing reels in the street for whoever is willing to put a paycheck in their hand. They all police uncultured reality, whether from the towers of Hoover, the 1879 hall at Princeton, the corridors of Yale Law School, or the sunlit prospects of Afro-American studies at Harvard. They are all, implicitly or explicitly, advocates for free market capitalism as an escape route (sort of a new north star) from the ghetto for earnest black majority laborers who are not afraid of getting their hands dirty. Yet, consider the following:

> Some of the responsibility for narrowing wealth inequality must rest with the black community itself. Debt is unacceptably high. Ownership of financial assets is low as compared to consumption of goods—such as depreciable assets like automobiles. But, responsibility also rests with industry and government that share some of the culpability for racial gaps in credit markets and entry points to acquisition of wealth. In an era when many state and local governments are abandoning programs designed to assist minority-owned businesses, there is no concomitant effort to eradicate the general societal conditions that lead to wide disparities in business ownership and ownership of other assets in the first place.[5]

If such wisdom about the near impossibility of the average black majority Joe gaining access to or even knowledge of entry points of prospective wealth is in wide and respectable circulation, why have our post–Civil Rights black intellectuals not surveyed this news? (Surely they would report it in the offices of intellectual integrity and rigor if they had.) Why have they not put the facts of very structurally bad and trying times squarely on the policy table? Why have they persistently given themselves over disingenuously to touting free market opportunities available to black folks in the racial majority? The answer is that the current crop of black public intellectuals is not created nor paid to deliver the hard facts about our national irresponsibility with respect to the poor. Nor are they given gratuities when they serve up their conservative soul food gumbo or minstrel shouts to provide sober, documented evidence about *who* precisely is accountable for the plight of the black majority. Their job description is, simply stated, to be black myth-enhancing entertainers. They have performed well, seldom turning their eyes or prose to the big issues, or wrestling with their abject betrayal of the very best we have as a culture—the black public intellectual legacy of Dr. Martin Luther King Jr. They have abetted the grand myth purveyors and preservers of our infamous American times, including those who energetically argue that incarcerated black and brown women and men are in prison solely because they are criminals, guilty, and justly belong there. One wonders what Dr. King—peering between metal bars of a Birmingham jail cell many decades ago—would have felt had he known his moral and ethical legacy would be so perverted by black public intellectuals' tacit endorsement of the rough, racially determined justice that marks the U.S. prison-industrial complex in our era.

IT IS ONE THING to pretend that money and market opportunities exist in abundance for all Americans. Such myth and fantasy is a remainder of our Puritan origins and pilgrim wanderings in the wilderness. It is quite another matter, however, to close one's eyes to what today seems our greatest national domestic disaster and disgrace: the phantasmagoric, revenue producing gulag that is our nation's private prison-industrial complex. This gulag is a direct outcome of the Reagan/Bush compromise that devastated life in the United States like a plutocratic neutron bomb. The Reagan and Bush administrations (as well as Bill Clinton's) deregulated, de-welfared, crime-and-drug-warred hundreds of thousands of new police onto the streets to "tame down" all righteous opposition; tax-breaked bigots and businessmen by the thousands; and exported more jobs than the population of many a nation. They did these things in complicity with disingenuous neoconservative intellectuals, superrich corporations, political action committees (PACs), mass media compliance, and a racialized and demonizing set of propaganda initiatives that brought even the poorest and most dispossessed of white men on board. Those national patriarchs racialized crime through a series of stunningly callous crime bills and, at the same time, criminalized poverty. Once our nation had sought to make war on poverty; those chief executives seemed dedicated to making it spread like kudzu. Where are we now? As black gospel genius Pop Staples sings: "Trying times is what the world is talking about / Confusion running all across the land. ... A whole lot of things is wrong.... These are trying times!"

PRISON COLORED BODIES, PRIVATE PROFIT

The impoverished low-wage working-class and unemployed youth who have fallen below the statistical radar [are] . . . "social dynamite" [that] . . . cannot simply be swept aside. Controlling them requires both a defensive policy of containment and an aggressive policy of direct attack and destabilization. They are contained and crushed, confined to the ghetto, demoralized and pilloried in warehouse public schools, demonized by a lurid media, sent to prison, and at times dispatched by lethal injection or police bullets. This is the class—or more accurately the caste, because they are increasingly people of color—which must be constantly undermined, divided, intimidated, attacked, discredited, and ultimately kept in check with what Fanon called the "language of naked force."

CHRISTIAN PARENTI
Lockdown America

We are definitely in the throes of trying times. From Michael Jacobson's *Downsizing Prisons*, we read:

> In 2004, nearly 2.2 million people [were] incarcerated in United States prisons and jails. At current incarceration rates, almost one-third of Black men born today are likely to spend some time in prison, more than seven times the 4.4% of white men likely to serve prison time. ... Spending on corrections continues to grow, despite studies that show little relationship between increasing incarceration and crime reduction.[1]

The number of inmates in U.S. prisons is increasing. And those numbers are heavily skewed toward the black majority. Nearly one-third of all African American men between the ages of twenty and twenty-nine are under criminal justice supervision on any given day—in jail, detention, prison, or under the mandates of probation and parole. The number of black women in prison rose by a staggering 828 percent from 1986 to 1991.[2] Our nation incarcerates, detains, and surveils more citizens than any other country in the world except China.[3]

What is so deeply disturbing about our national domestic wars on crime and drugs (launched by the Reagan, Bush, and Clinton administrations) is the toll they have exacted on federal, state, and municipal budget allotments for what might be designated our national human and infrastructural services. Currently, we spend twenty-five thousand dollars a year to house an average prisoner. We spend more than a hundred thousand dollars a year to house a single occupant of a supermax prison facility, such as the one in Florence, Colorado. While our inner cities fester, the number of privately managed prison beds is increasing.

There is limited funding for our national infrastructure. Bridges fall down. Public transportation in a host of cities is little more than a joke, plagued by strikes, employee absences, aging vehicles, and little concern for punctuality. There is scant money for parks, recreational facilities, public libraries, public museums, street repair, and public restrooms. Money has been transformed into fluid, fast-moving global capital. Virtually everything operates under the edicts of global capital. This decidedly is *not* your father's strong labor union, affirmative action–oriented, socially compassionate, and free market opportunity world of the American dream.

When one considers the abjection and horrors of chattel slavery, the innumerable white betrayals of black interests, the dread convict leasing systems

of incarceration and labor in the American South, and the discrepancies in
life expectancies between my young grandsons and their white counterparts
in 2007, "death row" seems to be the default location of black men in America. And the only justice meted out to black men and women seems to be
criminal justice. Jerome G. Miller writes as follows:

> The matter of who ends up in the criminal justice system of any country has
> always carried racial and ethnic implications. While those who are confined in a
> country's jails or prisons are a rough measure of the types of criminal activity at a
> given time, they provide a sharper picture of who is at the bottom of the socioeco-
> nomic heap or on the political *outs* at the given time. Visit Berlin's jails and count
> the Turks. Visit France's prisons and see the Algerians.... Visit American prisons
> and jails and see the blacks and Hispanics. ... California sociologist John Irvin
> [contends] that the nation's jails exist less for purposes of crime control than as
> places of "rabble management."[4]

Reduced to uselessness by corporate downsizing, the outsourcing of American jobs, intimidation of national labor unions, deindustrialization (and the
customary rejection of black job applicants by the American service industry), black and Hispanic residents of U.S. inner cities have been criminalized
by a national racial politics that seeks to control and isolate them.

It is not a coincidence that capital punishment was embraced by more
and more states during the Reagan and Bush administrations. For the Reagan-Bush era witnessed the utter crushing of American middle-class dreams
of prosperity, which, in turn, led the rank-and-file white population to lose
compassion for and to condemn resource-distribution for the nation's neediest. Compassion fatigue led those who knew better to blame, say, the black
homeless for the collapse of their neighborhood infrastructure. "If we had
fewer race folks among us, the city would immediately have shored up that
Germantown Avenue Bridge in Philadelphia!"

What was once a war on poverty has become a war on the impoverished.
Where once our national mandate was to secure for the disadvantaged free
lunches, early intervention, and preschool education, now we seem intent
on putting behind bars all those do not live up to the mythical ideals of the
American dream. That they *cannot* do so has no part in the equation. The
nation's present-day mantra seems to be, "Send 'em to jail!"

From the passage of the Rockefeller drug laws in 1973 (which gave birth
to mandatory minimum sentencing in the United States) to the lamentable

brutalization of Rodney King in the 1990s, the only course that America has been able to envision for those who are out is incarceration. But if you begin by justifying, tidying up, and protecting slavery at your very founding, how can your national imagination ever hope to transcend what Frederick Douglass called "the prison house of American slavery"? Indeed, locking down those who are not white is the life force of this land that I love. I abhor the American paucity of creative imagination that might instruct us in finding new ways to solve this problem.

The rhetorical war on crime on which President Nixon rode to reelection finally took shape in the form of legislation passed in the state of New York in 1974. Named for the governor who proposed them, the Rockefeller drug laws mandated a prison term of fifteen years to life for convictions on the charges of possessing four ounces of an illegal drug or for selling two ounces; it included a provision for establishing a mandatory prison sentence for many second felony convictions, regardless of the crime or its circumstances.[5] The egregiously cynical and racist Rockefeller legislation was actually somewhat less severe than what the governor had originally proposed. He proposed that *all* drug dealers—even juvenile offenders—be punished with a mandatory sentence of life without parole and that plea-bargaining should be forbidden in such cases. Can all the philanthropy, carriage trails in Maine, libraries, and grants in existence ever erase from the Rockefeller name the stench of bigoted opportunism?

Rockefeller's opportunistic, political racism went national with President Reagan's Anti–Drug Abuse Act of 1986. The American war on drugs was a cynical designer strategy for going after those whose only hope of income in their zones of blighted urban confinement was the drug trade. So, black youth—mostly young black and brown and Asian immigrant males—began to be rounded up by the tens of thousands. And after California (in its traditional new age wisdom) decided to convert baseball's "three strikes and you're out" into a legal mantra governing felony-offense sentencing, even more bodies were available for the new American private prison-industrial business. Private prison corporations endorse the busting of souls and the warehousing of bodies.

There is, alas, a groaning library of books on the prison-industrial complex available, so it would be repetitive, and tedious, to recount numbers, speculations, conspiracy theories, and Marxist analyses—all readily available at local bookstores—here. But a bit of substantiation is in order. Since the 1980s, drug arrests have accounted for the largest increase in the prison inmate population in the United States. (A fact to illustrate the perduring nature of American incarceration: Large numbers of blacks were incarcerated in the United States when Alexis de Tocqueville made his famous pilgrimage to America to study our prison system. Inmate numbers then, as in our own era, were disproportionate to the representation of blacks in the nation's general population.)[6]

In today's United States, black and Hispanic men and women under the surveillance of the criminal justice system move from fetid living spaces that are socially, physically, and psychologically imprisoning to the packed, dehumanizing cells of the prison-industrial complex. Those who are released are sent back to the crumbling streets, disrupting even further possibilities for orderly civic life in their black and Hispanic majority 'hoods. "In 1992," writes Jerome Miller, "there were over 14 million arrests nationally. Virtually all of them resulted in a booking into a local jail or police lockup. As many as five million of them were African-American males, most accused of minor offenses."[7]

Black male incarceration is not a new American phenomenon. Nineteenth-century abolitionists frequently referred to the American South, which maintained a system of African American chattel slavery for more than two and a half centuries, in the same words used by Frederick Douglass: they called it the "prison house of slavery." While the catastrophic American Civil War brought some respite for the black majority, the close of Reconstruction and birth of the so-called New South, saw black men arrested in bulk to provide labor for a new economic order. From the aptly titled *Twice the Work of Free Labor*, we read: "The use of the [southern] penal system to recruit and control black labor stood at the cutting edge of southern politics and economic development, not in its dark corners. Far from representing a lag in southern modernity, convict labor was a central component in the region's modernization."[8]

The enforced and oft-times murderous incarceration of blacks is not new. What beggars the imagination in 2007 is the scale, malevolence, and economics of black subjugation. The notorious, racially coded Willie Horton campaign advertisement during George H. W. Bush's 1988 presidential campaign exemplifies the notion that crime in America has been massaged from drugs decisively into race. And the war on drugs has, in turn, morphed into a genocidal assault on the black and poor in America. For example, "In Bal-

timore, Maryland, 11,107 of the 12,965 persons arrested for 'drug abuse viola-
tions' in 1991 were African-Americans. In Columbus, Ohio, where African-
American males made up less than 11% of the population, they comprised
over 90% of the drug arrests and were being arrested at 18 times the rate of
whites."[9]

Thousands of blacks and poor people have been removed from American streets by antidrug laws. These are not the Mister Big drug wholesalers.
These are the low-level mules who move the product for the big guys. The
only drug that carries a felony sentence for simple possession is crack cocaine
(which is powder cocaine mixed with baking soda and water, cooked, and
sold as "rock"). Who is most likely to trade in this inexpensive—yet lethally
addictive—product? Of course, it is the black and Hispanic mule, the street
retailer, the pitiable user. When (in the titular phrase of William Julius Wilson) "work disappears," young men (and women) of color sell drugs. They get
busted. They receive mandatory minimum sentences. Their lives are ruined.
Anyone who believes that a dramatic or televised portrayal of a city's deterio-
rating crime problem and its corollary budget shortfalls and infrastructural
disasters, such as *The Wire*, is not a show about race has not, I think, followed
the American money or the politics of the past forty years.

Further light is shone on the drug war's logic and mode of justice when
one looks at the economics behind our prison system. Someone is turning
quite a profit warehousing all these inmates. It is the economic question that
moves our present-day criminal justice system into the provinces designated
by President Dwight Eisenhower as the military-industrial complex. (The
phrase "military-industrial complex" refers to the complex of money and influence transfers between private businessmen, congressmen and other politicians, national and local lobbyists, and policymakers that generally leads to
private money dictating the systematic terms of our national governmental
policy and the allocation of resources.) If each body subject to incarceration
is worth a substantial sum of money—and tripling the rates of incarceration in America demands more holding space for colored bodies—one turns
with economic savvy to supply solutions and the supply side of the American
economy: private enterprise.

Corrections Corporation of America (CCA) was launched (with a dash of
good old American racial irony) using Kentucky Fried Chicken profits in my
new home state of Tennessee. Wackenhut Corrections specialized in various
forms of surveillance and private security before the prison boom. Wackenhut rapidly expanded its services to warehouse those colored commodi-

ties identified as nonviolent offenders. Both CCA and Wackenhut have built scores of privately owned U.S. prisons at the cost of billions of American tax-payer dollars in the form of tax breaks from deindustrialized and economically bottomed out geographies (such as upstate New York, and Youngstown, Ohio). They have hired utterly untrained corrections officers and engaged in financial malfeasance and corruption. They have paid PACs scores of millions of dollars to lobby hypocritical politicians. CCA and Wackenhut are body snatchers for profit; they move undesirables of color (those who inhabit uncultured reality and are on the outs) far from family and friends, and treat them worse than slaves.[10]

These privately owned, government-subsidized corporations lease out (with ghostly shades of the New South) prisoners to other private industries. The inmates so leased earn—after expenses are deducted from their pay—from 65 cents to $1.10 an hour. It should thus surprise no one that the U.S. prison industry represents a $100 billion bonanza for the supply side. For the average black male between the ages of eighteen and forty, the "public sphere" is likely to be the concrete and steel cell of a private Wackenhut or CCA prison.

We are a long way from the agency and glory of a Civil Rights Movement cry of "jail, not bail!" The trick has been viciously turned upon us by American incarceration. Private dollars and federal and state politics have converged to transform black majority urban spaces into feeder zones for prison and profit.

The allowable space for the impoverished collective black population is captured by the contours of the newly operational federal facility at Florence, Colorado:

> The new prison [at Florence] is tightly subdivided into nine units by means of 1,400 electronically controlled gates and shuttles and 168 television monitors. Each unit is self-contained down to separate sick-call rooms, law libraries and barber chairs so that an inmate gets a minimum of travel leeway even with his chains and blazer-dressed escorts....
>
> The shaving mirror is of polished steel deeply riveted to the wall to prevent the making of prison shivs [knives] and other weapons. Matches and cigarette lighters, the proven stuff of explosives in other prisons, have been replaced by a simple hole-in-the-wall apparatus for lighting cigarettes. Meals are dispensed in separate heated trays through cell slots from airline-style carts.[11]

If young blacks are canny enough to avoid death at the hands of SWAT teams, Fresno paramilitary troopers, rival drug retailers, infection from rat bites, drive-by shootings, simple absence of health care, Florence is what awaits them should they get busted doing the only work available to them in super-blighted ghettos. Low-level drug trading is the economy of choice in zones such as South Central Los Angeles and North Philadelphia's Diamond Street provinces.

Those who have been labeled out and thus cast viciously and brutally into our country's prison-industrial complex are emblems of the American majority future. Do we really want to be complicit in constructing the death row fashioned by mythical patriarchs, oligarchic businessmen, corrupt congressional representatives, and prison suppliers who constitute a billion-dollar elite? I hope not. But if we do not begin to imagine and then construct safe spaces of black American majority life *now*, death row—the civic, social, economic, and psychological incarceration of our culture—will be our American future. Mumia Abu-Jamal (for whom Philadelphia, Pennsylvania, justice was a travesty) speaks on our national prison-industrial complex in his fascinating and lucid book *Live from Death Row*:

> Solitary confinement, around-the-clock lock-in, no-contact visits, no prison jobs, no educational programs by which to grow, psychiatric "treatment" facilities designed only to drug you into a coma; ladle in hostile, overtly racist prison guards and staff; add the weight of the falling away of family ties, and you have all the fixings for a stressful psychic stew designed to deteriorate, to erode, one's humanity—designed, that is, by the state, with full knowledge of its effects.[12]

The supermax prison at Florence, Colorado, seems to me a warning sign to all who should listen attentively to the valiant, brilliantly articulate voices of alternative black public intellectuals such as Angela Davis and Manning Marable. They have in public and in print—to audiences of thousands—condemned utterly our era's neoconservative and brutal economies of lockdown. They have heeded Mother Teresa's maxim that calls upon all who have voices, podiums, and means of public articulation—teaching jobs at elite institutions, fellowships with think tanks, access to the media—not to do great things but to do small things with great love. They are the answer to the disingenuous greed of those neoconservative black public intellectuals discussed in this book.

Angela Davis scarcely needs identification in the context of American criminal justice. "Free Angela!" was an ubiquitous rallying cry of the social revolutionary cadres of the seventies. Davis was charged with abetting the criminal courthouse rebellion of a group of young black men who came to be known as the Soledad Brothers. After a year in prison, she was acquitted. Upon her release, she immediately took up again the radical activism that had allied her to the Black Panther Party. A charismatic, deeply informed, and magnificently accessible public speaker as well as an intellectually challenging university professor at the University of California Santa Cruz, Davis has become one of the nation's foremost advocates for prisoners' rights and abolition of the American prison system. She has organized conferences that have drawn thousands. She has relentlessly urged that the abolition of prisons, not their reform, is a national humane necessity. Her idea is that alternative institutions must be created for nonviolent offenders in order to stem the tide of incarceration that has swelled the U.S. prison population. She has been tireless in her efforts in the United States and abroad. She is adamantly opposed to the profit accruing from each new prisoner (usually people of color and, increasingly, women) cast into the U.S. private prison-industrial complex. Her ideas are spelled out clearly in her scintillating book *Are Prisons Obsolete?* and her answer to the titular query is, unequivocally, yes.

Manning Marable is a prolific worker for radical scholarship, multimedia reclamations of black history and historical figures, and advance guard public forums and journalism. A founder and director of U.S. black studies programs at more than one university, he has devoted the past two decades of his life to analyses of a U.S. neoconservative politics of exclusion, welfare dismantlement, urban deterioration, failed criminal justice, racialized globalization, and a private prison-industrial complex. Like Angela Davis, he has been a high-profile participant in conferences and forums addressing issues of for-profit incarceration of women and of Afro-American and Latino men in the United States. He lectures widely, organizes (particularly in New York) astutely, and writes prolifically. His is one of the most accessible contributions to *States of Confinement*, the important collection of essays on incarceration edited by Joy James.

Clearly, then, not all black intellectuals have failed to address the issue of prisons in the United States. But those who are most famously rewarded as black public intellectuals usually fail to join company and voice with liberation workers such as Davis and Marable. Dr. King, perhaps more resolutely and courageously than any other public activist, knew as early as Montgomery that unless he could, as it were, get inside U.S. systems of incarceration there was no chance of his helping to set people free. Arrested more than thirty times and issuing his most brilliant Civil Rights statement from within the precincts of a Birmingham jail, Dr. King would certainly have looked askance at those who call themselves black public intellectuals but do not lift up—on every public occasion—their voices against a private prison-industrial complex that now holds more than 2 million people.

IT IS TEMPTING IN our technologically plugged-in era with its studied absence of attention to the plight of those farthest down to believe America is doing OK. We long desperately to believe our battles against the entrapments, denigration, and dangers of American racism have been won. This is understandable. Our diminished economic, educational, military, and diplomatic power to unilaterally affect global turns of events is dispiriting. Who among us does not wish to believe we Americans are doing OK at home? We can scarcely envision victory over future generations abroad, so why not, with a dulling amnesia, declare democracy a reality at home? Why not declare victory over a dark racial past of slavery, Jim Crow, spectacle lynching, and legal segregation? Such a declaration might help us maintain a certain moral swagger in the face of our global diminishment. Alas, the undeniable national truth is that thoroughgoing, redemptive victory over race in America—at least with respect to the black majority—is still a dream. No thinking black chorus is imminently available to sing with vigorous racial pride: "We stand at last / Where the white gleam of our bright star is cast."

There is scarcely any gleam in the life of even the American middle class today. In fact, lights, for the most part, are permanently out or speedily dimming in U.S. factories everywhere. As I write, American auto manufacturers have all but given up the ghost, admitting that foreign manufacturers such as Toyota have gotten it right. Ford Motor Company announced in January 2007 that it would soon eliminate forty-two thousand more American factory jobs.

Wealthy white America has taken our land down a perilous, costly, and destructive course during the past four decades. And black public intellectuals have abetted that decline. Our land is not—certainly not in matters of race, civil rights, living wages, and efficacious national attention to urgent matters of structural and infrastructural overhaul—either as progressively inclined or as personally optimistic as it was in the 1960s. This is, in part, a result of the terrorism of 9/11 and the ongoing slaughter in Iraq. But the general sense of malaise among the former American middle class and black American majority is, I think, as much a function of clear signals received from our national elites that, in a very real sense, democracy as we have known it is dead. Post–Civil Rights era black public intellectuals are certainly implicated in sending such a signal. They have championed behaviorist causations for poverty, advocated an end to affirmative action, named "black 'memic' pathology" as the premiere social threat to civilized society, supported the dismantling of social safety nets, and relentlessly and disingenuously disparaged race as a viable analytical category. Who can have faith, then, when even those who were resolutely excluded from speaking in the traditionally all-white American academy and American public spheres of the past now stand unashamedly before paying audiences, denigrating the intellectual performance of black college students while advocating the end of affirmative action? Why do the formerly excluded and now affirmative-action-employed commit such betrayal?

They do so in the first instance because speaking with fiery and self-righteous condemnation against the black majority has always been and seems to remain a popular, well-financed, and best-selling vocation in America. I do not want to discount, by any measure, the sincerity of black neoconservatives' faith in the accuracy of their pronouncements. Nor do I want to do anything more than vigorously critique in the name of a more productive and better resourced black majority and American middle class the efficacy of what they have written. I am a textual critic; mine is not a social scientific critique. Suffice it to say, however, when black men in a society as pervasively obtuse or indifferent to its racial dynamics as the United States have an opportunity to occupy national pulpits, one does wish they would not live by faith alone. We do wish they would more adequately heed the old song's injunction: "Rise and look around you!" And having done so, offer us written texts that will help us address in energetic ways the decline of our land and the incarceration of its people.

I can suggest several courses of action we might take to minimize effects of the great national neoconservative juggernaut that seems never to be done with its wars of intellectual terror, assaults on culture, and co-optation of black public intellectuals looking for an economic fix. What might a progressive agenda in the academy entail for those of us who are brave?

First, let me make it clear that I am a well-salaried black American. I obtained my first job not as the old advertisements used to declare through the *New York Times*, but as a direct result of affirmative action and my outstanding graduate school record. I am an energetic participant in the privileges and opportunities of the new black middle class. I serve on the faculty of an elite, formerly all white, southern university. I live in a spacious urban home among welcoming and generous white neighbors and their friendly children. I am blessed to spend entire days at my computer, and I do not scruple to call myself a black writer and tenured academic intellectual. I could never, during my wintry, cabbage-scented days in Little Africa, have dreamed of such a comfortable existence. So I do not, therefore, claim to be writing from the black majority trenches. No—my preeminently text-based critique is, I hope, that of a responsible black intellectual who holds race as an analytical construct firmly in the forefront of his analysis. As a trained interpreter of texts and the author of a number of scholarly books that have been endorsed in their rigor by the academy, I am as punctilious about historical accuracy and the necessity for social empathy and compassion as the most astute of the social scientists and historians who have informed our consciousness in efficacious ways. I now move to some final observations and recommendations.

"These are trying times." George W. Bush is the most antilabor president recently to walk White House corridors. "Confusion is running all over the land." The murderous slaughter that is the consequence of the Bush administration's mendaciously motivated invasion of Iraq grows exponentially with each passing day. Assaults on labor and invasions of foreign lands represent gargantuan malfeasance by our national political elites. To me, however, they scarcely seem within reach of any efficacious remedial acts of the merely academic mind and imagination. Their scale is, perhaps, too grand. But academic intellectuals really do not have to leave their backyards in order to do serious work at making a progressive difference in the world.

As a former president of the Modern Language Association of America (one of the largest professional associations in the world), I take pride in the fact that the American neoconservative right has directed harsh attacks in recent decades against me and the multicultural and inclusive humanities for which I hope I stand. Haki Madhubuti and other of my compeers in

216 CONCLUSION

the early days of my academic career during the 'sixties always enjoined: "If nobody significant is attacking you, my brother, then you know you are not doing anything right, certainly anything in the interest of the black majority." These compeers were themselves exemplary in following the injunctive title of one of Madhubuti's recent volumes *Run Toward Fear*. What then must we do?

We must forge connections (secular and sacred) with so-called local communities that provide labor for our intellectual home institutions. We must also, I think, work to understand privatization, especially the same higher-education/corporatist nexus between business and the university to which we were first alerted by Clark Kerr during the sixties. Today, not only is government really business, but so too is the consumer university. However, concern with privatization—evident in the ever-spiraling influence of the corporate sector on college and university trustees, as well as the shaping of curricular and athletic priorities—should extend beyond campus. How can we not take measure of a private prison-industrial complex and remain socially responsible intellectuals? We must also analyze the sharp decline in intellectual standards and accountability for accurate and adequate analysis that is privately financed by the archipelago of neoconservative think tanks across the land.

At the level of pedagogy and scholarship, we must, I think, encourage a new imaginativeness in both slavery studies and critical media studies. We must break the hold of a standard, sometimes outdated, and booked history, and direct our students' attention to alternative media. We must join them even in small efforts to ameliorate the monopolistic stranglehold on all modes of intellectual and cultural distribution by corporations such as Viacom, AOL/Time Warner, and others. We need to foster some studious unplugging, rather than offering students free iPods as an inducement to enrollment.

We might seek to lead our students, colleagues, administrators, and local community participants to understand the costs of globalization. Today, the World Bank and International Monetary Fund glibly destroy colored local economies. Trade treaties such as NAFTA are designer-produced for white power and colored abjection. We know this when twenty-five cents in a demographic of color is held to be a sensible daily wage for those employed in exported and outsourced American jobs.[1]

Finally, we must encourage student fieldwork that pulls the covers off of university employment practices (from janitors to adjunct professors). In this vein we must also encourage our students and colleagues to get beyond the media hype and seemingly informed treatises of such black public intellectuals discussed in this book. It is important for those within our limited sphere of influence to encourage audiences to figure out precisely what such black public intellectuals are up to, even in their own backyards. And why, we might also want to discover, are these folks so welcome as racial heralds in these trying times?

The black public intellectual mission of the present day—as glorious workers such as Lani Guinier, Manning Marable, Angela Davis, Patricia Williams, Troy Duster, Elijah Anderson, Greg Thomas, and others know so well—is not to do great things, but to do small, racially specific, analytical work in the interest of the black majority. And to do such work with great love. If "It is the poets who run toward fear," we should perhaps labor always to be one of their number.[2]

INTRODUCTION: LITTLE AFRICA

1. *Report of the National Advisory Commission on Civil Disorders* (New York: Bantam Books, 1968), vii; commonly called the Kerner Commission Report.
2. W.E.B. Du Bois, *Dusk of Dawn: An Essay Toward an Autobiography of a Race Concept* (New York: Schocken, 1968), vii.
3. Juan Williams, *Enough: The Phony Leaders, Dead-End Movement, and Culture of Failure That Are Undermining Black America—and What We Can Do About It* (New York: Crown, 2006).
4. For an overview of the scandal, see "Mess at U. Mass," March 17, 1975, Time in Partnership with CNN, www.time.com/time/magazine/article/0,9171,912994-1,00.html.

JAIL: SOUTHERN DETENTION TO GLOBAL LIBERATION

1. Diane McWhorter, *Carry Me Home: Birmingham, Alabama: The Climactic Battle of the Civil Rights Revolution* (New York: Touchstone-Simon & Schuster, 2001), 90.
2. Quoted in Stewart Burns, *To the Mountaintop: Martin Luther King Jr.'s Sacred Mission to Save America, 1955–1968* (New York: HarperSanFrancisco/Harper Collins, 2004), 35.
3. Burns, *To the Mountaintop*, 74–75.
4. Quoted in McWhorter, *Carry Me Home*, 343.
5. Quoted in McWhorter, *Carry Me Home*, 341.
6. Quoted in McWhorter, *Carry Me Home*, 342.
7. Burns, *To the Mountaintop*, 169.
8. Martin Luther King Jr., *A Testament of Hope: The Essential Writings of Martin Luther King, Jr.*, ed. James Melvin Washington (San Francisco: Harper & Row, 1986), 10. Hereafter cited in text as *Testament*.
9. Quoted in McWhorter, *Carry Me Home*, 346.
10. Quoted in Burns, *To the Mountaintop*, 225.
11. Taylor Branch, *Parting the Waters: America in the King Years, 1954–63* (New York: Simon and Schuster, 1988), 392.

12. Branch, *Parting the Waters*, 393.
13. McWhorter, *Carry Me Home,* 355.
14. Quoted in Burns, *To the Mountaintop*, 26.
15. W.E.B. Du Bois, *The Souls of Black Folk: Three Negro Classics* (New York: Avon Books, 1969), 339.
16. Carol Jenkins and Elizabeth Gardner Hines, *Black Titan: A. G. Gaston and the Making of a Black American Millionaire* (New York: One World-Ballantine Books, 2004), xiii.
17. Quoted in McWhorter, *Carry Me Home*, 441.
18. James Baldwin, "Everybody's Protest Novel," *Notes of a Native Son* (Boston: Beacon Press, 1984), 17.
19. James R. Ralph, *Northern Protest: Martin Luther King, Jr., Chicago, and the Civil Rights Movement* (Cambridge, MA: Harvard University Press, 1993).
20. Ralph, *Northern Protest*.
21. King, *Where Do We Go from Here: Chaos or Community?* (New York: Harper & Row, 1967), 112. Hereafter cited in text as *Where Do We Go?*
22. Quoted in James H. Cone, "Martin Luther King, Jr., and the Third World," *We Shall Overcome: Martin Luther King, Jr., and the Black Freedom Struggle*, ed. Peter J. Albert and Ronald Hoffman (New York: Pantheon Books, 1990), 206.

FRIENDS LIKE THESE: RACE AND NEOCONSERVATISM

1. Ralph Ellison, *Shadow and Act* (New York: Vintage/Random House, 1964), 128.
2. See Christian Parenti's *Lockdown America: Police and Prisons in the Age of Crisis* (New York: Verso, 1999) for an account of the "criminalization" and attribution of inherent (race specific) "criminality" of those who, in the United States, stand outside the precincts of acceptability. Parenti's discussion of the massive buildup of studies and purported evidence from sociology, political science, and criminology (much of it from the neoconservative camps) that have buttressed American "lockdown" in recent decades is thorough and persuasive. His in-depth discussions of specific urban police forces and their logistics are spectacular.
3. Amiri Baraka [LeRoi Jones], "THREE MOVEMENTS AND A CODA," *Black Magic Poetry, 1961–1967* (New York: Bobbs-Merrill, 1969), 103.
4. Eric Foner, *Reconstruction: America's Unfinished Revolution, 1863–1877* (New York: Perennial-Harper & Row, 1988), 109.
5. James Baldwin, *Notes of a Native Son* (Boston: Beacon Press, 1984), xv–xvi; emphasis in original.
6. Eric Schlosser, "The Prison-Industrial Complex," *Atlantic Monthly* (Dec. 1998): 52; Marc Mauer, *Race to Incarcerate* (New York: New Press, 1999), 9.
7. Irving Kristol, *Neoconservatism: The Autobiography of an Idea* (New York: Free Press, 1995), 471.
8. Kristol, *Neoconservatism*, 472.
9. Thomas Reeves, "Open Admissions at Parkside," History News Network, George Mason University, 7 Oct. 2002, http://hnn.us/articles/1020.html.

10. Kristol, *Neoconservatism*, 472–475.

11. Kristol, *Neoconservatism*, 12.

12. "Neocon 101," Christian Science Monitor online (2004), www.csmonitor.com/specials/neocon/neocon101.html.

13. Robert Westbrook, "The Counter Intelligentsia: How Neoconservatism Lived and Died," *Lingua Franca* 6, no. 7 (Nov. 1996): 66; my emphasis.

14. Calloway, "I Wanna Be Rich," performed by Reginald and Vincent Calloway, *All the Way*, Sony, CD, 1990.

15. Donald Reilly, cartoon, *New Yorker*, 3 June 1974.

16. Quoted in Gary Dorrien, *The Neoconservative Mind: Politics, Culture, and the War of Ideology* (Philadelphia: Temple University Press, 1993), 150.

17. The "drug laws" endorsed and supported by New York governor Nelson Rockefeller carried mandatory minimum sentencing and harshly differential sentences for low-level drug trafficking in crack cocaine (the stuff of ghetto commerce, addiction, and violence) as opposed to powder cocaine. The unintended consequences of the new drug laws included an exponential increase in the prison population, which led to the need for new, privately financed prison construction. Presidents Ronald Reagan and George H. W. Bush promulgated, at the federal level, a heavily funded War on Drugs, complete with the neoconservative William Bennett as America's drug tsar. With the new "three strikes" mandates in judicial sentencing that were considered critical to the war's success, even more prisons were required. And neoconservative law-and-order advocates such as John Dilulio—former aide in the George W. Bush White house and redoubtable political science professor at the University of Pennsylvania—massaged statistics and engaged in hyperbolic rhetoric that included the term "superpredators" to foster an aggressive "tough on crime" politics and policies as the national norm.

Vincent Schiraldi captures much of what is indicated about direct and tacit support of neoconservatism for the funding and construction that has produced an enormous private prison-industrial complex. He singles out Dilulio in particular. "The 1990s were a punishing decade for America, with nearly as many people added to our prisons and jails as in [the country's] entire history prior to 1990. These policies were particularly devastating to the black community as one in three young African American males was put under criminal justice control and *states shifted funds from higher education into prisons*. Fittingly, the number of adults and juveniles locked up in America topped the 2 million mark at the decade's end. While many politicians competed for top honors in the tough-on-crime sweepstakes, academia's acknowledged king of crime hype was John Dilulio. In 1996 he authored an incendiary report warning of a 'rising tide of juvenile superpredators' waiting to engulf America. Bob Dole picked up on the 'superpredator' epithet in a radio address during his presidential campaign. Rep. Bill McCollum (R-Fla.) dubbed legislation that jailed juveniles alongside adults 'The Violent Predator Act of 1996'" (Vincent Schiraldi, "Will the Real John Dilulio Please Stand Up," Common Dreams.org News Center, published on Monday, February 21, 2001, in the *Washington Post*, www.commondreams.org/views01/0205-02.htm; my emphasis).

18. Sterling Brown, "Old Lem," Oldpoetry.com Poetry Archives, www.oldpoetry.com/opoem/36386.

19. Lawrence Ferlinghetti, "I Am Waiting," *A Coney Island of the Mind* (New York: New Directions, 1958), 51–56.

20. Michael Bérubé, *Public Access: Literary Theory and American Cultural Politics* (New York: Verso, 1994), 62.

21. Quoted in Dorrien, *Neoconservative Mind*, 191.

22. Dorrien, *Neoconservative Mind*, 9–10.

23. Quoted in Dorrien, *Neoconservative Mind*, 11.

24. Dorrien, *Neoconservative Mind*, 102. Dorrien discusses the imbrication of neoconservative projects and corporate backing on pp. 100–102.

25. See Bérubé, *Public Access*, 62.

26. Dorrien, *Neoconservative Mind*, 102.

27. Gary North, "An Introduction to Neoconservatism," LewRockwell.com, 10 June 2003, www.lewrockwell.com/north/north180.html.

28. James Baldwin, *The Fire Next Time* (New York: Vintage International, 1993), 19.

29. Baldwin, *The Fire Next Time*, 87.

30. Baldwin, *The Fire Next Time*, 96.

31. Baldwin, *The Fire Next Time*, 106.

32. Norman Podhoretz, "My Negro Problem—and Ours," *Commentary* (Feb. 1963): 93.

33. Podhoretz, "My Negro Problem," 101.

34. Podhoretz, "My Negro Problem," 101.

35. Dorrien, *Neoconservative Mind*, 382.

36. Schuyler, *Black and Conservative*, 121–122.

AFTER CIVIL RIGHTS: THE RISE OF BLACK PUBLIC INTELLECTUALS

1. Bart Landry, *The New Black Middle Class* (Berkeley: University of California Press, 1987), 72.

2. Robert Harris, "The Rise of the Black Middle Class," The World and I, www.worldandi.com/public/1999/February/middle.cfm.

3. Landry, *New Black Middle Class*, 2, 86.

4. Orlando Patterson, "The Paradox of Integration," *New Republic* (6 Nov. 1995): 24–25.

5. Michael Bérubé, "Public Academy," *New Yorker* (9 Jan. 1995): 75.

6. Alan Wolfe, "The New Pamphleteers," *New York Times Book Review* (11 July 2004): 12.

7. Cornel West, *Race Matters* (New York: Vintage, 2001), 20. Hereafter cited in text as *Race*.

8. Michael Eric Dyson, *The Michael Eric Dyson Reader* (New York: Basic Civitas, 2004), 412–413.

9. Dyson, *Michael Eric Dyson Reader*, 411.

10. See Tricia Rose, *Black Noise: Rap Music and Black Culture in Contemporary America* (Hanover, NH: Wesleyan University Press, 1994).

11. Dyson, *I May Not Get There with You: The True Martin Luther King, Jr.* (New York: Free Press, 2000), 174.

12. Richard A. Posner, *Public Intellectuals: A Study of Decline* (Cambridge: Harvard University Press, 2001), 165.

HAVE MASK, WILL TRAVEL: CENTRISTS FROM THE IVY LEAGUE

1. Quoted in Barbara Stock, "Bill Cosby and Clarence Thomas: The New Odd Couple?" IntellectualConservative.com, 6 July 2004, www.intellectualconservative.com/article3581.html.

2. Henry Louis Gates Jr., "Breaking the Silence," New York Times Archives, 1 August 2004, www.nytimes.com/2004/08/01/opinion/01gates.html.

3. Peter Irons, *Jim Crow's Children: The Broken Promise of the* Brown *Decision* (New York: Penguin, 2002), 344.

4. William Julius Wilson, *When Work Disappears: The World of the New Urban Poor* (New York: Knopf, 1996), 87.

5. Irons, *Jim Crow's Children*, 345.

6. Irons, *Jim Crow's Children*, 345–346.

7. Wilson, *When Work Disappears*, 52.

8. Wilson, *When Work Disappears*, 34–35.

9. Wilson, *When Work Disappears*, 73; Irons, *Jim Crow's Children*, 326.

10. Quoted in Wilson, *When Work Disappears*, 68.

11. Anne Makepeace, "Edward Curtis: Dialogue," *American Masters*, "Did He Show Us What Was Really Happening?" www.thirteen.org/americanmasters/curtis/show_us_about.html.

12. Makepeace, "Edward Curtis: Dialogue."

13. Henry Louis Gates, *Colored People: A Memoir* (New York: Knopf, 1994), xi. Hereafter cited in text as *Colored*.

14. Paul Laurence Dunbar, "Chrismus on the Plantation," in *Selected Poems* (New York: Penguin, 2004), 109–110.

15. Henry Louis Gates Jr. and Cornel West, *The Future of the Race* (New York: Knopf, 1996), 24. Hereafter cited in text as *Future*.

A CAPITAL FELLOW FROM HOOVER: SHELBY STEELE

1. Schuyler, *Black and Conservative: The Autobiography of George S. Schuyler* (New Rochelle, NY: Arlington House, 1966), 121.

2. Shelby Steele, *The Content of Our Character: A New Vision of Race in America* (New York: Harper Perennial, 1990), 40–41. Hereafter cited in text as *Content*.

3. Schuyler, *Black and Conservative*, 351.

4. Washington, "Atlanta Exposition Address," in *Booker T. Washington Papers*, ed. Louis Harlan (Urbana: University of Illinois Press, 1974), 3:586.

5. Edmund Burke, "Change and Conservation," in *Reflections on the Revolution in France: The Portable Conservative Reader*, ed. Russell Kirk (New York: Viking Press, 1982), 11–12.

6. Burke, *Reflections*, 12.

7. Thomas Jefferson, *Notes on the State of Virginia*, ed. William Peden (Chapel Hill, N.C.: Institute of Early American History and Culture, 1955), 141, 143.

8. Jefferson, *Notes*, 143.

9. Burke, *Reflections*, 33, 15.

10. F.A. Hayek, "Why I Am Not a Conservative," LewRockwell.com, www.lewrockwell.com/orig6/hayek1.html, from *The Constitution of Liberty* (Chicago: University of Chicago Press, 1960).

11. Marianne Moore, "Poetry," *Complete Poems* (New York: Penguin, 1994).

12. Manthia Diawara, "Malcolm X and the Black Public Sphere: Conversionists versus Culturalists," in *The Black Public Sphere*, ed. Black Public Sphere Collective (Chicago: University of Chicago Press, 1995).

13. Diawara, "Malcolm X and the Black Public Sphere," 41; my emphasis.

14. Shelby Steele, *White Guilt: How Blacks and Whites Together Destroyed the Promise of the Civil Rights Era* (New York: HarperCollins, 2006), 20. Hereafter cited in text as *White Guilt*.

REFLECTIONS OF A FIRST AMENDMENT TRICKSTER: STEPHEN CARTER

1. For a discussion of the tale "A Prophet Vindicated," see Houston A. Baker Jr., *Long Black Song: Essays in Black American Literature and Culture* (Charlottesville: University Press of Virginia, 1972), 25–26.

2. Jeanne Rosier Smith, *Writing Tricksters: Mythic Gambols in American Ethnic Fiction* (Berkeley: University of California Press, 1997), 2.

3. Suzy Hansen, review of *The Emperor of Ocean Park*, by Stephen L. Carter, http://dir.salon.com/story/books/review/2002/06/24/carter/index.html.

4. Stephen L. Carter, "Stephen L. Carter's Summer Job," interview with Dave Welch, Powells Author Interviews, 17 July 2002, www.powells.com/authors/carter.html.

5. Amiri Baraka [LeRoi Jones], *Home: Social Essays* (Hopewell, N.J.: Ecco Press, 1998), 79. For an extended discussion, see Houston A. Baker Jr., *The Journey Back: Issues in Black Literature and Criticism* (Chicago: University of Chicago Press, 1980).

6. Justice Oliver Wendell Holmes, *Abrams v. United States* 250 U.S. 616 (1919), introduction to Justice Holmes's dissenting opinion on the *Abrams v. United States* case, http://usinfo.state.gov/usa/infousa/facts/democrac/43.htm.

7. Stephen L. Carter, *Reflections of an Affirmative Action Baby* (New York: Basic Books, 1991), 139; my emphasis.

8. Carter, *Reflections*, 171.

9. Carter, *Reflections*, 187.

10. Carter, *Reflections*, 112.

11. Quoted in Ronald Turner, "The Dangers of Misappropriation: Misusing Martin Luther King Jr.'s Legacy to Prove the Colorblind Thesis," *Michigan Journal of Race and Law* 2, no. 101 (Fall 1996): 120; emphasis in original.

12. Turner, "The Dangers of Misappropriation," 123.

13. Carter, *Reflections*, 82.

14. Carter, *Reflections*, 82.

15. Carter, *Reflections*, 6.

16. Carter, *Reflections*, 119; my emphasis. Carter's comparison of himself to Du Bois along with his characterization of them both as dissenters appears throughout the book as a recurring refrain; see, for example, 115, 122, 129, 140–141, and 252–253.

17. Carter, *Reflections*, 6.

18. Carter, *Reflections*, 60, 86, 95, 178, 216.

19. Connie Aitcheson, "Corporate America's Black Eye," from *Black Enterprise*, April 1997, reprinted at Look Smart Find Articles, http://findarticles.com/p/articles/mi_m1365/is_n9_v27/ai_19262620/pg_1.

20. Stephen L. Carter, "Just Be Nice," *Yale Alumni Magazine*, May 1988, http://www.yalealumnimagazine.com/issues/98_05/Stephen_Carter.html.

MAN WITHOUT CONNECTION: JOHN MCWHORTER

1. John McWhorter, *Losing the Race: Self-Sabotage in Black America* (New York: Free Press, 2000), 37. Hereafter cited in text as *Losing the Race*.

2. I use the word "interpellation" as it has been employed in recent years by the French scholar Louis Althusser.

3. John McWhorter, *Authentically Black: Essays for the Black Silent Majority* (New York: Gotham, 2003), xv. Hereafter cited in text as *Authentically Black*.

4. Booker T. Washington, *Up from Slavery: Three Negro Classics* (New York: Avon Books, 1969), 37–38.

5. Booker T. Washington, *Up from Slavery*, ed. William L. Andrews (New York: Norton, 1995), 23–24.

6. John McWhorter, *Winning the Race: Beyond the Crisis in Black America* (New York: Gotham Books, 2005), 199. Hereafter cited in text as *Winning the Race*.

7. Derrick Bell, *Silent Covenants: Brown v. Board of Education and the Unfulfilled Hopes for Racial Reform* (New York: Oxford University Press, 2004).

8. Nell Irving Painter, *Soul Murder and Slavery* (Waco, Tex.: Baylor University Press, 1995).

9. Amiri Baraka [LeRoi Jones], *Black Magic Poetry, 1961–1967* (New York: Bobbs-Merrill, 1969).

10. Sudhir Alladi Venkatesh, *Off the Books: The Underground Economy of the Urban Poor* (Cambridge, Mass.: Harvard University Press, 2006), xiii.

AMERICAN MYTH: ILLUSIONS OF LIBERTY AND JUSTICE FOR ALL

1. Christian Parenti, *Lockdown America: Police and Prisons in the Age of Crisis* (New York: Verso, 1999), 239.
2. James Baldwin, *Notes of a Native Son* (Boston: Beacon Press, 1984).
3. Lee A. Daniels, ed., *The State of Black America: The Complexity of Progress, 2004,* (New York: National Urban League, 2004), 59.
4. Alfred J. Sciarrino, "Civil Rights: Religion in the Public Sphere," *Howard Law Journal* 30, no. 4 (1987): 1127.
5. Daniels, ed., *State of Black America,* 67.

PRISON: COLORED BODIES, PRIVATE PROFIT

1. Michael Jacobson, *Downsizing Prisons: How to Reduce Crime and End Mass Incarceration* (New York: New York University Press, 2005), 215.
2. Christian Parenti, *Lockdown America: Police and Prisons in the Age of Crisis* (New York: Verso, 1999), 239.
3. Eric Schlosser, "The Prison-Industrial Complex," *Atlantic Monthly* (December 1998): 52; Marc Mauer, *Race to Incarcerate* (New York: New Press, 1999), 9.
4. Jerome G. Miller, *Search and Destroy: African American Males in the Criminal Justice System* (New York: Cambridge University Press, 1998), 49–50; my emphasis.
5. Schlosser, "Prison-Industrial Complex," 51–77.
6. Gustave de Beaumont and Alexis de Tocqueville, *On the Penitentiary System in the United States and Its Application in France* (1833; Carbondale: Southern Illinois University Press, 1964).
7. Miller, *Search and Destroy,* 107.
8. Alex Lichtenstein, *Twice the Work of Free Labor: The Political Economy of Convict Labor in the New South* (New York: Verso, 1996), xvii.
9. Miller, *Search and Destroy,* 81–82.
10. Schlosser, "Prison-Industrial Complex," 66; Parenti, *Lockdown America,* 217–227.
11. Francis X. Clines, "A Futuristic Prison Awaits the Hard-Core 400," *New York Times,* 17 October 1994, B10.
12. Mumia Abu-Jamal, *Live from Death Row* (Reading, Mass.: Addison-Wesley, 1995), 29–30.

CONCLUSION: WHAT THEN MUST WE DO?

1. Tom Hayden and Charles Kernaghan, "Pennies an Hour, and No Way Up," *New York Times,* 6 July 2002, A13; Benjamin Powell and David Skarbek, "Sweatshops and Third World Living Standards: Are the Jobs Worth the Sweat?" Independent Institute Working Paper 53 (27 September 2004): 5; Jay R. Mandle, *Globalization and the Poor* (New York: Cambridge University Press, 2003), 108.
2. Haki R. Madhubuti, "Fear," in *Run Toward Fear: New Poems and a Poet's Handbook* (Chicago: Third World Press, 2004).

Abu-Jamal, Mumia. *Live from Death Row.* Reading, Mass.: Addison-Wesley, 1995.

Aitcheson, Connie. "Corporate America's Black Eye." From *Black Enterprise*, April 1997. Reprinted at Look Smart Find Articles, http://findarticles.com/p/articles/mi_m1365/is_n9_v27/ai_19262620/pg_1.

Baker, Houston A., Jr. *Black Studies, Rap, and the Academy.* Chicago: University of Chicago Press, 1993.

——. *The Journey Back: Issues in Black Literature and Criticism.* Chicago: University of Chicago Press, 1980.

——. *Long Black Song: Essays in Black American Literature and Culture.* Charlottesville: University Press of Virginia, 1972.

Baldwin, James. "Everybody's Protest Novel." *Notes of a Native Son.* Boston: Beacon Press, 1984. 13–23.

——. *The Fire Next Time.* New York: Vintage International, 1993.

——. *No Name on the Street.* New York: Dial, 1972.

Baraka, Amiri [LeRoi Jones]. *Black Magic Poetry, 1961–1967.* New York: Bobbs-Merrill, 1969.

——. *Home: Social Essays.* Hopewell, N.J.: Ecco Press, 1998.

Beaumont, Gustave de, and Alexis de Tocqueville. *On the Penitentiary System in the United States and Its Application in France.* 1833. Carbondale: Southern Illinois University Press, 1964.

Bell, Derrick. *Silent Covenants:* Brown v. Board of Education *and the Unfulfilled Hopes for Racial Reform.* New York: Oxford University Press, 2004.

Bérubé, Michael. "Public Academy." *New Yorker* (9 January 1995): 73–80.

——. *Public Access: Literary Theory and American Cultural Politics.* New York: Verso, 1994.

"Booker T. Washington." In *Norton Anthology of African American Literature*, ed. Henry Louis Gates Jr. and Nellie Y. McKay, 488–521. New York: Norton, 1997.

Branch, Taylor. *Parting the Waters: America in the King Years, 1954–63.* New York: Simon and Schuster, 1988.

Brown, Sterling. "Old Lem." Oldpoetry.com Poetry Archives. www.oldpoetry.com/opoem/36386.

Burke, Edmund. *Reflections on the Revolution in France: The Portable Conservative Reader*, ed. Russell Kirk, 7–35. New York: Viking Press, 1982.

Burns, Stewart. *To the Mountaintop: Martin Luther King Jr.'s Sacred Mission to Save America, 1955–1968*. New York: HarperSanFrancisco/Harper Collins, 2004.

Calloway. "I Wanna Be Rich." Perf. Reginald and Vincent Calloway. *All the Way*. Sony, 1990.

Carter, Stephen L. "Just Be Nice." *Yale Alumni Magazine*, May 1988. http://www.yale-lumnimagazine.com/issues/98_05/Stephen_Carter.html.

——. *Reflections of an Affirmative Action Baby*. New York: Basic, 1991.

——. "Stephen L. Carter's Summer Job." Interview with Dave Welch. 17 July 2002. Powells Author Interviews. www.powells.com/authors/carter.html.

Clines, Francis X. "A Futuristic Prison Awaits the Hard-Core 400." *New York Times*, 17 October 1994.

Cone, James H. "Martin Luther King, Jr., and the Third World." In *We Shall Overcome: Martin Luther King, Jr., and the Black Freedom Struggle*, ed. Peter J. Albert and Ronald Hoffman, 197–221. New York: Pantheon, 1990.

Cosby, William H., Jr. "An Integration of the Visual Media via 'Fat Albert and the Cosby Kids' into the Elementary School Curriculum as a Teaching Aid and Vehicle to Achieve Increased Learning." EdD diss., University of Massachusetts, 1976.

Daniels, Lee A., ed. *The State of Black America: The Complexity of Progress, 2004*. New York: National Urban League, 2004.

Dawkins, Richard. *The God Delusion*. New York: Houston Mifflin, 2006.

Diawara, Manthia. "Malcolm X and the Black Public Sphere: Conversionists Versus Culturalists." In *The Black Public Sphere*, ed. Black Public Sphere Collective, 39–52. Chicago: University of Chicago Press, 1995.

Dorrien, Gary. *The Neoconservative Mind: Politics, Culture, and the War of Ideology*. Philadelphia: Temple University Press, 1993.

Du Bois, W.E.B. *Dusk of Dawn: An Essay Toward an Autobiography of a Race Concept*. New York: Schocken, 1968.

——. *The Souls of Black Folk: Three Negro Classics*. New York: Avon, 1969.

Dunbar, Paul Laurence. *Selected Poems*. New York: Penguin, 2004.

Dyson, Michael Eric. *I May Not Get There with You: The True Martin Luther King, Jr.* New York: Free Press, 2000.

——. *The Michael Eric Dyson Reader*. New York: Basic Civitas, 2004.

Eisenhower, Dwight D. "Military-Industrial Complex Speech, Dwight D. Eisenhower, 1961." The Avalon Project at Yale Law School. www.yale.edu/lawweb/avalon/presiden/speeches/eisenhower001.htm.

Ellison, Ralph. *Shadow and Act*. New York: Vintage/Random House, 1964.

Executive Committee of the Third Communist International. "The 1930 Comintern Resolution on the Negro Question in the United States." In *The 1928 and 1930 Comintern Resolutions on the Black National Question in the United States*. Washington, D.C.: Revolutionary Review Press, 1975. From Marx to Mao. 1998. Ed. David J. Romagnolo. www.marx2mao.com/Other/CR75.html.

Eyes on the Prize. American Experience. PBS. 1987.

Ferlinghetti, Lawrence. *A Coney Island of the Mind.* New York: New Directions, 1958.

Foner, Eric. *Reconstruction: America's Unfinished Revolution, 1863–1877.* New York: Perennial/Harper & Row, 1988.

Gates, Henry Louis, Jr. "Breaking the Silence." *New York Times.* www.nytimes.com/2004/08/01/opinion/01gates.html.

——. *Colored People: A Memoir.* New York: Knopf, 1994.

Gates, Henry Louis, Jr., and Nellie Y. McKay, eds. *Norton Anthology of African American Literature.* New York: Norton, 1997.

Gates, Henry Louis, Jr., and Cornel West. *The Future of the Race.* New York: Knopf, 1996.

Giddings, Paula. *When and Where I Enter: The Impact of Black Women on Race and Sex in America.* Rev. ed. New York: Quill-William Morrow, 1996.

Hansen, Suzy. Review of *The Emperor of Ocean Park*, by Stephen L. Carter. http://dir.salon.com/story/books/review/2002/06/24/carter/index.html.

Harlow, Jennifer N. "The Compromise of 1877." In United States of America Chronology. Ed. David Koeller. WebChron Project. www.thenagain.info/WebChron/USA/1877Comp.html.

Harris, Joel Chandler. "How Mr. Rabbit Was Too Sharp." In *Norton Anthology of African American Literature*, ed. Henry Louis Gates Jr. and Nellie Y. McKay, 121–123. New York: Norton, 1997.

——. "The Wonderful Tar-Baby Story." In *Norton Anthology of African American Literature*, ed. Henry Louis Gates Jr. and Nellie Y. McKay, 120–121. New York: Norton, 1997.

Harris, Robert. "The Rise of the Black Middle Class." *The World and I.* www.worldandi.com/public/1999/February/middle.cfm.

Hayden, Tom, and Charles Kernaghan. "Pennies an Hour, and No Way Up." *New York Times*, 6 July 2002.

Hayek, F.A. "Why I Am Not a Conservative." LewRockwell.com. www.lewrockwell.com/orig6/hayek1.html. From *The Constitution of Liberty.* Chicago: University of Chicago Press, 1960.

Himmelfarb, Dan. "Conservative Splits." In *Conservatism in America since 1930*, ed. Gregory L. Schneider, 383–394. New York: New York University Press, 2003.

Holmes, Justice Oliver Wendell. *Abrams v. United States.* 250 U.S. 616 (1919). Introduction to Justice Holmes' Dissenting Opinion on the *Abrams v. United States* Case. http://usinfo.state.gov/usa/infousa/facts/democrac/43.htm.

Irons, Peter. *Jim Crow's Children: The Broken Promise of the Brown Decision.* New York: Penguin, 2002.

Jacobson, Michael. *Downsizing Prisons: How to Reduce Crime and End Mass Incarceration.* New York: New York University Press, 2005.

James, Joy, ed. *States of Confinement.* New York: St. Martin's Press, 2000.

Janken, Kenneth Robert. *Rayford W. Logan and the Dilemma of the African-American Intellectual.* Amherst: University of Massachusetts Press, 1993.

Jefferson, Thomas. *Notes on the State of Virginia*. Ed. William Peden. Chapel Hill, N.C.: Institute of Early American History and Culture, 1955.

Jenkins, Carol, and Elizabeth Gardner Hines. *Black Titan: A. G. Gaston and the Making of a Black American Millionaire*. New York: One World-Ballantine, 2004.

King, Martin Luther, Jr. *A Testament of Hope: The Essential Writings of Martin Luther King, Jr.* Ed. James Melvin Washington. San Francisco: Harper & Row, 1986.

——. *Where Do We Go from Here: Chaos or Community?* New York: Harper & Row, 1967.

Kristol, Irving. *Neoconservatism: The Autobiography of an Idea*. New York: Free Press, 1995.

Landry, Bart. *The New Black Middle Class*. Berkeley: University of California Press, 1987.

Lichtenstein, Alex. *Twice the Work of Free Labor: The Political Economy of Convict Labor in the New South*. New York: Verso, 1996.

Madhubuti, Haki. Address. Black Writers Conference. Howard University Institute for the Arts and Humanities, 1978.

——. *Run Toward Fear: New Poems and a Poet's Handbook*. Chicago: Third World Press, 2004.

Makepeace, Anne. "Edward Curtis: Dialogue." *American Masters*. "Did He Show Us What Was Really Happening?" www.thirteen.org/americanmasters/curtis/show_us_about.html.

Mandle, Jay R. *Globalization and the Poor*. New York: Cambridge University Press, 2003.

Mauer, Marc. *Race to Incarcerate*. New York: New Press, 1999.

McWhorter, Diane. *Carry Me Home: Birmingham, Alabama: The Climactic Battle of the Civil Rights Revolution*. New York: Touchstone-Simon & Schuster, 2001.

McWhorter, John. *Authentically Black: Essays for the Black Silent Majority*. New York: Gotham, 2003.

——. *Losing the Race: Self-Sabotage in Black America*. New York: Free Press, 2000.

——. *Winning the Race: Beyond the Crisis in Black America*. New York: Gotham, 2005.

"Mess at U. Mass." March 17, 1975. Time in Partnership with CNN. www.time.com/time/magazine/article/0,9171,912994-1,00.html.

Miller, Jerome G. *Search and Destroy: African American Males in the Criminal Justice System*. New York: Cambridge University Press, 1998.

Moore, Marianne. *Complete Poems*. New York: Penguin, 1994.

"Neocon 101." 2004. Christian Science Monitor Online. 17 November 2004. www.csmonitor.com/specials/neocon/neocon101.html.

North, Gary. "An Introduction to Neoconservatism." 10 June 2003. LewRockwell.com. 17 November 2004. www.lewrockwell.com/north/north180.html.

Painter, Nell Irving. *Soul Murder and Slavery*. Waco, Tex.: Baylor University Press, 1995.

Parenti, Christian. *Lockdown America: Police and Prisons in the Age of Crisis*. New York: Verso, 1999.

Patterson, Orlando. "The Paradox of Integration." *New Republic* (6 November 1995): 24–27.

Podhoretz, Norman. "My Negro Problem—And Ours." *Commentary* 35 (February 1963): 93–101.

Posner, Richard A. *Public Intellectuals: A Study of Decline.* Cambridge, Mass.: Harvard University Press, 2001.

Powell, Benjamin, and David Skarbek. "Sweatshops and Third World Living Standards: Are the Jobs Worth the Sweat?" Independent Institute Working Paper 53 (27 Sept. 2004).

Ralph, James R. *Northern Protest: Martin Luther King, Jr., Chicago, and the Civil Rights Movement.* Cambridge, Mass.: Harvard University Press, 1993.

Reeves, Thomas. "Open Admissions at Parkside." History News Network. George Mason University. http://hnn.us/articles/1020.html.

Reilly, Donald. Cartoon. *New Yorker* (3 June 1974).

Report of the National Advisory Commission on Civil Disorders. New York: Bantam Books, 1968.

Rose, Tricia. *Black Noise: Rap Music and Black Culture in Contemporary America.* Hanover, N.H.: Wesleyan University Press, 1994.

Schiraldi, Vincent. "Will the Real John Dilulio Please Stand Up." Common Dreams. org News Center. Published on Monday, February 21, 2001, in the *Washington Post.* www.commondreams.org/views01/0205-02.htm.

Schlosser, Eric. "The Prison-Industrial Complex." *Atlantic Monthly* (December 1998): 51–77.

Schuyler, George S. *Black and Conservative: The Autobiography of George S. Schuyler.* New Rochelle, N.Y.: Arlington House, 1966.

Sciarrino, Alfred J. "Civil Rights: Religion in the Public Sphere." *Howard Law Journal* 30, no. 4 (1987): 1127–1139.

Smith, Jeanne Rosier. *Writing Tricksters: Mythic Gambols in American Ethnic Fiction.* Berkeley: University of California Press, 1997.

Steele, Shelby. *The Content of Our Character: A New Vision of Race in America.* New York: Harper Perennial, 1990.

——. "Under the Skin: Shelby Steele on Race in America." Uncommon Knowledge. 2000–2001. www.hoover.org/publications/digest/3467461.html.

——. *White Guilt: How Blacks and Whites Together Destroyed the Promise of the Civil Rights Era.* New York: HarperCollins, 2006.

Stock, Barbara. "Bill Cosby and Clarence Thomas: The New Odd Couple?" 6 July 2004. IntellectualConservative.com. www.intellectualconservative.com/article3581.html.

Turner, Ronald. "The Dangers of Misappropriation: Misusing Martin Luther King Jr.'s Legacy to Prove the Colorblind Thesis." *Michigan Journal of Race and Law* 2, no. 101 (Fall 1996): 101–130.

Venkatesh, Sudhir Alladi. *Off the Books: The Underground Economy of the Urban Poor.* Cambridge, Mass.: Harvard University Press, 2006.

Washington, Booker T. "Atlanta Exposition Address." In *Booker T. Washington Papers*, vol. 3, ed. Louis Harlan, 583–587. Urbana: University of Illinois Press, 1974.

——. *Up from Slavery.* Ed. William L. Andrews. New York: Norton, 1995.

——. *Up from Slavery: Three Negro Classics.* New York: Avon, 1969.

West, Cornel. *Race Matters.* New York: Vintage, 2001.

Westbrook, Robert. "The Counter Intelligentsia: How Neoconservatism Lived and Died." *Lingua Franca* 6, no. 7 (Nov. 1996): 65–71.

Williams, Juan. *Enough: The Phony Leaders, Dead-End Movements, and Culture of Failure That Are Undermining Black America—and What We Can Do about It.* New York: Crown, 2006.

Wilson, William Julius. *When Work Disappears: The World of the New Urban Poor.* New York: Knopf, 1996.

Wohlgelernter, Elli. Irving Kristol and Neoconservatism. "The Godfather of Conservatism." Free Republic.com. www.freerepublic.com/forum/a3830066a52a3.htm. From the *Jerusalem Post*, 25 June 1999.

Wolfe, Alan. "The New Pamphleteers." *New York Times Book Review* (11 July 2004): 12–13.

betrayal, xi–xiii, xvii–xviii, 15, 51, 94, 115,
    186, 190, 201–203
Between God and Gangsta Rap (Dyson),
    83–85
Bevel, James, 31–32, 34
biology, evolutionary, 186–187
Birmingham Civil Rights campaign,
    16–33; "Letter from a Birmingham
    Jail," 25–28, 31, 33
Black Atlantic, The (Gilroy), 161
blackface minstrelsy, 158–159
black intelligentsia, xvii, 79. *See also* black
    public intellectuals
black majority, 5–8, 131–132; black middle
    class's rejection of, 91–92; Black Power
    as voice of, 38; "disappearance" of, 42,
    191, 198; global nature of, 11–12; King's
    alliance with, xi–xii, 36, 38–39, 133,
    160, 200–201; lack of wealth, 199–200;
    leadership and, 22–23
black mind, concept of, 137, 138–139, 141–142
black nationalism, 34–37, 139; militarism
    of, 40–41
Black Noise (Rose), 85
Black Panther Party, 35, 40, 182
black party line, 160, 163–165, 167–169, 184
Black Power, xiii, xiv–xv, 35–38; accom-
    plishments of, 40, 139–140; global
    influence of, 160–161; neoconservative
    denunciation of, 132, 136–140, 160; po-
    licing against, 40–41
Black Power (Carmichael and Hamilton),
    35
black public intellectuals: categories of,
    xi–xii; emergence of, 79–80; evidence,
    lack of, 83, 135, 175–176, 180, 193, 199;
    first wave of (1980s), 94–96; ideo-
    logical precursors, xv–xvi, 79, 181–183;
    intellectual shallowness, 80–84,
    124, 146–147, 152, 175–176, 180–181;
    as pamphleteers, 80–84, 91, 138; as
    self-serving, 15, 177–179, 187–188. *See
    also* centrist black public intellectu-

als; neoconservative black public
    intellectuals
"Black Striving in a Twilight Civilization"
    (West), 121–125
black studies programs, 40, 95, 118–120,
    140; British, 160–161
Black Studies, Rap, and the Academy
    (Baker), 87
black/white alliance, demise of, 48–49
blues people, 9
body, black, 28; white fears projected
    onto, 65–66, 137; white violence
    against, 47–48. *See also* prison-indus-
    trial complex
Boyz in the Hood, 88
British black cultural studies, 160–161
Brown, H. "Rap," 35
Brown, Sterling, 59
Brown v. Board of Education, 25, 65, 91,
    99, 189
Bryce-Laporte, Roy, 118, 119
Burke, Edmund, 129–131
Burns, Stewart, 18, 21
Bush, George Herbert Walker, 151–152,
    184; Willie Horton campaign, 62, 297
Bush, George W., 149–150, 152, 215

Carmichael, Stokely (Kwame Toure), 35,
    48
Carter, Bunchy, 41
Carter, Stephen, 69–70, 159–172; affirma-
    tive action, opposition to, 167–168;
    awareness of effects of writing,
    159–160; First Amendment, view of,
    161–167, 169–171; intellectual, view of,
    169–170; natural black aristocrat, doc-
    trine of, 163–165, 171
Carville, James, 151
censorship, 162
center: economics of, 105–109; as no posi-
    tion, 104–105
centrist black public intellectuals, xi–xii,
    xv, 94, 99–101; avoidance of policy

Abbott, Louis, 36–37
Abernathy, Ralph, 21, 31
Abrams v. United States, 163
abstraction, 161
Abu-Jamal, Mumia, 210
affirmative action, 23, 38, 75, 77, 145, 153; as affront to black
    aristocracy, 163–164, 171; neoconservative view of,
    60, 62–63, 132–138, 145–146, 152, 163–164; successes of,
    167–168
agoraphobia, 2, 5, 10, 145
Aid for Dependent Children, 62
Albany Civil Rights campaign, 19–20
Alexander, Elizabeth, 74
allegory, as strategy, 134–139, 141, 169, 199
Amendments to the Constitution: Fifteenth, 76–77, 177;
    First, 161–167, 170–171
American Enterprise Institute, 61
American way, metaphor of, 59–60
Amos 'n' Andy, 109, 112–114
anti-Communism, 54–55
Anti-Drug Abuse Act of 1986, 206
anti-intellectualism, 176
Apology (Plato), 26
Are Prisons Obsolete? (Davis), 211
aristocracy, black, 163–165, 171
Army of Northern Virginia, 50
Asian Americans, 135
assimilation, 68, 91–93
audience, 80, 90–91
Authentically Black (McWhorter), 174, 195
autobiography, 10–12
Autobiography of an Ex-Colored Man, The (Johnson), 91
Autobiography of Malcolm X (Diawara), 143

backlash, 45–46
"Backlash Blues" (Simone), 45
Baker's Market, 1–2, 4, 8
Baldwin, James, 142, 199; *The Fire Next Time*, 65–66; *Go
    Tell It on the Mountain*, 82; *Notes of a Native Son*, 51
Baraka, Amiri, 9, 49, 162, 192
behaviorism, 97, 100–101, 104–105, 117–118, 214
Benito Cereno (Melville), 66
Bérubé, Michael, 60, 79

issues, 116–117; behaviorism vs. struc-
turalism debate, 97, 100–105, 117–118;
Civil Rights movement, view of,
105, 108, 110–114, 125; liberalism, view
of, 117, 120. *See also* Dyson, Michael
Eric; Gates, Henry Louis, Jr.; West,
Cornel
Chicago, 36–37
Chicago Defender, 36–37
Chicago liberation campaign, 39
"Chrismus on the Plantation" (Dunbar),
113–114
Christian justice, 25–26
Chuck D, 87
citizenship, second-class, as phrase, 3, 13
City College of New York (CCNY),
52–53
civil disobedience, 18–19
civil obedience, 18
Civil Rights Act of 1964, 33, 74–75, 135–137,
176
Civil Rights movement: Birmingham
Civil Rights campaign, 16–33; centrist
black view of, 105, 108, 110–114, 125;
neoconservative black view of, 48–49,
63, 69, 132–137, 145, 147–148, 152, 161,
169, 176, 209; incarceration as strategy
of, 16–18; strategies and techniques,
21–22, 72; white view of, 72, 76, 193. *See
also* black nationalism; Black Power;
King, Martin Luther, Jr.
Clinton, William Jefferson, 146, 149, 151
codes of conduct, 146–147
colorblindness, doctrine of, 68, 69
Colored People (Gates), 108–116, 119
Coltrane, John, 124
Columbian Orator, The, 174
Come Hell or High Water (Dyson), 93–94
Commentary, 58
confession, rhetoric of, 146
Connor, Theophilus Eugene "Bull," 17, 19,
25, 31, 32
consciousness, black, 181–183

conservatism: origins of, 129–131; superiority, belief in, 131–132, 163. *See also*
centrist black public intellectuals;
neoconservatism; neoconservative
black public intellectuals
Constitution, U.S., 76, 77, 160–163
Content of Our Character, The (Steele),
128–129, 132–145; McWhorter's epiphany and, 174, 176
conversionist discourses, 143
convict leasing, 209
corporate sector, 180
Corrections Corporation of America
(CCA), 208–209
Cosby, Bill, 12, 91, 99–100, 155
Cosby Show of assimilators, 92
counterculture, sixties, 181–183, 192
credit, 6–7
criminality, alleged as innate, 49, 59, 135,
151, 220n. 2
critique, autobiography as platform for,
11–12
Cruse, Harold, xvii
cultural conflict, 77
culture, black, 142–143
culture wars, 58
Curtis, Edward, 106–107, 125, 134

Davis, Angela, 210–211
Dawkins, Richard, 186
DeChabert, Glen, 119, 120–121
democracy, demise of, 214
Democratic National Convention, 99
deregulation, 85, 151
Diawara, Manthia, 143
Dickens, Charles, 117–118
DiIulio, John, 221n. 17
disorder, politics of, 136–137
domestic Marshall Plan, 23, 77
Dorrien, Gary, 68–69
Douglass, Frederick, 114, 174, 192, 207
Downsizing Prisons (Jacobson), 204
drug laws, 151, 205, 221n. 17

drum major metaphor, 29–30

Du Bois, W. E. B., xii, 10–11, 15, 30, 79, 169; in *The Future of the Race*, 116–117, 121–122; "Of the Death of the First Born," 122–123; Victorian ideals of, 123–124

Dunbar, Paul Laurence, 105, 113–114

Dusk of Dawn: An Essay Toward an Autobiography of a Race Concept (Du Bois), 10–11

Dyson, Michael Eric, 80–85, 96; *Come Hell or High Water*, 93–94; *Between God and Gangsta Rap*, 83–85; *I May Not Get There with You: The True Martin Luther King, Jr.*, 80, 89–91; *Is Bill Cosby Right?*, 91

Ebonics/vernacular, 100

economic focus of neoconservatism, 72–76, 144–145, 152–153, 159, 179–180

economy, 85, 102–103, 194

education: *Brown v. Board of Education*, 25, 65, 91, 99, 189; failures of, 77–78, 151, 183–184; inner-city realities, 100–101; international competitiveness, 183–184; racial quotas, 52–53

Eisenhower, Dwight David, 146

Elijah Muhammad, 34, 35

elite blacks, 9, 20, 34; as aristocracy, 163–165, 171

Elkins, Stanley, 142

Ellison, Ralph, 47, 53, 109, 135, 169

Emancipation Proclamation (1863), 135, 177

Emperor of Ocean Park, The (Carter), 159

England, response to French Revolution, 129–130

Enlightenment ideals, 122–123

entertainment, blacks as, 73–74, 143

Equal Employment Opportunity Commission, 74–75

estates, balance of, 129–130

ethnic cleansing metaphor, 64

eugenics, rhetoric of, 137, 141, 164

Executive Order 11246, 63, 77

Eyes on the Prize (movie), 134

family, as model for society, 130

family, black, neoconservative view of, 61–62

Fanon, Frantz, 4

Faubus, Orville, 198

Ferlinghetti, Lawrence, 59

films, 191

Fire Next Time, The (Baldwin), 65–66

fitness, as term, 64

Florence, Colorado prison, 209–210

Florida A&M, 29–30

forbearance, 32, 33

forty acres and a mule syndrome (FAMS), 50–51, 58, 61, 68

Forty-Million-Dollar Slaves (Rhoden), 73

Foucault, Michel, 93

freedom: as economic, 75; First Amendment and, 161–167; linked to white supremacy, 147–149

freedom songs, 25, 29, 46

Freedom Summer (1964), 76

French Revolution, 129

"Fuck tha Police" (NWA), 88

Future of the Race, The (Gates and West), 108, 116–125; "Black Striving in a Twilight Civilization," 121–125

gangsta rap, 83–85, 87–90

"Gangsta Rap and American Culture" (Dyson), 84

Gaston, Arthur G., 20

Gates, Henry Louis, Jr., 80, 87, 94, 100; autobiographical essay, 119–121; *Colored People*, 108–116, 119; *The Future of the Race* (with West), 108, 116–125; "W. E. B. Du Bois and the Talented Tenth," 116

George, Nelson, 86

ghettos, 1–2; King moves to, 39; North and West, 36–37; white implication in, 10

Gilroy, Paul, 161
Gissing, George, 80
global era, King's view of, 34, 36, 39
globalization, 85, 102–103, 184, 213
global nature of black majority, 11–12
good life, black, 142–143, 164–165
good man, as calling, 8–9, 14
goodwill, white pretense to, 65–66
Go Tell It on the Mountain (Baldwin), 82
governmentality, 93–94
Graves, Earl, 78
Great Society, 63–64
Greenwood, Mississippi, 35

Hamilton, Charles, 35
Harlem Renaissance, xvii
Harper, Michael, 47
Harrington, Michael, xv, 55
Harris, Joel Chandler, 188
Hartford, Huntington, 58
hate speech, 166–167
Hayek, F. A., 132
hip-hop, 74, 83–85
Holmes, Oliver Wendell, 163
Holocaust, 182
Hoover, J. Edgar, 40, 182
Hoover Institution, 128
Horton, Willie, 62, 207
House Un-American Activities Committee, 55, 74
Huggins, John, 41
Hughes, Cathy, 78
Hughes, Langston, xiii, 45

ideology, white, 46–48, 51–52
I May Not Get There with You: The True Martin Luther King, Jr. (Dyson), 80, 89–91
immigration, myth of, 37–38
Indiana, 188–190
Indians, American, 106–107
individualism, 169
institutions, black, 22–23, 78

intellectual, Carter's view, 169–170
intellectual shallowness, 80–84, 124, 146–147, 152, 175–176, 180–181
internships, 118–119
Invisible Man (Ellison), 109
Iraq wars, 77, 151–152
Irons, Peter, 100–102
Is Bill Cosby Right? (Dyson), 91

Jackson, Jesse, 125
Jacobson, Michael, 204
jazz, 87
Jefferson, Thomas, 130–131
Jim Crow's Children: The Broken Promise of the Brown Decision (Irons), 100–102
Johnson, Andrew, 50, 51
Johnson, James Weldon, 91
Johnson, Lyndon, 63, 77
Jordan, Michael, 73
justice, 26–27, 131, 197–198; Christian, 25–26; King's demands for, xvii, 22, 29–30, 43, 152, 168, 186
Justice Department, 31

Karenga, Ron, 41
Katrina disaster, 93–94, 150
Kennedy, Robert F., 31
Kerner Commission, 10
Kerr, Clark, 216
Kerry, John, 51
King, Martin Luther, Jr., 195–196, 202; as antiwar partisan, 56; assassination of, xiii, 42–43; Birmingham Civil Rights campaign and, 16, 21; black majority, alliance with, xi–xii, 36, 38–39, 133, 168, 200–201; on black nationalism, 35; Carter's view of, 168; as Christian martyr, xv, 72, 132–134; demands for world justice, xvii, 152, 186; on effects of nonviolent action, 33–34; eulogy, suggestions for, 29; gangsta rappers equated with, 89–91; global era, view of, 34, 36, 39; government,

King, Martin Luther, Jr. (*continued*)
  relationship to, 94; "I Have a Dream"
  speech, xiv–xv, 41, 44–45, 132–133, 161;
  as intellectual, 152; "Letter from a
  Birmingham Jail," 25–28, 31, 33; moves
  to public housing, 39; Nobel Peace
  Prize awarded to, 22; on nonviolent
  action, 26–28, 31; peaceful life denied
  to, 42–44; plans for arrest, 16; public
  speaking and writing style, 28–29; as
  structuralist, 97; as *Time* Man of the
  Year, 19; *Where Do We Go from Here:
  Chaos or Community*, 39, 41–42, 76–78;
  on white liberals, 49
King, Rodney, 91, 153–154, 205–206
Kors, Charles Alan, 96
Kristol, Irving, 52–54, 57, 60–61, 96

Landry, Bart, 75
language, manipulation of, 157–158
law, idealized, 176–177, 181
leadership, black, 29, 72; black public and,
  22–23; spirit and, 30–31
"Letter from a Birmingham Jail" (King),
  25–28, 31, 33
liberalism, 117, 120
Lichtenstein, Alex, 207
Little Africa (Louisville, Kentucky), 1–15
Little Africa reality, 191
Live from Death Row (Abu-Jamal), 210
local communities, 216
*Losing the Race: Self-Sabotage in Black
  America* (McWhorter), 173–179
lottery tickets, 103
Louisville, Kentucky, 1–15
love, prescription of, 65, 67

Macolm X, 143
Madhubuti, Haki, 69, 215–216
Madison, James, 161
Malcolm X, 34, 143, 182
Marable, Manning, 211
March Against Fear, 35

March on Washington (1963), 33, 44, 77
Marley, Bob, 25
McCarthy, Joseph, 55
McCollum, Bill, 221n. 17
McWhorter, John, xv, 12, 173–196; biologism of, 186–187; *Losing the Race:
  Self-Sabotage in Black America*, 173–179;
  progress-through-immigration myth,
  189–190; victimology, discourse of,
  173–176; *Winning the Race*, 179–195
media, 35, 56, 77, 79, 94; Civil Rights
  movement coverage, 19–21, 31
Meet the Press, 90
Melville, Herman, 66
memes, cultural, 186–187, 189
Memphis sanitation workers' strike, xi,
  xiii, 35–36
men, black, pathology attributed to, 62
mental illness, allegations of, 155
Meredith, James, 35
middle class, black, 7, 40, 75, 78, 91–92, 198
middle class, white, 7
militarism, black nationalism and, 40–41
military-industrial complex, 208
Miller, Jerome G., 205, 207
Milton, John, 136
ministers, black, 82
miscegenation, 68
Miss Evers' Boys (film), 191
modernism, black, 36–37
Modern Language Association of America, 215
Mohammad, Khalid Abdul, 166
Montgomery bus boycott, 18–19
Montgomery Improvement Association
  (MIA), 18
moral authority, 146–150
moral law, 26–27
Morehouse University, 30
Morrison, Toni, 124, 140
Moynihan, Daniel Patrick, 61–64
My Bondage and My Freedom (Douglass),
  114

"My Negro Problem—and Ours" (Pod-horetz), 65–68
myths, xii, 197–203; progress-through-im-migration, 189–190

Narrative of the Life of Frederick Douglass: An American Slave (Douglass), 174
National Association of Scholars (NAS), 96
National Interest, The, 61
National Public Health Service, 191
National Urban League, 23, 199–200
Nation of Islam, 34, 166
Native Son (Wright), 36–37
nature, state and, 129–130
Neal, Mark Anthony, 86
Negro Family, The: The Case for National Action (Moynihan), 61–62
neoconservatism, xv–xvi; abandonment of black America by white allies, 51–52; affirmative action, view of, 60, 62–63, 132–138, 145–146, 152, 163–164; as com-munity, 158; Constitution, view of, 161–163; disorder, politics of, 136–137; economic focus of, 72–76, 144–145, 152–153, 159, 179–180; forty acres and a mule syndrome (FAMS), 50–51, 58, 61, 68; historical background of, 48, 54–55, 63; prison-industrial complex and, 58–59; race politics and, 61–65, 72–73. *See also* conservatism
neoconservative, as label, 55–56
neoconservative black public intellectu-als, xi–xii, xv, 12, 69, 128–129; allegory as strategy, 134–139, 141, 169; black family, view of, 61–62; black party line, view of, 160, 163–165, 167–169, 184; Civil Rights movement, view of, 128, 134–138, 145–148, 168–170, 176–177; conversionist discourses, 143; oppression, view of, 147–148; as race-aversive, 72–73; rhetorical strate-gies of, 133; slavery, view of, 147–148,

178–179, 191–192; social reform, view of, 149–151
neo-Reconstructionism, 188
new class, 60
New Grub Street (Gissing), 80
new New York intellectuals, 80
"New Pamphleteers, The" (*New York Times Book Review*), 81
nigger, white use of term, 146
nihilism, 82–83
nonviolent action, 21–22, 26–28, 31
North, Gary, 61
North American Indian, The (Curtis), 106–107
North and West, urban dwellers in, 36–37
North Lawndale, Chicago, 102–103
Notes of a Native Son (Baldwin), 51
Notes on the State of Virginia (Jefferson), 130–131
NWA (Niggaz with Attitude), 88

Obama, Barack, 83, 99–100, 200
O'Connor, Sandra Day, 153
Off the Books (Venkatesh), 194
"Old Lem" (Brown), 59
Olin Foundation, 60, 61
oppression, neoconservative black view of, 147–148
Osucha, Eden, 61
ownership, 130

Page, Thomas Nelson, 188
Painter, Nell Irving, 191
pamphleteers, black intellectuals as, 80–84, 91
Paradise Lost (Milton), 136
Parenti, Christian, 198–199, 220n. 2
Parks, Rosa, 16–17
pathology: activism as, 120, 132, 137–143, 145, 173, 214; American, 50
patriotism, 189
Patterson, Orlando, 78
Pax Americana, 64

periodicals, 60
Plantation School, 188
Plato, 26
Plessy, Homer, 153
Plessy v. Ferguson, 153
Podhoretz, Norman: black violence against, 66–67; "My Negro Problem—and Ours," 65–68
police, 40–41, 153–154, 199–200
Posner, Richard, 95
poverty: culture of, 2–3, 192–193; feminization of, 62
prior restraint, 162
prison, 16–19; ghettos as, 37; as public arena, 24; testimonies from, 25–27; women, incarceration of, 185, 204
prison-industrial complex, 9, 42, 151, 203–212; demographics, 52, 204; historical context, 206–207; mandatory sentencing, 151, 206, 221n. 17; neoconservative interest in, 58–59; private enterprise and, 208–211, 216; war on drugs and, 206–208, 221n. 17
Pritchett, Laurie, 19–20
privatization, 208–211, 216
professional groups, separatist, 40
Project C. *See* Birmingham Civil Rights campaign
property, 129–130
public activism, black studies departments and, 118–120
Public Enemy, 87
Public Intellectuals: A Study in Decline (Posner), 95

quarter educated, metaphor of, 80

race, dismissal of, xii–xiv, 23, 25
race man, King as, xi–xii, 23
Race Matters (West), 80, 82–83
race people, 9
race politics, neoconservatives and, 61–65
racial quotas, 52–53

Rainbow/PUSH Coalition & Citizenship Education Fund, 99
Ralph, James, 38
Rap Attack: African Jive to New York Hip Hop (Toop), 86
rap music: gangsta rap, 83–85, 87–90; hip-hop, 74, 83–85; mythology in, 84–87; as news, 85, 87, 88; origins of hip-hop, 85–87
Reagan/Bush compromise, 117, 151, 184–185, 203, 205
Reagon, Bernice Johnson, 25
Red Cross Hospital (Louisville), 8–9
Redding, Jay Saunders, 40
Reed, Adolph, xvii
Reflections of an Affirmative Action Baby (Carter), 159–172
Reflections on the Recent Revolution in France (Burke), 129–131
reparations, 23, 145
Republican Party, 59
Republican response to Civil Rights movement, 42
restoration, politics of, 50
results, equality of, 63
reverse racism, 63, 137
Rhoden, William C., 73
Rice, Condoleezza, 200
riots, 34, 38
Robeson, Paul, 74
Robinson, Armstead, 119, 120–121
Robinson, Jackie, 74
Rock, Chris, 200
Rockefeller drug laws, 151, 205, 221n. 17
Rock Hill, South Carolina, 24
Rose, Tricia, 85
Rosenberg, Julius, 55
Run Toward Fear (Madhubuti), 216
Rustin, Bayard, 43

Schiraldi, Vincent, 221n. 17
schizophrenia, as term, 155
Schuyler, George, 69, 127–128

SCOPE, 128
Seale, Bobby, 162
second-class citizenship, as phrase, 3, 13
self-examination, white refusal of, 65
self-help networks, 6–9
September 11, 2001, attacks, 214
service economy, 85
Sherman, William Tecumseh, 50
Shuttlesworth, Fred, 16
Simone, Nina, 45
Simpson, O. J., 152–153
slave narratives, 174, 175
slavery, 9, 50, 137; blacks as property, 129,
    130; neoconservative black view of,
    147–148, 178–179, 191–192
Slavery (Elkins), 142
Smith, Jeanne Rosier, 157
social sciences, xvi, 117
Soledad Brothers, 211
soul murder, 191–192
Souls of Black Folk, The (Du Bois), 117
Southern Christian Leadership Confer-
    ence, 16, 21, 128
spirit, leadership and, 30–31
standardized testing, 101
Staples, Pop, 203
state, nature and, 129–130
State of Black America (Daniels, ed.),
    199–200, 202
States of Confinement (Marable), 211
Steele, Shelby, xv, 12, 69, 96, 127–155, 168;
    allegory as strategy, 134–139, 141; black
    mind, concept of, 137, 138–139, 141–142;
    Black Power, view of, 132, 136–140;
    Civil Rights activism of, 128; *The Con-
    tent of Our Character*, 128–129, 132–145,
    174, 176; disorder, politics of, 136–137;
    King, view of, 132–134; oppression,
    view of, 147–148; as terminator figure,
    140, 141–143; *White Guilt*, 146–155
Stowe, Harriet Beecher, 32
Straight Outta Compton (NWA), 88
structuralism, 97, 100–105, 117–118

Student Nonviolent Coordinating Com-
    mittee (SNCC), 24
students, black, 140, 167
suffering, as redemptive, 30
superpredator epithet, 221n. 17
surveillance, 40, 85, 93

"Talented Tenth, The" (Du Bois), 117
Taylor, Otis, 58
terror: caused by white supremacy, 3– 5,
    14–15; as fear of white man's jail, 18,
    23–24; theology of, 32–33, 142
textual evidence, xviii
*That's the Joint: The Hip-Hop Studies
    Reader* (Neal), 86
theology, black, 40
theology of terror, 32–33, 142
There Ain't No Black in the Union Jack
    (Gilroy), 161
think tanks, xv, 60, 68–69
Title VII (Civil Rights Act of 1964),
    74–75
Tocqueville, Alexis de, 207
Toop, David, 86
trickster figure, 157–159
Trotskyists, 53
Turner, Ronald, 168
Tuskegee Institute, 191
12 Million Black Voices (Wright), 189
Twice the Work of Free Labor (Lichten-
    stein), 207
2 Live Crew, 87

Uncle Tom, image of, 32–33
underground economies, 103, 194
university, 216–217
University of Massachusetts School of
    Education, 12–13
University of Pennsylvania, 96
Up from Slavery (Washington), 104, 179
urban dwellers, 36–37
Urban Poverty and Family Life Study, 103
urban rebellions, 34–35

utilitarianism, 64

Venkatesh, Sudhir, 194
victimization/victimology, 138–139, 173–176
Victorian ideals, 123–124
violence: black, psychology of, 3–4; ideological, 46–48; white, 4–5, 46–48
visual blackness, 64–65, 130–131
Voting Rights Act of 1965, 76, 176, 177

"W. E. B. Du Bois and the Talented Tenth" (Gates), 116
Wackenhut Corrections, 208–209
Walker, Wyatt T., 28
war on drugs, 206–208, 221n. 17
War on Poverty, 64
Washington, Booker T., 8, 69, 70, 82, 104, 113; neoconservative black view of, 169–170; opposition to activism, 127–128; self-congratulatory writing, 178–179; Up from Slavery, 104, 179
Watts Riot, 34, 38
Weldon Johnson, James, xvii
welfare, open-ended, 187, 192
welfare queen label, 62
welfare "reform," 184–185
West, Cornel, 80–83, 94, 96, 97; "Black Striving in a Twilight Civilization," 121–125; Race Matters, 80, 82–83; The Future of the Race (with Gates), 108, 116–125
Westbrook, Robert, 55–56

Westvaco Paper Mill, 113
When Work Disappears (Wilson), 102–103
Where Do We Go from Here: Chaos or Community (King), 39, 41–42, 76–78
white allies, abandonment of black America, 51–52
white guilt, concept of, 146–155
White Guilt (Steele), 146–155
white supremacy: black freedom linked to, 147–149; contemporary manifestations of, 13–14; goodwill, white pretense to, 65–66; ideology of, 46–48; neoconservative black view of, 137–138, 140–141, 166; psychological effect of, 3–4; response to call for justice, 43; white guilt and, 146–155
white trauma speak, 67
Wilkins, Roy, 40
Williams, Juan, 12, 81
Wilson, William Julius, 101, 102–103, 117
Winning the Race (McWhorter), 179–195
Wire, The (show), 208
Wolfe, Alan, 81
Woodard, Alfre, 191
Wright, Richard, 3, 7, 36–37, 189

Yale Summer High School, 120
Yale University, 119–121
Young, Andrew, 16, 21
Young, Whitney, 23
younger generations, 34–35
youth audience, 86